D1519475

River of the Carolinas: The Santee

❧ ❧ ❧ ❧ ❧ *River of the Carolinas: The Santee*

BY *Henry Savage, Jr.*

ILLUSTRATED BY *Lamar Dodd*

THE UNIVERSITY OF NORTH CAROLINA PRESS • CHAPEL HILL

Contents

CONTENTS

❧ ❧ ❧ ❧ *Introduction to the 1968 printing*

Some fifteen years have passed since this book was written. For a river that rises in mountains as old as any on earth and flows through the red hills of the world's oldest land mass, a mere decade and a half is but a tick of the cosmic clock, little different from those preceding or those to follow. But this book is the story of man and the river—in that order. From the standpoint of man in a dynamic, fast-changing region, those fifteen years have provided a welter of pertinent new material appropriate to that story. So we, the publishers and I, thought we should take this opportunity to at least briefly mention the more significant latter day happenings.

The account of the development of the river as a source of power is given in Chapter 30. The principal addendum to that account is Duke Power Company's vast, newly created Lake Norman at Cowans Ford on the Catawba. The map on page 347 has been revised to include this 33,000 acre lake, the largest of all North Carolina lakes, with a power capability three-quarters that of all thirteen of Duke's other hydro-electric installations up and down the Catawba and Wateree and over on the Broad. However, on the scale of present day power generation even an installation of that magnitude is but a puny thing as a power producer, compared to a modern steam generation plant like Marshall Station, built on the shore of Lake Norman so that it might use its waters, essential to the steam plant's operation.

More and more, through the years, hydro-generation of electricity has been relegated to the performance of the single role it performs best because of its instant availability at the throw of a switch—supplying the peak power demands. Although an essential part of an economical power system, all that string of lakes and hydro-generating plants extending two hundred miles or more along the Wateree Catawba, "the world's most electrified river", together now account for but 7 per cent of Duke's power production. Far down the river even the mammoth Santee-Cooper hydro facilities have been relegated to auxiliary status, producing now less than a third of the power sold by the state-owned facility. Recently the United States Army Engineers revealed a $35,000,000 plan to remedy the silting problem in Charleston harbor where the great flow of the Santee water diverted into the Cooper river has been adding $2,500,000 annually to the harbor's maintenance. The plan calls for the water diverted into Lake Moultrie in the Cooper river basin to be channeled back into the lower Santee—a modification that will substantially reduce Santee-Cooper's water-generated power potential.

There remains another new paragraph in the story of electric power and the river. A few years ago at Parr Shoals on the Broad River in central South Carolina, the pioneer atomic power plant in the Southeast was put into operation. A few days ago its closing was announced. Built solely as

INTRODUCTION

an experimental research facility, it has already served its purpose. Now it is planned that the $45,000,000 installation, with its great white masonry sphere, will be left standing there beside the river—a monument to the advent of atomic power.

In Chapter 31 I dealt with the phenomenal industrial growth of the region since World War II. That growth has continued unabated. In the past decade alone some six billion dollars in new industrial investment have located in the Carolinas, creating directly some 400,000 new industrial jobs.

This mounting industrialization is having its effect on the region's agriculture, speeding the changes which have been in progress for a generation or more. The resulting labor shortages and higher wage standards tend to accelerate the liquidation of the little farm that can't afford or fully employ modern farm machinery. So farms continue to get fewer in number and larger in size. The "soil bank" program and the increased market for pulpwood to supply the expanding paper mills have given added impetus to tree farming. Every day the pulp and paper mills of the Carolinas consume the entire annual growth on 15,000 acres of forest. Even so, thanks to more intelligent forest management growth still exceeds the harvest. In furtherance of the effort to keep it that way both public and private programs have been inaugurated to breed super trees for the future. To that end a sixty-acre seed tree orchard has been established on the upper Catawba near Morganton. There strains of especially superior forest trees of several species are being developed through selective breeding.

To supplement my account in Chapter 34 of the near death and resuscitation of the river, I recently inquired as to the current health of Santee waters. The pollution control authorities of both Carolinas reported the river biologically more healthy today than it was fifteen years ago. This is news of enormous import to the millions of Carolinians

INTRODUCTION

whose health, happiness and economic well being, whether they realize it or not, are intimately dependent on the continuing health of those waters. Those good reports represent a signal victory for intelligent conservation, for year after year the river has been asked to do more work, cool more condensers, carry away more domestic and industrial wastes, and at the same time serve as recreation mecca for hundreds of thousands.

So that the magnitude of that victory may be fully appreciated, let me point out that of the 2,500 new industries which located in the Carolinas in the past decade hundreds located on Santee tributaries, dozens doing so to use their waters. A single one of those, albeit the giant among them, Bowater's big paper mill on the lower Catawba, requires as much water as a city of a quarter of a million people, although every gallon is used successively to do many jobs, to cool condensers, convey logs, wash pulp and carry away waste chemicals. That the river is successfully digesting its ever mounting load of industrial and domestic effluent and still is able to keep its waters biologically alive marks the Santee, particularly its Wateree-Catawba reaches, as a superb example of the rescue and rejuvenation of a once all but ruined river—an extraordinary object lesson in the care and use of a river.

Henry Savage, Jr.

Camden, S. C.
October, 1967

❦ ❦ ❦ ❦ ❦ ❦ ❦ *River of the Carolinas: The Santee*

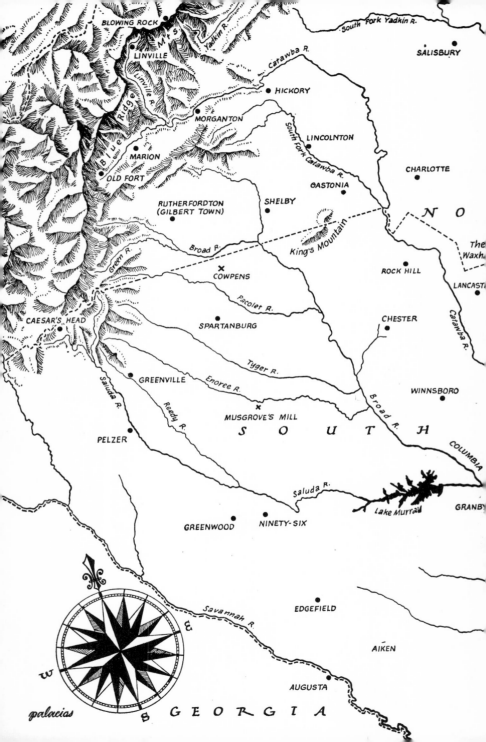

❧ ❧ ❧ ❧ ❧ *Foreword*

*L*ife is full of drama in which
we ourselves are both the actors and the audience. For those
who take the pace in sufficient leisure or hesitate and con-
template frequently enough, it is the personal dramas,
whether they be great or small, that provide the flavor of living. Soon after I began my study of the Santee I realized that
in this experience I was involved in a particularly fascinating
one of these personal dramas. For there is something about a
river that speaks to the hearts of all men in a language each
can understand, in a song of endless significance and beauty.
As the river winds its watery way from mountain source to
lonely marsh, it seems to run like a green, resilient thread
through the world's history, speaking to man of the days of
the earth before his coming, of his slow beginnings and turbulent progress, of his eternal kinship with the spirit of the
universe, of his ancient heritage and his infinite promise.
Sometimes it has seemed to me that this river drama

should have a musical background for fullest appreciation, like the movement of a great symphony; and I, myself, have liked to identify it with my favorite symphony, Dvořák's *From the New World,* which seems to me as perfectly the story of the Santee in musical form as it could have been had it been studiedly composed to tell that story. I see this symphony as the Song of the Santee. To me its music tells the history of this romantic and dramatic stream from that faraway day when the Indian's cypress dugout was silently gliding along its green expanse between high, moss-hung forest walls to the accompaniment of the slither and plunk of the water moccasin, dropping from the low-hanging branches, and the thumping of the great woodpeckers, to this day when nature's diminished sounds are buried under the tonal overburden of whirring generators and the rasping staccato of the construction drill. I hear the calls and songs of the wild creatures, the drums of the red men, the homesick plaints of the black men, the troubled days that ushered in the new era which knit together all these and from them made the stirring and triumphant melody that is the song of the Santee today.

In another mood I see that stream as a sinuous yellow monster, deceptively sleeping through peaceful summer days only to rouse suddenly in destructive fury. Then I see it as the rampaging beast that swept away my father's bridge across its muddy waters and hurled him and the workers who were struggling to save it into the midst of the loosed mass of rolling and pitching debris. For several that day it was death at the hands of the beast. For my father it spelled harrowing hours of struggle in the swirling current among the pitching and crashing flood rafts until at last, a dozen miles downstream, he was able to reach a treetop and eventual rescue. Meanwhile the insatiable monster was roaring in through wide breaches in the dykes that protected his plantation's alluvial fields and covering them deep beneath sterile sand.

FOREWORD

With the hope that I can impart to the reader the beauty and excitement, the tragedy and frustration, the discouragement and the hope flowing through its history, I begin this story of time and of man and this river.

❦ ❦ ❦ ❦ ❦ *1. As it was in the beginning*

A half billion years ago when the still warm original rocks of the earth were half as old as they are today, a great range of mountains, higher than the present-day Alps, was born as a result of the shrinking and rumpling of the earth's surface as it cooled. These mountains, known to geologists as the Ocoees, formed the lofty backbone of a continent which extended from northeast Virginia to the Gulf of Mexico. Millions of years of violent weather, running the gamut from centuries of almost ceaseless torrential rain to long periods of desert conditions and high winds, and periods productive of great alpine glaciers at length well-nigh leveled the peaks of the Ocoees. The red piedmont hills of the Carolinas and Georgia are all that remain of them today. The rocks that lie under these hills are among the oldest on earth, and these hills themselves are among the oldest of the world's land masses.

It took three hundred million years to transform the

great Ocoees into the modest red hills of the Carolina up-country—and then another great revolution in the earth's rocks took place. To the west of the reduced Ocoees rose a new great mountain range more lofty than the Rockies of to-day. Only yesterday in the geologic timetable the remnants of these mountains were misnamed the Appalachians, a mis-nomer which was further perpetuated and given scientific dignity by being adopted by geologists to designate a geolog-ical period—the Appalachian revolution—descriptive of the period during which were born the oldest mountain ranges of North America.

In colonial times these mountains were appropriately called the Cherokee Mountains. However, a fabricated ac-count by one Brigstock, published in 1644, describing a visit in 1622 to the "king of Appalachia" near these mountains, was sufficient to change the name of this range despite the fact that, had there been a king of Appalachia, he would properly have resided with his people in northwest Florida and would surely never have ventured anywhere near the do-main of the formidable Cherokees in their mountain citadel.

Getting back to the fascinating story that the stones about us have revealed to those who know their language, we are told that during the next one hundred million years after the Appalachians were born along the eastern edge of our ancient continent the sea moved out to what is now called the continental shelf, 150 miles or more beyond where it is today. The streams carrying the runoff from the new mountains cut their ways through and across the ancient foundations of the now reduced Ocoees, became organized into river systems carrying the surplus rain water and the very substance of the mountains themselves, then unprotected by plant growth, eastward to the faraway ocean. These rivers were to be the direct ancestors of our rivers of today.

Along the riverbanks, forests of fern, fernlike trees and rushes dominated the scene, supporting a varied population of reptiles and multitudes of insects even as today. The much-publicized great Brontosaurus took to the river to escape the terror of that embodiment of a nightmare, the great-toothed Tyrannosaurus rex. Remaining to us today as our heritage from this period, and remarkably little changed in all intervening millions of years, are the turtles and alligators which still hold fast to the home that nature chose for them back in the age of the dinosaurs.

Another fifty million years, and, as a result of the melting of ice which had held great quantities of water in plateaus of ice at either end of the earth, the oceans rose and moved in on the land some three hundred miles to the very foot of the ancient Ocoees where the easterly primeval rocks outcrop along a line roughly parallel with today's shore line and the mountains to the west, and lying about halfway between them. This is the line known to us as the fall line, where the rivers reach their last rapids and begin their lethargic meanders across the flat coastal plains.

For a very long time the ocean stayed at that level, during ages of weather far more violent than anything we know today. It stayed there so long that the beach dunes were built into sand hills, thousands of square miles of them that stretch in a band at the fall line across the Southeast, but most pronounced in their sweep across the Carolinas. At this time there was no Santee River. Its bed all lay under the full-blown ocean of that day. Its two principal tributary rivers, the Congaree and the Wateree, were then completely separate streams, entering the ocean through deep bays running back into the hills to where Columbia and Camden, South Carolina, now stand.

During this period the great dinosaurs passed from the scene, and the first small mammals began to take up the living space the reptiles were having to surrender from causes as yet unknown. In the air the flying lizards were being displaced by the true birds which had evolved from them. In the rivers the first bony fishes appeared. Today's fantastic-looking garfish with his long, toothed, scissors beak and the worthy sturgeon, so famous for its eggs, are living fossils of this age, persisting oblivious of their good luck in being by-passed by nature's scythe when most of their fellow creatures of that age were effectively liquidated.

Meanwhile the vegetation was becoming more special-ized, adapting itself to more varied environments. The leafed trees appeared. Generally speaking, after this period, the over-all appearance of our area was not greatly different from its appearance when men first laid eyes upon it. Geo-logically speaking our area was mature. It was almost the dawn of our day. But as man measures time it was still a long, long time ago. Many younger parts of the world bore no resemblance to their present appearance. The Alps and Himalayas had not yet risen from the plains which extended across their present sites. Central United States was still in-termittently a great shallow sea. Several times the polar ice-cap pushed southwardly, always stopping short of Carolina, thereby enormously affecting the flora of the Carolina moun-tains even to this day. On visiting the Far East, people famil-iar with the Carolinas have frequently noted with astonish-ment a striking similarity between the Carolina mountain flora and that of Japan, Okinawa, and parts of eastern Asia, and botanists confirm those impressions. They explain that a growth similar to that of the Southern Appalachians and the Asiatic mountains once covered most of the land areas of the northern hemisphere. As the icecap pushed southward, this flora was pushed southwardly. When the icecap receded, only the mountain areas of southeastern North America and eastern Asia remained hospitable to that flora. Thus these kindred islands were left on opposite sides of the world, so that even now the blossom of the Carolina rhododendron is almost identical with the Japanese pink azalea even to the spots on the top of the corolla, and these widely separated areas are the homes of the wild azaleas, ginseng, galax, the catalpas, wisterias, and many others. During the period between fifty million and twenty million years ago, mammals became the dominant land fauna. Primates moved in, stayed for several million years and then abandoned the area, leaving their descendants to occupy tropical America. The varied mammal population was mostly miniature in stature. Horses the size of terriers, camels the size of cats, waist-high elephants and rhinoceroses the size of pigs abounded. As the millions of years passed, this teeming herbivorous population stimulated the evolution of predatory species such as the great saber-toothed tiger. Size then became a protection and many species adopted increased size to permit survival, culminating in the great mastodon and giant sloths which drank from our river only yesterday in the geological timetable. During these millions of years, the sea repeatedly moved up to the piedmont, only to recede again to far beyond its present location, reflecting the recurring ice ages.

When the sea receded, the Congaree and Wateree meandered to a merger in what had been the alluvial bottom of the ocean, and the great Santee became a river. The stage was set for man—a creature who would not be evolved for another million years and who would not arrive on this stage until another lapse of time equal to a thousand Christian eras.

We have now reached almost the end of the life history of the Santee. All but the last tick of the cosmic clock has been covered. But the story with which we are concerned, that of man and the river, has yet to begin.

❧ ❧ ❧ ❧ ❧ 2. The coming
of man

*I*t was thousands of years ago
that men first came to these parts. No one knows just when
they came, who they were, and what they looked like. But
from the tiny bits of evidence they left behind them, some
very likely guesses have been made about these prehistoric
Carolinians.

The warm, moist climate of southeastern United States
has effectively obliterated most of the remaining traces of
these early people, but here and there throughout the area of
hilltop sites crude, leaf-shaped white arrow points and other
stone artifacts are still to be found. As often as not these spots
are far from the rivers and navigable streams. Usually no
pottery remains are to be found with the stone implements.
That is about the sum total of the evidence. From this meager
evidence students of these people deduce a picture of early
Stone Age nomads, living by gathering the nuts and fruit
of the countryside and by hunting. Such cooking as they may
have done must have been toasting and broiling before the

fire or baking in the coals. No crops were planted. Since they appear to have shunned the riverbanks, it is reasonable to assume that they did not look upon streams as assets and, consequently, that they did not navigate them. Probably for them the rivers were but impediments to cross-country travel. Being likewise impediments to the flight of game, bends in the rivers were no doubt utilized as corrals. Only in these respects did the rivers have significance for them. Since earlier remains of human habitation have been found in western United States, it is assumed that the first Easterners came here out of the West.

The question as to whether or not these people were the ancestors of those who had this region during much later times no one can answer.

After them—but long after them, centuries ago rather than millenniums ago—there were other vanished people who had been here and left behind more substantial evidences of their occupancy. They, however, appear to have been similar in culture to the Indians who were found here when the first Europeans arrived on the scene. They left, for us to remember them by, mounds and other earthworks here and there all up and down the Santee and its tributaries— many of which works were being used by the Indians of the sixteenth century. But those later tenants of these earthworks had no knowledge or tradition of their construction. So the assumption is made that a vanished race of "Mound Builders" lived by these rivers before the Catawbas, the Cherokees and the other tribes we know came on the scene.

And so we skip down through the ages to the people who possessed this fair land when the first white men came—to the dawn of the written history of Carolina.

From a combination of legend, tradition and diggings in the relatively recent remains of the Indians, it is known that generally speaking the same tribes that were found here had been in this region for some two or three centuries. During all this time Carolina had been a frontier, a bloody Indian frontier, where several powerful language groups—and consequently people of mutual enmity—abutted. The Blue Ridge in North Carolina and the piedmont hills of South Carolina were the eastern boundaries of the formidable Cherokee Nation who had left the lands of their Iroquois kinsmen in the region of the Great Lakes to make their home in the Southern Appalachians. The great group of Muskhogean tribes were supreme in Georgia and to the west. Of this group the Creeks were involved in almost ceaseless warfare where they were in contact with the Cherokees in North Georgia, and as Yamassees and Cusabos they spilled over the Savannah into southern South Carolina. To the north, in eastern North Carolina, were the Iroquoian Tuscarora and several coastal tribes representing the southernmost extension of the Algonquin group.

Right in the middle of this ring of perpetually hostile groups, occupying almost all the Santee and Peedee watersheds, were the river people, the tribes of Siouan stock—the Sewees, the Winyahs, the Santees, the Congarees, the Waterees, the Catawbas, the Waxhaws and others. They professed to have come here from the Middle West, leaving their kinsmen to migrate to the Dakota region, there to make a latter-day reputation as warriors under the fearsome name of the Sioux. Had there been historians to record the martial exploits of the Carolina part of the Siouan family, there is little doubt but that there their reputation as fighters would be no less brilliantly crimson, for whatever else is said of them in what history has recorded no one has ever disparaged their bravery and ability in that foremost aspect of Indian life. One of the early legends of these people tells of their moving down the Catawba River into the Cherokee territory west of the river, undaunted by the much greater numbers and the acknowledged ability of the Cherokee warriors. After a fierce battle lasting all day, a truce was arranged whereby the Broad River was made the boundary between the two nations. Thereafter, until it was renamed by the English, it was known as Eswa Huppeday—the line river.

Being the frontier of four powerful Indian groups, enemies of one another with a fanatical devotion to warfare, through the centuries the Carolinas were the scene of almost perpetual war. So ceaseless and so bloody were these conflicts that the total population of the area remained always numerically very small. In view of the frequent references to extensive abandoned Indian fields in the accounts of the early explorers of the interior, it may be assumed that the Indian population had already substantially declined because of that much earlier history-making transoceanic swap of diseases, smallpox for syphilis, each proving devastating to the receiver. Even so the Indian population had always been unbelievably sparse by our standards. At the time of the first English colonization there were no more than twenty-five thousand Indians in the whole of the two Carolinas. Add the Cherokees of Georgia and Tennessee and we still have less than half as many people in our entire area as there are now in the city of Columbia. The Indian population of the whole southeastern United States at that time is comparable to the present population of Charlotte.

For a people so few in numbers, so widely scattered and so divided among themselves to have loomed so large in history and exerted such an influence on Colonial America during its first full century is tribute indeed to their enormous vitality and their unmatched talent in that field of their special skill—warfare. Their great impact on history in relation to their numbers must place these simple Stone Age barbarians in the high company of the tribes of Israel and the early Greeks. To them we owe much of our daily diet, also tobacco, cocaine, quinine, a large and particularly colorful segment of our language, and the frontier spirit which made America great.

❦ ❦ ❦ ❦ ❦ *3. As it is now*

*W*ithout names for mountains and hills, rivers, and streams, and other features of the landscape, it is practically impossible to communicate any intelligible description of an area of the earth. It was the dearth of such names, together with subsequent name changes, that has made it so difficult to trace from their accounts the routes followed through our region by its early explorers, de Ayllón, De Soto, Pardo, Lederer, Henry Woodward and even the articulate and observant John Lawson in his detailed account of his trip from Charleston to the upper reaches of the Catawba in 1700.

But, of course, at last men did come to the region and successively attempt to possess themselves of it, and, as a byproduct of their possession, give names to the various aspects of the landscape. First there were the nomad hunting-and-gathering people, who probably gave names to the features about them, but, unless the Indians whom the white men found here adopted some of their names from those early people, there is probably no trace of those names. But their successors, the Indians who peopled these parts for at least four or five hundred years prior to the coming of the white man, supplied the region with a rich heritage of fascinating and beautiful names—names which in most instances remain today the only monuments to these vanished people.

After them came the Spaniards who mostly modified the Indian names they came upon. As the years rolled on, the English came and contributed a major portion of the names which eventually stuck. But they were soon followed by French, Scots and Germans, all of whom erected verbal monuments to themselves here and there across the landscape by dubbing this or that physical feature with a name from their own languages.

It is the sum total of these names that makes it possible for us now to give an intelligible description of our river valley and identify the principal features of the valley and its environs.

The Santee River system drains a watershed area which outlined on a map has the appearance of a great oak tree, bent northwardly by a south wind, rooted in the coast line between Bull's Bay, north of Charleston, and Winyah Bay, south of Georgetown. Include the watershed of the Cooper River, which in recent years has been grafted onto the Santee by the latter's diversion into the Cooper River and Charleston Harbor, and the tree simile still holds, modified only by adding flaring buttresses at the base of the trunk. Some seventy-five miles inland the "tree" branches at a "crotch" where the Congaree and Wateree watersheds commence. From there, northward and westward, the great tree branches and rebranches to its topmost twigs, the mountain brooks and streams which drain the southern and eastern slopes of the Blue Ridge Mountains all the way from Table Rock and Caesar's Head, near where North Carolina, South Carolina, and Georgia meet, to the neighborhood of the Brushy Mountains, Grandfather Mountain and Blowing Rock, 150 miles to the northeast.

This vast area embracing more than seventeen thousand square miles is bounded northwest by the Blue Ridge Mountains, separating the watershed of the Tennessee River, north and northeast by the Yadkin-Peedee watershed to the fall line and that of the Black River in the Low Country, while to the southwest there is first the watershed of the Edisto River to the piedmont hills and then the watershed of the Savannah River up to the mountains.

If the names of three centuries ago are employed, a description of the watershed would still be recognizable. The Indians would have told of the great Zantee or Seretee (the Santee), meaning in their language "the river," by telling of its formation by the flowing together of the river of the Congarees (meaning "deep river people") with that of the Guatari (Wateree, meaning "people of the river with broken banks"). Upstream the Wateree was known as the Catapaw, that being the name of a tribe of the Iswa (river) people who lived along it. Going back to the Zantee and up the deep river of the Congarees we would learn of its formation by the flowing together of the river of the Saludas and a very wide river bisecting the watershed and lying about midway between the river of the Catapaws and that of the Saludas. To this river (the Broad), the Indians gave the name Eswa Huppeday (meaning the line river dividing the lands of the Catawbas and the Cherokees). The length and difficulty of that name no doubt accounts for the fact that the Broad is the single major portion of the whole Santee system which does not have a name of Indian origin. In Indian times the Santee basin would have been described as rising in the mountains of the Chalaque (the Cherokee, but not then a name, "Chalaque" simply meaning people speaking a different language); to the northeast was the land of the Enos,

Waxhaws and Joaras or Saras (Cheraws) and of the Pee-
dees; the Zantee's waters entered the sea between the bay of
the Winyahs (people of the bend) and the bay of the Sowes
or Sewees (Bull's Bay) or an island people, while southwest
lay the lands of the Adusta (the Edisto, or people who sprin-
kle themselves with river water) by the river of the Savanos
and by the Oconee or "place of springs" in the hills of the
Cherokee.

Rivers and waters, riverbanks and springs—by their
words and names we see what a momentous place the river
had in the lives and cultures of these early Americans and
how appropriate they are to this relation. However obsessed
we may be today with the significance and importance of
rivers in our culture and economy, to them they were of even
greater import.

Let us return from this digression into the past to give
some mundane details of our subject. From its farthest
reaches in the Blue Ridge Mountains to the sea, the waters
of the Santee system flow some 450 miles to cover a bee-
line distance of about 250 miles. So much water falls on its
high rainfall watershed that it discharges into the sea an
average of about twenty thousand cubic feet per second—a
flow greater than that of any other Atlantic coast river except
the Susquehanna. As Eastern rivers go, this flow is subject to
great and occasionally violent change, sometimes multiplying
this average flow more than twentyfold. When such floods
occur, usually several times a year, the Santee and the lower
reaches of both the Wateree and the Congaree attain in
many places a width exceeding ten miles, and a half million
acres of river swamp forests are submerged.

Perhaps the most outstanding characteristic of the Santee
system as it is today is its utilization to turn the wheels of industry. In hydroelectric installations it far exceeds any other
river east of the Mississippi, excepting only its neighbor
across the mountains, the Tennessee. More than half of the

hydroelectric projects on all the Atlantic seaboard rivers south of the Potomac are on the Santee system. Thirty-eight of the seventy-five major installations on the coastal rivers from the Potomac southward and westward to the Mississippi are on the Santee and its tributaries. Its forty-seven dams with their forty-nine powerhouses develop some 1,150,000 horsepower. Most of these installations are on the Santee-Wateree-Catawba reach of the river, virtually transforming that river into a chain of lakes, extending from within a few miles of the Atlantic to Lake James which backs water up into remote mountain coves. A traveler by water from the river mouth to Old Fort, in the center of the Blue Ridge Mountains of North Carolina, would travel most of the intervening four hundred miles on the still waters of the lakes of these power projects.

People who are interested in rivers always want to know where they rise, and usually a river's source can be pretty definitely ascribed to a certain stream, brook, or even a particular spring. But not so with the Santee. Its source is simply the broad eastern ramparts of the Carolina Blue Ridge. The Santee is a multisource river, and nothing like a satisfactory case can be made out on behalf of any particular location as being its primary source.

It might be said (and it is said) that the Santee has its source in the brooks that drain the frequent rains from the southern slope of lofty Grandfather Mountain and those of his nearby, appropriately more delicate mate, Grandmother Mountain. These and other mountain brooks join to form the Linville River, which winds its way through the picturesque alpine village of Linville, North Carolina, a bare ten miles from the Tennessee line. From there it fairly tumbles southward into Linville Gorge where it cascades ninety feet over the lower falls and rushes on between Jonas Ridge and the Linville Mountains, deep beneath the sheer walls of the narrow Linville Gorge, which, incidentally, is said to be the only box canyon east of Grand Canyon. Emerging from this spectacular canyon, the Linville roars beneath the sheer west side of Shortoff Mountain into that man-made gem among Southern lakes, Lake James. From there the waters of the Linville, now merged with those of the Catawba entering the lake from the west, continue as the Catawba their eastward and then southward course successively passing through Rhodhiss Lake, Lake Hickory, Lookout Shoals Lake, Mountain Island Lake, Catawba Lake, Fishing Creek Pond, the Dearborn and Cedar Creek reservoirs; after which for no good reason, the Catawba River suddenly becomes the Wateree, flowing through Wateree Lake and down the Wateree to its junction with the Congaree, where these two become the Santee.

A few more lazy miles and these combined waters enter the Santee Reservoir or Lake Marion as it is more lately known, the largest artificial lake east of the Appalachians. In wet seasons, after making their imperceptible way through the thirty-five-mile length of Lake Marion, much of these waters spill over the Santee Dam into the pristine channel of the Santee to follow a lethargic, twisting course between almost uninterrupted moss-draped forest walls for seventy-five miles to the Atlantic. But ordinarily most of the river's flow is channeled from Lake Marion through a great canal into wide, man-made Lake Moultrie, from which it is released through the great turbines of the Santee-Cooper powerhouse into the artificially widened upper reaches of the Cooper River. So most of the Santee's waters now flow down the Cooper, beneath the towering double spans of the fantastic, roller-coasterlike Cooper River bridge past the eastern waterfront of Charleston, and on between Fort Moultrie and Fort Sumter to the sea.

More continuity of name, together with the greatest channel distance to the sea, gives support to the claim that the source of the Santee is the rugged watershed of the upper

Catawba near the village of Ridgecrest, North Carolina. There numerous clear mountain brooks quickly combine to form a stream of sufficient size to be called the Catawba River. In its rush down the ravine it leaps five hundred feet over the steep staircase of incredibly beautiful Catawba Falls, rushes on through cavernlike arches of rhododendron, hemlock and tulip trees, through a washed-out early power installation, past small grassy openings here and there which were the homesites of isolated mountain folk in days gone by, and on to a junction with Swannanoa Creek in the town of Old Fort—which as Davidson's Fort was for decades the North Carolina settlers' farthest penetration into the Cherokee country. The nearest approaches to these roaring waters of the upper Catawba, in their descent from the divide at Ridgecrest, are the cuts and fills of the country's most costly mountain highway, which fairly leaps from Ridgecrest to Old Fort. South of this awe-inspiring highway, over the Catawba gorge, people sometimes see the great bulk of Mystery Mountain, all clothed in forests as its surrounding neighbors, only to have it disappear with a shift of the wind or an attempt to approach it for closer examination. From Old Fort the Catawba Gorge widens into a delectable fertile valley through which the river winds, passing close by the home of the Revolutionary hero, Colonel Joseph McDowell, whose father, "Hunting John," had appropriately named the valley "Pleasant Gardens." A little farther on, the Catawba joins the North Fork Catawba, which has come down from Humpback Mountain parallel to the Linville, passing on its way the entrance to the as yet not fully explored Linville Caverns. Together these streams form the headwaters of Lake James, there mix with the waters of the Linville, and, thus mingled, travel their long, lake-interrupted journey to the Atlantic.

But a few miles away on the opposite side of the ridge

from where the Catawba rises, a dozen miles east of Asheville, other brooks join to make the upper Broad River. Rapidly picking up volume from other mountain streams, it tumbles through the narrow confines of Hickory Nut Gap, past Bat Cave and beneath the towering majesty of Chimney Rock and on into the deep still waters of Lake Lure. Below Lake Lure, the Broad is joined by the Green River flowing in from the west, a river which, after rising on Standing Rock Mountain, has passed through Lake Summit and Lake Adger. Together they continue eastwardly just north of the line between the Carolinas to the neighborhood of Shelby where the Broad bends to take a due south course into South Carolina and continues through Ninety-Nine Islands Lake, picks up the Pacolet and continues through the Lockhart reservoir, over the prehistoric rock fish dam near Carlisle, and then adds the waters of the Tyger and the Enoree rivers and flows on into Parr Shoals reservoir—and then on to Columbia, where the Saluda River comes in from the west to form the Congaree. Another fifty miles and the Congaree will meet the Wateree where the Santee begins.

Up in the Blue Ridge Mountains of far northwest South Carolina, under the eternal surveillance of the great stone visage of Caesar's Head, flows the newborn Saluda River, which comes in from Pickens County to the west and, after resting awhile in Table Rock Lake, passes beneath the great, boxlike bulk of three-thousand-foot-high Table Rock. Turning south, it runs fifty miles southeast through many a turbine to the head of Lake Greenwood, a relatively new, more elegant name for what was once well known as the Buzzards' Roost Power Project. Ten miles below the Buzzards' Roost dam, the Saluda enters the headwaters of Lake Murray, a man-made lake with a shore line of 520 miles, impounded by one of the largest earthen dams in the world, creating a head of 180 feet. Through the penstocks and turbines of the

powerhouse below the dam, the entire Saluda River flows, as it continues on its way to its confluence with the Broad at Columbia where the Congaree begins.

Hidden in the fastness of their wide swamp and walled off from view by the tall, thick swamp forests, the Congaree below Columbia, the Wateree below Camden, and the whole Santee, except where it is impounded in Lake Marion, are best seen from the air.

Through their swampbound courses, crooked as the proverbial blacksnake, in an endless series of duplicated meanders, the Congaree and the Wateree coil and wind their separate ways for fifty miles to their junction where they impart to the Santee, but on a larger scale, the same tortuous pattern.

Here and there, all along its course, lie shining crescents of water and crescent-shaped differences in the shades of the green of the forests. With Islamic prevalence, these green-and-silver crescents are spread at random through the swamp forest on either side of the meandering ribbon of the great stream. These crescents are the remains of sharp curves in the river, where the channel was cut deep during ages gone by, and later left isolated from the river when some freshet of the past caused it to cut suddenly across the neck of a meander, which had gradually extended itself too far to be tenable in the face of the mad, seaward rush of floodwaters. The older and shallower of these abandoned river bends gradually filled with the sediment of floods and the debris of the forest, until shallow enough to permit the water-loving, bell-bottomed tupelo gums and cypresses to take possession of them. From the air we can still discern these by the contrast of their lighter green against the neighboring sweet gums and oaks. Those which have not filled to such a degree remain as isolated swamp lakes.

Even beneath the surface of thirty-five-mile-long Lake Marion, the former river bed is still discernible, like a great dark sea serpent, lying on the bottom, twisting its way to the straight line of the lake's eastern shore, where stands the great bulk of the Santee Dam, so high that it turns the waters of the Santee out of its pristine bed, into another inland sea, Lake Moultrie, and thence into the Cooper River and the harbor at Charleston.

Beyond the Santee Dam, the Santee, itself, becomes an emaciated monster. The bulk of its substance is now, by government order and decree, drawn off to the south to turn the wheels of industry. As it approaches tidewater, after sluggishly winding another fifty miles, the swampbound Santee divides into the North Santee and the South Santee. In the wide marshes above the North Santee lie the neat grids of a multitude of abandoned canals, all that remains of the once great rice plantations of this area.

A few miles below the South Santee lies Cape Romain, the long sea island that has given its name to the Cape Romain Migratory Bird Refuge, which extends some twenty miles along the coast and includes fifty thousand acres of sea islands. This teeming birdland is becoming an increasingly impelling Mecca for bird lovers from all parts of the country. Its headquarters, Bull Island at the farther end of Bull's Bay, is, from nature's standpoint, one of the few unspoiled areas on the Atlantic Coast.

To the reader of this description of the Santee system, one paramount attribute of the river is apparent—inherent variety and contrast—contrasts especially remarkable in the face of the fact that they are all presented within a distance of three hundred airline miles: contrasts epitomized by the clear rushing waters of Catawba Falls, as against the sluggish, tawny lower Santee, as it approaches the sea through the dolorous, moss-hung forest of the Low Country. These contrasts stem from the fact that the sources of the river system are located in the cool Southern Appalachians, the heaviest rainfall region in the country, where a rainfall as high as twenty-two inches in twenty-four hours was recorded in 1916, while its mouth is in the subtropical coastal Carolina where the growing season is three and a half months longer than it is in the region of its source—a climatic contrast sufficient to account for the fact that in Carolina there are found far more plant species than in all of Europe, and more than in any other comparable area of America.

The wide coastal plain through which the Santee flows is a relatively featureless land. To an observer on the ground it presents only a flat expanse of forests and fields. But from the air it presents a very different picture. Either side of the swamp through which the great river snakes its way, the

whole countryside presents an astonishing pattern of rectangles and ellipses—rectangles man created by his farm clearings. But the origin of those endless successions of elliptical formations is one of the world's most baffling geological enigmas.

Locally they are known as "savannas," "pocosins," or, more commonly, as "bays"—probably because of the frequent growth about them of the sweet bay trees. They are shallow elliptical-shaped depressions, all oriented so that the longer axis has approximately a northwest-southeast direction. Generally a crescent-shaped mound of white sand runs around the southeastern end. They vary in length from a hundred or so feet to more than three miles. It was practical to drain some of them, so those now appear as fertile fields amid the surrounding forests. Others have remained boggy areas, supporting mainly tupelos and cypresses. The deeper ones appear as perfect elliptical pools, as if created by a formal garden designer for a gargantuan garden. Sometimes they intersect and overlap. Sometimes it appears that there are smaller ones within large ones. Frequently they are lined up as if marching abreast.

Occupying the flat coastal plain in a band about eighty miles wide, of which the course of the Santee is about the center, they are so numerous that they are termed countless. Authorities estimate them in the hundreds of thousands. These facts only came to light when the airplane permitted people to look down on them and see their outlines. Soon after, of course, geologists began to study them in detail in an effort to explain when and how they came to be.

Along about 1933, several investigators fascinated the scientific world and then succeeded in completely captivating the popular imagination by describing them as the scars made when a comet struck Carolina. Several scientific and many popular articles set forth the theory that in prehistoric times a comet, made up of a swarm of meteors of various sizes, plowed into the Carolinas from the northwest, each meteor plowing an elliptical crater and throwing up a sandbank around the southeastern edge of the crater. Without going into details, suffice it to say that serious defects were found in this glamorous theory, and few scientists now accept it as a satisfactory explanation of the origin of the bays.

Since then numerous other theories have been suggested. They have been explained as the result of a receding sea under the action of a prevailing southeast wind. Complicated explanations involving wind, artesian springs, and the caving in of the underlying limestone rock strata have been expounded. None of these explanations has proved satisfactory enough to receive any general acceptance. The geologist who probably knows more about these formations than any man living today, on being asked for his theory of the origin of the bays, stated simply that he had none, that no explanation yet proposed has provided a satisfactory answer.

So the Carolina Bays, those very simple, common, and easily observed formations, remain as one of the most puzzling enigmas of geology.

❧ ❧ ❧ ❧ ❧ 4. "The Span-iards passed here"

A decade after Columbus first set foot on Santo Domingo, one Lucas Vásquez de Ayllón became infected with the wanderlust which was sweeping Spain in response to the colorful propaganda of the Admiral. Leaving his native Toledo, he set forth for the New World to see for himself its wonders. By 1520 in Hispaniola he was a colorful grandee of proportions, having accumulated wealth and high position in the island government. During his years there, the Spanish had so rapidly "developed" the island that under their gentle hand half the native population had died of disease and hardship. A serious shortage of slaves for the plantations had developed.

Exploration rather than slave hunting, however, appears to have been the mission of a ship which de Ayllón outfitted and dispatched that year to the American mainland under the command of Francisco Gordillo. After running up the continental coast, perhaps as far as New York, Gordillo was homeward bound through the Bahamas when he met up with another vessel, outward bound from Hispaniola on a slave-hunting expedition. This ship had been sent out by a court associate of de Ayllón under the command of Captain Quexos, a cousin of Gordillo's. A conference between the captains and the two joined forces, Gordillo turning back to return to the continent with Quexos. In June, 1521, they sailed into a bay at the mouth of a considerable river, which they named Saint John the Baptist; but they neglected to draw a map of the area, thus leaving its identity for later historians to dispute. Such identifying evidence as they did leave suggests that their River Saint John the Baptist is our Winyah Bay which lies at the mouth of the Peedee a few miles north of the mouth of the Santee. To the natives this was the land of Chicora.

At the sight of the ships, the Chicorans fled in terror, but a landing party succeeded in capturing two of the laggards, a man and a woman. These captives were taken aboard one of the ships and were there treated with a great show of kindness. Flattered, lionized and splendidly adorned in European clothes, they were returned to shore. While awaiting the results from the snare thus set, the captains occupied themselves by conducting a ceremony by which they took formal possession of the territory in the name of the King of Spain, thereby establishing a claim by right of discovery which was to hound England and her Southern colonies for the next two centuries, a claim which was destined to cost the succeeding generations thousands of lives before title by right of conquest and possession finally prevailed. During the ceremony, as symbols of their possession both for the king and for Christianity, crosses were hewn on the trunks of the great spreading live oaks which formed the canopy of the low-lying land beyond the marshy fringe of the River Saint John the Baptist.

Thus fortified in the good graces of both the powers terrestrial and celestial, they extended an invitation to the now unsuspecting Chicorans to come aboard the ships to partake of the hospitality which had been heaped upon the captive couple a few days before. When 150 of their guests had arrived aboard, the Spaniards hoisted their sails and set out to sea. Quexos' vessel was lost during a storm and most of the captive Indians on the other deliberately starved themselves to death. Upon his vessel's return to Hispaniola, de Ayllón condemned the slaving activities of his captain and took steps to have the few survivors returned to Chicora. But it seems he never got around actually to doing it. Instead he hurried off to Spain to get His Majesty's permission to explore and settle the Carolina-Virginia mainland, carrying with him for stage effect one of the captive Indians who had been converted and named Francisco. This Francisco of Chicora was quite a character. He inextricably entwined fact and fiction in tales which have come down to us as the earliest accounts of life back home in Chicora.

With Francisco's help de Ayllón got his royal permit. And so it came to pass that after many vicissitudes he set sail from Santo Domingo in the summer of 1526, with a fleet of three ships and a tender. Aboard he had eighty-nine horses and some five hundred men and women, including several Negro slaves and, of course, a supply of Dominican friars to convert the natives. One of these friars appears to have been pretty much of a radical—the account tells of his being persecuted for speaking out against enslaving Indians. Reaching the Carolina coast, the fleet sailed around Cape Romain and entered the bar-obstructed mouth of the River Jordan. On the maps of today there is no River Jordan in Carolina. In its place they show the Santee.

Dropping anchor in the quiet waters of the sluggish river behind the shoals, the sea-weary colonists landed on the low, mosquito-infested shore to reconnoiter the area for a suitable location for what they hoped would be the first European colony north of Mexico. While scouts explored the country around, the colonists busied themselves replacing one of the ships, which had been lost in crossing the bar as they entered the river, and adding another of shallow draft for navigating these coastal waterways. The scouts returned with discouraging reports. They had found no suitable spot.

So they put to sea again, sailing southwestwardly along the coast to the neighborhood of the Savannah River where under a blazing August sky they began their town. Before the first frosts of fall, they were decimated by those fevers

that were to curse the Low Country through the ages until the advent of the window screen and quinine. De Ayllón himself was one of the victims. The scourges of the summer fevers were followed by a particularly severe winter. Then mutiny and a slave rebellion filled to overflowing their cup of misery. Before the winter was over, the handful of survivors gave up the struggle and set sail for home. The tender, carrying the mortal remains of their leader, symbolically sank in the wintry storm-driven sea they encountered on their passage back to Santo Domingo.

After the star of de Ayllón's dream of empire set beneath

his horizon of time, thirteen years were to pass before the out-pouring vitality of sixteenth century Spain would thrust another band of its amazingly courageous, blindly fanatical, shockingly ruthless, insatiably avaricious minions into Carolina fields and forests. It was 1540 when the indomitable De Soto, followed by his five hundred armor-clad soldiers, some mounted and some on foot, a dozen priests, and shackled Indian burden bearers, as well as bloodhounds and droves of pigs, was greeted by the Indian chieftainess, known to history as the Lady of Cofitachequi. Striving to please, she presented him with the great string of pearls she was wearing about her neck. With Spanish courtesy in return for the gift of these pearls and for her generosity in provisioning his army—which, incidentally, exceeded in size those used by the Spaniards in their conquests of Mexico and Peru—he made her a captive when he set out for the Cherokee country, where he thought he might find the gold he was seeking. Somewhere along the way she made her escape, as he pressed on into the hills, over the Blue Ridge, off our stage and on over into the Tennessee country—to discover that the yellow metal the natives had been telling him could be found there was only copper. Driven on by his gold hunger, he carried his dauntless army on into the West to his own burial beneath the waters of the Mississippi two years later.

While most historians trace De Soto's march across South Carolina along the Indian path which ran from the coast to the mountains between the Saluda and the Savannah, there are authorities who present convincing arguments that the town of the Lady of Cofitachequi was located on the Congaree River about where Columbia now stands and that his march to the mountains was up the Broad River.

Yet another seal was formally affixed to Spain's title to what is now southeastern United States by an expedition under a man bearing the fancy name of Angel de Villafane and the title of Governor of Florida. Bent on protecting his title in order to counter the persistent claims and settlement attempts of rival France, Philip II had determined to take actual possession of the region and to this end the expedition of Villafane set out from Vera Cruz, Mexico, in the spring of 1561. The governor was to select suitable locations for the settlements ordered by the king. By June, with a force greatly reduced by heavy desertions which occurred when he touched at Havana (even then apparently a seductive place), he successively entered the likely-looking river estuaries of the Carolinas. After stopping at Santa Elena (Saint Helena) on Port Royal Sound, he ran on up the coast past Cape Saint Romain and entered the Santee. There, by yet another formal ceremony, the region was claimed for his Spanish Majesty. But these wild regions were far from hospitable. The condition of his force rapidly became desperate and after pushing up the coast as far as Cape Hatteras he was forced to seek the settled haven of Santo Domingo.

By 1566, carrying forward the plans of their king, the Dons had planted a string of settlements from southern Florida to Saint Helena, all under the command of Don Pedro Menendez de Aviles, whose ruthless fanaticism can scarcely be matched in all the pages of history. These posts combined forts and missions to serve their dual purpose of securing the continent for his king and his God. The coast thus secured, the next step was to explore, conquer and convert the interior. But this was vastly more difficult to accomplish in these verdant, roadless wilds than had been the ventures of his fellow countrymen in the lands of the Aztecs and Incas.

Nevertheless, with the undaunted confidence of Don Quixote, he planned an expedition to discover and conquer the interior country from there to Mexico. To the accomplishment of this bold undertaking he assigned Captain Juan Pardo with an "army" composed of 125 volunteers, with orders to seek alliance with the natives, spread the gospel among the heathen and open a borderland trail all the way from Santa Elena to Zacatecas. No doubt it was with the glorious examples of Cortez and Pizarro in their minds that on November tenth, Saint Andrew's day, Captain Pardo and his equally dauntless sergeant, Hernando Boyano, at the head of their armor-clad handful of volunteers, marched forth from the palisaded safety of San Felipe to conquer a subcontinent.

Ten days later they had pressed fifty leagues northwestward into the wilderness, resting near "one of two large rivers," the extensive clearings being described as well suited to maize and grapes. Pardo declared it a splendid land "in which to plant a chief town." The distance and his direction of travel would put him on the banks of the Congaree River where the Indian trading post of later years, known as the Congarees, was located. No doubt the other large river he mentions was the Wateree, which joins the Congaree about a day's travel downstream.

To this bountiful land they were given a generous welcome by the warriors of Cofitachequi, the people of the "pearl queen" of De Soto. But this time there was no longer a dusky queen but only a hospitable village, generous with their supplies of meat and corn. However tempting it may have been to linger in this happy spot beside the full-flowing river, the magnitude of Pardo's assignment spurred him on. He stayed long enough to tell them as best he could of his God and his king and to require of them an oath of allegiance. Pressing on northward up the Broad River, he came to a place he called Tagaya, an even fairer land of "springs and Brooks." Eliciting the required oaths of allegiance along the way, he continued upstream to the foothills of the mountains and into the domain of the Essaws (Catawbas), reluctantly leaving behind "three very good crystal mines." They were very excited by these, believing that the fine quartz they had come upon were *"los diamantes."*

Pushing on over the ridges separating these Santee tributaries, they descended into the Catawba valley, probably in the neighborhood of Pleasant Gardens west of the present city of Marion. They called the place Xualla, a mountain name which has come down to us as Qualla. Here they were forced to halt, for the mountains ahead were deep in snow, and the friendly Catawbas told awesome tales of the mountain people. So arrangements were made to build a fort here on the banks of the east-flowing Catawba, "in a land as fair as there is in the best of Spain." To garrison this fort, Pardo assigned thirty of his men under his doughty Sergeant Boyano with orders to hold the frontiers against attack.

Stymied by the snowy mountain barrier, Pardo decided to head back towards the coast for the winter. So from Xualla he headed eastwardly down the Catawba and then turned southward, following approximately the Wateree-Catawba valley. Along the way he visited the great town of the Guatari (Waterees), "a rich land" ruled by two queens with "pages and ladies-in-waiting." The town was located on the river and was composed of many "good houses and round huts of earth." So pleased was Pardo with the hospitality of the Waterees and so successful were his efforts to convert these children of the wilderness that he lingered for fifteen days. To continue his missionary work, he left his own padre and four of his men when he was hastened on by news from Santa Elena of fears of French attack there. To expedite his return, he struck back over to the route he had followed coming into these parts and so came back through Tagaya and Cofitachequi. Conquistador Pardo must have been of a very different brand from his more famous fellow countrymen of the period, for his account tells of enthusiastic welcomes at each town as he revisited it. Instead of with animosity and terror, his little army was greeted by throngs bearing gifts of maize, venison, chestnuts and other delicacies. The braves were "all painted in many colors" for the occasion and would run, leap and dance in the ecstasy of their greeting.

Back at Santa Elena, the continuing apprehension at the post prevented Pardo from resuming his great undertaking until the next fall. September, 1567, finds him retracing his route of the previous year. By now he was so idolized by his Indian friends that they carried him by litter from village to village, clearing before them the route he was to pass, and opening their storerooms of maize, beans, pumpkins and chestnuts for his men.

When the captain reached Xualla again, he learned that his superb sergeant had been far from idle during the year which had elapsed since he and his thirty-man army had been left to hold the mountain frontier. By the current Spanish standards Boyano had gone magnificently beyond the call of duty! The sergeant, unlike his captain, was definitely of the Cortez-Pizarro school of conduct when dealing with the natives. But it was all clearly the fault of the aggressive-minded native leaders of the mountain tribes. Merely because Boyano had made a foray into the mountains and destroyed a town and killed a thousand Indians, one of the mountain caciques sent the sergeant a grossly disrespectful message to the effect that he was coming down and eat both the sergeant and his dog. To defend himself, Boyano was forced to muster an army of twenty of his men (re-enforced by an unspecified number of his river Indian allies) and take to the warpath. After four days' travel they reached the fortified town of the insolent one, successfully stormed the wooden palisades and burned the dwellings enclosed. According to his statistics, fifteen hundred Indians were put to the sword and burned in this glorious victory for king and God. Boyano's losses—none.

The way thus paved by such exemplary lessons, Boyano with little difficulty pushed halfway from the mountains to the Gulf of Mexico before his captain arrived at the Xualla and set out to follow him. After penetrating well into northern Alabama, Pardo realized the necessity of establishing strong points along the extended trail from Santa Elena. He therefore retraced his route, stopping here and there to construct forts and blockhouses, at each of which he left part of his group to garrison it pending his return in a few months.

Fate intervened, however, and Pardo never returned. Starvation and Indian troubles had already weakened Spain's continental settlements. The challenge of the Fleur-de-lis had meanwhile grown so strong that only with difficulty could Spain maintain even her coastal posts, and she could no longer divert any of her energies to conquering the interior.

Of the fate of the men which these expeditions had dropped here and there along the thousand-mile trail Pardo had opened, little is definitely known. Some were killed. Some drifted back down the trail when the captain failed to return. Others, including "a fifer with his wife and children," stayed and threw in their lot with their native hosts. Boyano returned to Santa Elena only to meet the richly deserved tomahawk of a neighborhood Edisto Indian who resisted his attempt to seize a withheld corn levy.

The mystery in the exploit was Pardo himself. Whence did he come? What was he like? What became of him after these expeditions? His impersonal accounts give no answer to these questions.

Across Carolina, history records: "The Spaniards passed here."

❦ ❦ ❦ ❦ ❦ 5. "A fair and spacious province"

For a full century and a half after the first Spanish galleons sailed the Carolina coasts, Spain effectively played the part of the dog in the manger with that whole vast territory extending from Virginia down to Florida. Unable really to possess herself of the inhospitable wilderness, she effectively prohibited it to all others with emphasis written in the blood of all who dared to trespass on this reserved domain. By 1570 the overextended Spanish reach had begun to fail. Another score of years and her Invincible Armada was at the bottom of the sea, the riches she had plundered from the Aztecs and Incas had been squandered in her efforts to dominate Europe, and her failing hands lost their tenuous hold on Carolina. The outposts had been pulled in to Saint Augustine. The stranded missions soon afterward faded from the scene. Spain had nothing left in the Carolina portion of Florida but bare legal title, feebly protected by threat of force and unsupported by possession. For almost another century no forest creature was startled by gunfire in all that vast land from the Carolina coast to the Mississippi. New generations of red men were born and grew to old age without knowing the fear which their ancestors had known in the days of De Soto and Boyano. For this long hiatus in threats from abroad, the Indians, had they been versed in seventeenth-century world politics, could have thanked a providential shift back from America to Europe. For more than the three decades of its extent, the Thirty Years' War and the multitude of issues involved, wracking and distracting all the leading powers, so heavily taxed their strength that their colonizing efforts slowed to a mere trickle.

But on the far side of the wide ocean, plans were being made, plans of momentous import to the unsuspecting Indians. War weariness, the Revolution, and perpetual religious strife were turning many a mind to thoughts of flight from it all. Bearing more than their full share of the suffering caused by the politico-religious strife of the times were the French Huguenots. To escape annihilation in Catholic France, many of them had fled to the refuge of Protestant England. Their plight there continued pitiful, for they were not assimilated and remained refugees in spite of the generous hospitality of many of the English, who raised large funds for their relief. Carolina, as a legal entity, at least on paper, came into being as a result of an effort to solve this seventeenth-century refugee problem. To provide a new home for these people, Charles I in 1629 granted to his attorney general, Sir Robert Heath, a charter to the territory between Virginia and Florida, naming it Carolana. The next year the *Mayflower*, of Pilgrim fame, sailed for Carolina with a shipload of Huguenots, but for some obscure reason landed them in Virginia instead.

Another generation was born and grew to middle age while the rivers of Carolina felt no burden save that of red men's cypress dugouts.

But the strength of England continued to wax, and again

plans were being made to unfurl the cross of St. George along those Carolina shores to forestall any return of the far-flung Maltese Cross. Oliver Cromwell and his Roundheads were out and the Stuarts were back. Rewards were now due those who had prepared the way for their return. To meet some of these obligations in the face of an empty treasury, the proposal was made to Charles II that generous grants of the American Spanish domain might serve the dual purpose of satisfying the claims of his supporters and extending the frontier of the rising empire.

Among the throngs who had claims upon the bounty of the king were Edward Hyde, Earl of Clarendon, who had turned from his early espousal of the Parliament party to support the return of Charles II and to sponsor the "Clarendon Code" for the persecution of dissenters; George Monck, Duke of Albemarle, distinguished general under Cromwell, who turned his powerful coat at the right time; William, Lord Craven, and John, first Baron Berkeley, of unswerving loyalty to the House of Stuart; Anthony Ashley Cooper, Earl of Shaftesbury, brilliant, liberal father of that fundamental of personal liberty, the *Habeas Corpus Act;* Sir George Carteret, who, as governor of the Isle of Jersey, made it the last stronghold of the Stuarts during the Revolution; Sir John Colleton of the Barbados, who had given liberally of his fortune in the Stuart cause and with whom the idea of the Carolina charter originated; and Sir William Berkeley, the colorful governor of Virginia, who had attempted to hold that colony for the Stuarts during the Revolution and had invited Charles II to seek asylum there. So it came to pass that by royal charter in 1663 these eight noblemen became the absolute owners, as far as England was concerned, of a territory of imperial dimensions embracing a wide strip of North America from the coast of Georgia and Carolina across the continent to the Pacific Ocean. Plans for colonization and development were immediately begun.

From the beginning the versatile Shaftesbury played a leading part in planning. He engaged his protégé, the renowned Whig philosopher, John Locke, to prepare a fundamental constitution for the projected colony. The amazing document he produced is a classic illustration of how very conservative, by twentieth-century standards, was the thinking of the liberal of the seventeenth century. On the liberal side there were provisions for complete religious freedom for all except such as deny the existence of God and provisions for a popularly elected Assembly to represent the people. On the other hand, "that we may avoid erecting a numerous democracy" an elaborate system of colonial nobility was established. The colonial lords were to carry the title of landgrave, while the knights were given the title customarily given the native Indian headmen, caciques. To these noblemen, baronies of twelve thousand acres were to be allotted to be worked by serfs, known as leetmen. "All children of leetmen shall be leetmen, and so to all generations." The representatives of the proprietors together with these noblemen were constituted the Council or upper house with veto power over the Assembly. For, as Shaftesbury wrote later to the young colony, "for men without estates to make laws for men of estates is as bad as a state of war." And while even slaves were guaranteed complete freedom in their choice of religion, the master was given "absolute authority over his negro slaves, of what opinion or religion soever."

Planted in the provisions of the Fundamental Constitutions, side by side, were seeds that were to blossom into the future glory of Carolina and seeds of the malignant growth that was to be the curse of the region for generations. From the nobility established by the document stemmed the brilliant aristocracy which was to dominate South Carolina for the next two centuries, based upon the institution of Negro slavery which was to be the nemesis of the Entire South.

Armed with this "sacred and unalterable form and rule

of government of Carolina forever," the proprietors aggressively set about the task of securing a colonial population to utilize that paper government. The assurance of religious freedom and the alluring firsthand accounts of several recent visitors to Carolina were widely broadcast in their efforts to recruit prospective *émigrés* to the colony.

A sample of the Carolina promotion literature was Robert Horne's *Brief Description of Carolina on the Coasts of Florida, etc.*, published in 1666 following his visit to the ephemeral Barbados settlement on the Cape Fear River:

> *Carolina* is a fair and spacious Province on the Continent of *America:* so called in honour of His Sacred Majesty that now is, *Charles the Second,* whom God preserve; and His Majesty hath been pleas'd to grant the same to certain Honourable Persons, who in order to the speedy planting of the same, have granted divers privileges and advantages to such as shall transport themselves and Servants in convenient time; This Province lying so neer *Virginia,* and yet more Southward, enjoys the fertility and advantages thereof; and yet is so far distant, as to be freed from the inconstancy of the Weather, which is a great cause of the unhealthfulness thereof; also, being in the latitude of the *Barmoodoes* may expect the like healthfulness which it hath hitherto enjoy'd, and doubtless there is no Plantation that ever the *English* went upon, in all respects so good as this: for though Barmoodoes be wonderful healthy and fruitful, yet is it but a Prison to the Inhabitants, who are much streightned for want of room, and there-fore many of them are come to *Carolina,* and more intend to follow. . . . there is plenty of as rich ground as any in the world; It is a blackish mold upon a red sand, and under that a clay, but in some places is rich ground of a grayer colour, they have made Brick of the Clay, which proves very good; and Lime they have also for building. The whole Country consists of stately Woods, Groves,

Marshes and Meadows; it abounds with variety of as
brave Okes as Eye can behold, great Bodies tall and
streight from 60 to 80 foot, before there be any Boughs,
which with the little under-wood makes the Woods very
commodious to travel in, either on Horse-back or a foot.
In the barren sandy ground grow most stately *Pines,*
white and red *Cedars, Ash, Birch, Holly, Chesnut* and
Walnut-trees of great growth and very plentiful; There
are many sorts of fruit Trees, as *Vines, Medlars, Peach,*
Wild Cherries, Mulbury-Trees, and the *Silk-worm* breeding naturally on them, with many other Trees for Fruit
and for Building, for Perfume and for Medicine, for
which the *English* have no name; also several sorts of
Dying Stuff, which may prove of great advantage; The
Woods are stored with Deer and Wild Turkeys of a great
magnitude, weighing many times 50 l. a piece, and of
a more pleasant tast than in *England,* being in their
proper climate; other sorts of Beasts in the Woods that
are good for food, and also Fowls, whose names are not
known to them. . . .

The Marshes and Meadows are very large from
1500 to 3000 Acres, and upwards, and are excellent food
for Cattle, and will bear any Grain being prepared; some
Cattle both great and small, will live well all the Winter,
and keep their fat without Fodder; Hogs find so much
Mast and other Food in the Woods, that they want no
other care than a Swine-herd to keep them from running
wild. The Meadows are very proper for *Rice, Rape-seed,*
Lin-seed, &c. and may many of them be made to over-
flow at pleasure with a small charge. Here are as brave
Rivers as any in the World, stored with great abundance
of *Sturgeon, Salmon, Basse, Plaice Trout,* and *Spanish*
Mackrill, with many other most pleasant sorts of Fish,
both flat and round, for which the *English* Tongue hath
no name. Also, in the little Winter they have, abundance
of *Wild Geese, Ducks, Teals, Widgeons,* and many other
pleasant Fowl; and (as it is said before) the Rivers are
very deep and navigable above 100 miles up; also there

are wholsom springs and Rivulets. Last of all, the Air comes to be considered, which is not the least considerable to the well being of a plantation, for without a wholsom Air all other considerations avail nothing; and this is it which makes this Place so desireable, being seated in the glorious Light of Heaven brings many advantages, and His convenient distance secures them from the Inconvenience of his scortching beams. The summer is not too hot, and the Winter is very short and moderate, best agreeing with *English* Constitutions. . . .

If therefore any industrious and ingenious persons shall be willing to pertake of the Felicities of this Country, let them imbrace the first opportunity, that they may obtain the greater advantages. . . .

Such as are here tormented with much care how to get worth to gain a Livelyhood, or that with their labour can hardly get a comfortable subsistance, shall do well to go to this place, where any man what-ever, that is but willing to take moderate pains, may be assured of a most comfortable subsistance, and be in a way to raise his fortunes far beyond what he could ever hope for in *England*. . . .

If any Maid or single Woman have a desire to go over, they will think themselves in the Golden Age, when Men paid a Dowry for their Wives; for if they be but Civil, and under 50 years of Age, some honest Man or other, will purchase them for their Wives.

Those that desire further advice, or Servants that would be entertained, let them repair to *Mr. Matthew Wilkinson, Ironmonger,* at the Sign of the *Three Feathers,* in *Bishopgate-Street,* where they may be informed when the Ships will be ready, and what they must carry with them.

🌷 🌷 🌷 🌷 🌷 *6.* *"Bony conraro*
Angles"

*A*bout a dozen miles down
the coast from the South Santee mouth lies a spacious bay girt
on three sides by low-lying sea islands. Into this bay, now
known as Bull's Bay, in March of 1670 sailed two ships with
the British flag flying from the masthead in the soft spring
breeze. One of the passengers of the *Carolina,* the larger of
the two vessels, in graphic language reported to Lord Shaftesbury their reception by the Sowee (Sewee) Indians who occupied this part of the coast:

> ye Longe boate went Ashoare. . . . vpon its approach
> to ye Land few were ye natives who vpon ye Strand
> made fires & came towards vs whooping in theire own
> tone and manner making signes also where we should
> best Land, & when we came a shoare they stroaked vs
> on ye shoulders with their hands saying Bony Conraro
> Angles, knowing us to be English by our Collours (as

we supposed) we then gave them Brass rings & tobacco
at which they seemed well pleased, & into ye boate after
halfe an howre spent with ye Indians we betooke our
selves, they liked our Company soe well that they would
haue come a board with us. . . . A day or two after ye
Gouernor whom we tooke in at Barmuda with seuerall
others went a shoare to view ye Land here. Some 3
Leagues distant from the shipp carrying along with us
one of ye Eldest Indians who accosted us ye other day,
& as we drew to ye shore A good number of Indians appeared clad with deare skins haueing with them their
bows & Arrows, but our Indian calling out Appada they
withdrew & lodged theire bows and returning ran up to
ye middle in mire and watter to carry us a shoare where
when we came they gaue us ye stroaking Complimt of
ye country and brought deare skins some raw drest to
trade with us for which we gaue them knives beads &
tobacco and glad they were of ye Market. by & by came
theire women clad in their Mosse roabs bringing their
potts to boyle a kinde of thickening which they pound
& made food of, & as they order it being dryed makes a
pretty sort of bread, they brought also plenty of Hickery
nutts, a wall nut in shape, & taste onely differing in ye
thickness of the shell & smallness of ye kernell. The Gouernor & seu'all others walking a little distance from ye
water side came to ye Hutt Pallace of his Ma^{ty} of ye
place, who meeteing us took ye Gouernor on his shoulders & carryed him into ye house in token of his chearfull
Entertainment. here we had nutts & root cakes such as
their women useily make as before & watter to drink for
they use no other lickquor as I can Learne in this Coun-
trey. while we were here his Ma^{tyes} three daughters en-
tred the Pallace all in new roabs of new mosse which
they are neuer beholding to ye Taylor to trim up, with
plenty of beads of diuers Collours about their necks: I
could not imagine that ye sauages would so well deport
themselues who coming in according to their age & all
to sallute the strangers, stroaking of them.

Spring fairly bursts upon coastal Carolina in March. The soft beauty of the landscape, the tender fragrance of the surrounding forests, and the sincere hospitality of these simple natives must have filled with gladness the hearts of the sea-weary passengers after the storms, shipwrecks and frustrating delays which they had endured during the seven long months since they had hopefully set sail from England to make yet another brave attempt to establish a settlement in a land where so many before them had tragically failed.

Certainly another very potent source of encouragement for them as they first looked upon this strange land was the presence among them of the fabulous Dr. Henry Woodward, for to him this was not a strange land at all. Four years previously when a Barbadian official, Robert Sandford, was exploring the region for a suitable site for a settlement, Woodward had volunteered to remain with the natives, to learn their languages and to explore the country around the lower Carolina coast. He was adopted as a son by the cacique of one of the native tribes of the Port Royal area and soon became adept in the native tongues and accomplished in Indian diplomacy, attributes which in the years to come were to prove indispensable to the infant colony. What followed reads like a Saturday movie thriller: When the Spaniards at Saint Augustine heard of the trespassing Doctor's presence among the Carolina natives an expedition was dispatched to capture him. Their mission was successfully accomplished and Woodward was carried back to Saint Augustine a prisoner. Some time later the English buccaneer Robert Searle surprised and captured the town and released all the prisoners confined there. Searle carried Woodward to the Leeward Islands. From there he shipped out as the surgeon on a British privateer and was shipwrecked and cast upon the Island of Nevis by the same hurricane which had wrought such damage to the ships carrying the Carolina settlers. From Nevis he had the opportunity to return to Carolina by joining the passengers on the *Caro-lina*.

While the ships lay at anchor at Sewee, disturbing news was brought to William Sayle, the Bermudian who had been named governor of the projected colony. The plans had called for establishing their settlement at ill-starred Port Royal, site of an early tragic French settlement attempt and a later unsuccessful Spanish post. But before they sailed from Sewee, this determination was shaken by the arrival of the cacique of Kiawah, the headman of the Indian tribe which occupied the region around Charleston harbor. The cacique told the governor that the terrible Westos, who were reputed to be bloodthirsty cannibals, had laid waste the whole coast all the way from their villages near the Savannah River up to Kiawah. He argued that it would be a grave mistake to settle at Port Royal right under the Westo tomahawks and urged instead that the English settle at Kiawah, hoping no doubt for the assistance of the colony in keeping the Westos from his towns. That he might continue to press his invitation and to pilot the ships through the shallow coastal waters, the cacique sailed with the colonists when they left Sewee for Port Royal.

A growing realization of the vulnerability of Port Royal to both Spanish and Westo attack, a discouraging inspection of the possible sites there, and the continued urging of the determined cacique finally turned the ships back northward to the land of Kiawah; and in early April they sailed into Charleston harbor and several miles up the Ashley River to a high spot, protected by a creek on the south, which they named Albemarle Point. When they counted heads after they disembarked there were 148. If this handful was to survive in a region where so many before them had failed, fortune would have to smile upon them.

Fortune did indeed smile upon them. For more than a decade they prospered mightily. Not that they were not beset

by immediate and frequent grave problems and serious
threats to their very existence, but they were able to surmount
these difficulties capably and were thereby quickly strengthened. Before the summer was out, Dr. Woodward's Indian
friends reported an invading party of two hundred Spaniards with three hundred Indian allies a few miles away, but
these enemies were afraid to attack the settlers and their native friends. A year later the colony was involved in a war
with the neighboring Kussoes and bettered its position with
the other nearby tribes by effecting a prompt and complete
victory. The Kussoe captives were sold as slaves in the West
Indies, thereby starting a tragic trade which in the years to
come would prove well-nigh disastrous both to the Indians
and the colony.

An early frost took much of the crops, including some
cotton, which were late being planted the first year. Ice an
inch thick shocked the colony into the realization that they
were not in the tropical clime they had expected. Then followed a spring drouth which killed their plantings of provisions and indigo.

The going was rough. It was soon obvious that Carolina
was no Garden of Eden. But back home in England and especially in the British West Indian colonies, the Lords Proprietors were doing a good selling job. A steady stream of glamorous reports and descriptions of Carolina was being published
and circulated. Generous offers of land grants were being
widely publicized. And repetitive advertising, then even as
today, brought results. The catchall offerings of free fertile
land, perfect climate, wifeless men, duty-free trade, popular
government, possible colonial peerage, easy living, free transportation and, above all, freedom of religion appealed one
way or another to a wide variety of people. Consequently,
Carolina soon emerged as America's first human melting pot.
Scotchmen, Englishmen, aristocrats, bond servants, Dissenters, Quakers, criminals and husband seekers—French

Huguenots, Lutherans from the Rhineland, crowded-out Swiss, New England Puritans, expansion-seeking Barbados planters and their younger sons, and eventually the motley pirate crews, all became imbued with the conviction that Carolina was the place they wanted to be. A liberal, cultivated, international atmosphere soon pervaded the colony. The agglomeration of diverse religious sects attracted by Locke's clauses insuring religious freedom made Carolina perhaps the most tolerant spot in the whole seventeenth-century world. From the Barbadians came the slave-based plantation system that would dominate the South for almost two centuries. The Huguenots gave illustrated lessons in industrious and rapid adaptation to a strange environment. The unique architecture of Charleston is primarily a Barbadian contribution with a strong French flavor.

By 1680 the heart of the settlement had been moved down from Albemarle Point to what was then known as Oyster Point, the peninsula lying between the Ashley and Cooper rivers at their confluence, and had been named Charles Town. The town itself was laid out facing east on the Cooper River which, like the Ashley, was but a small Low Country river, very wide, however, in its seaward reaches. But a century and a quarter later through a great canal, connecting its headwaters with the Santee, the Cooper would carry the water-borne traffic between the interior and the important port city this settlement was to become. And in our day it was to come to pass that the flow of the great Santee itself would be diverted into the Cooper and flow past East Bay Street and the Battery on its way to the Atlantic, lending substantially more credence to the popular dogma of a latter-day proud Charleston that here the Ashley and the Cooper flow together to form the Atlantic Ocean.

During the next score of years after the settlement at Oyster Point, the colony surged ahead, more in power, prosperity and prestige than in population for, as the eighteenth century opened, the total white population of the colony was only about five thousand. Timber and naval stores from the forests, an active trade in Indian slaves and, most important of all, a highly profitable barter system with the natives along trade paths radiating out from Charles Town, up the river valleys, around and over the mountains, even to the waters of the Gulf of Mexico and the Mississippi, were the fountainheads of that prosperity. However, quick wealth promised by the Indian trade retarded to a serious degree the more stable prosperity that was later to flow from agriculture. The early colonial fortunes were mostly mercantile fortunes.

The prestige enjoyed by the colony was all out of proportion to its population. Its frontier position against the long-seated Spanish in Florida and the aggressive French who had begun to flow into the Mississippi, both from the North and the South, gave it a special place in the halls of empire back in England. Its mounting trade in skins, forest products, rice and slaves, coupled with a pleasing paucity of manufacturing, made it the favorite colony in London's influential halls of trade.

The ever increasing expansion which the colony was experiencing during these latter years of the century brought with it an amazing vitality. It was only this vitality, born of expansion, which made it possible for the tiny colony to survive the devastating blows which fate dealt it at this time. This concentration of calamities was ushered in by a violent smallpox epidemic in 1698 which spread out from Charles Town to the neighboring Indian tribes, almost exterminating them. While that scourge was still raging, a fire destroyed nearly half the city. An unidentified cattle disease at the same time was decimating the colonists' herds. The terror of an earthquake convinced many that the colony was damned. The smallpox epidemic had not died out before the colony was visited by its first yellow fever invasion which continued to wrack the populace through 1699 and was so devastating in its effect that but half of the colonial assembly survived. In the fall of that year one of the most violent hurricanes in history bore down on the miserable town, forcing the residents into the upper floors of their homes to escape the accompanying high seas. All the while cargo after cargo was being lost to the bands of bold pirates who had chosen the Carolina coast both as a haven and a happy hunting ground.

Truly this colony was built of heartwood, else it could not have struggled to its feet again after such trials by ordeal. The years to come and the even greater ordeals they would bring would reveal the amazing strength of those tested timbers.

❧   ❧   ❧   ❧   ❧ *7. John Lawson*

'Tis a great Misfortune that most of our Travelers, who go to this vast Continent of America, are Persons of the meaner Sort, and generally of a very slender Education; who being hired by the Merchants to trade amongst the Indians, in which Voyages they often spend several Years, are yet, at their Return, uncapable of giving any reasonable Account of what they met withal in those remote Parts; though the Country abounds with Curiosities worthy of nice Observation.

*T*his quite justified lament was penned by an educated young Yorkshireman in the prefatory remarks to the account of his eight years of travel and observation in Carolina which was dedicated to the Lords Proprietors and published in England in 1709. Although white men were regularly penetrating far into the back country long before he came on the scene, in England and even in the coastal settlements the impressions of that vast interior and its inhabitants were hazy indeed until Lawson's accounts were published under the title of *A New Voyage to Carolina; etc.*

That we may see this back country through his observant eyes and to retain the savor of the salt of his sprightly and picturesque style, which would surely be lost by paraphrasing, what follows is a brief account of his journey up the Santee-Wateree-Catawba River, largely in his own words:

> In the Year 1700, when People flocked from all Parts of the Christian World, to see the Solemnty of the Grand Jubilee at Rome, my Intention at that Time being to travel, I accidentally met with a Gentleman, who had been Abroad, and was very well acquainted with the Ways of Living in both Indies; of whom having made Inquiry concerning them, he assured me that Carolina was the best country I could go to; and, that there then lay a Ship in the Thames in which I might have my Passage. I laid hold of this Opportunity.

At length he arrived in Charles Town on a

> . . . commodious Harbor . . . being seated between two pleasant and navigable Rivers. . . . The Inhabitants, by their wise Management and Industry, have much improved the Country, which is in as thriving Circumstances at this Time as any Colony on the Continent. . . . This Colony was at first planted by a genteel Sort of People, that were well acquainted with Trade, and had either Money or Parts, to make good use of the Advantages that offered, as most of them have done, by raising themselves to great Estates. . . .
>
> They have a well disciplined Militia; their Horse are most Gentlemen and well mounted, and the best in America, and may equalize any in other Parts . . . which shows the Richness and Grandeur of this Colony. They are a Frontier, and prove such troublesome Neighbors

to the Spaniards, that they have once laid their Town of Saint Augustine in Ashes. . . . What the French got by their Attempt against South Carolina, will hardly ever be ranked amongst their Victories. . . . They are absolute Masters over the Indians, and carry so strict a Hand over such as are within the Circle of their Trade, that none does the least Injury to any of the English, but he is sent for and Punished with Death, or otherwise according to the Nature of the Fault. . . .

On December the 28th, 1700, I began my Voyage from Charles-Town . . . in a large Canoe. . . . The first place we designed for was Santee River, on which is a Colony of French Protestants. . . .

As we went up the River we heard a great Noise as if two Parties were engaged against each other; seeming exactly like small shot. When we approached nearer the Place we found it to be some Sewee Indians firing the Cane Swamps, which drives out the Game, then taking their particular Stands, kill great Quantities of both Bear, Deer, Turkies, and what wild Creatures the Parts afford.

Among the Sewees he observed:

Rum, a Liquor, now so much in use with them that they will part with the dearest Thing they have, to purchase it; and when they have got a little in their Heads, are the Impatientest Creatures living, till they have enough to make them quite drunk, and the most miserable Spectacles when they are so, some falling into the Fires, burn their Legs or Arms, contracting their Sinews, and becoming cripples all of their Lifetime. . . .

He told of the expedition that began their downfall:

They, seeing several Ships coming in, to bring the English Supplies from Old England, one chief Part of Their Cargo being for a Trade with the Indians, some of the craftiest of them had observed that the Ships came always in at one Place, which made them very confident

that Way was the exact Road to England; and could not
be far thither, esteeming the English that were among
them no better than Cheats, and thought that if they
could carry the Skins and Furs they got themselves to
England, which were inhabited with a better Sort of
People than those sent amongst them, that then they
should purchase twenty times the Value for every Pelt
they sold Abroad, in consideration of what Rates they
sold for at Home. The intended Barter was exceeding
well approved of, and after a general Consultation of the
ablest Heads amongst them, it was *nemine contradicente*
agreed upon, immediately to make an addition of their
Fleet, by building more Canoes, and those to be of the
best Sort and the biggest Size, as fit for their intended
Discovery. Some Indians were employed about making
the Canoes, others to hunting, every one to the Post he
was most fit for, all endeavors tending towards an able
Fleet and Cargo for Europe. The Affair was carried on
with a great deal of Secrecy and Expedition, so as in a
small Time they had gotten a Navy, Loading, Provisions,
and Hands, ready to set Sail, leaving only the Old, Impotent, and Minors at Home, 'til their successful Return.
The Wind presenting, they set up their Mat-Sails, and
were scarce out of Sight, when there rose a Tempest,
which it is supposed carried one Part of these Indian
Merchants by way of the other World, whilst the others
were taken up at Sea, by an English Ship, and sold for
Slaves to the Islands. The Remainder are better satisfied
with their Imbecilities in such Undertaking, nothing af-
fronting them more than to rehearse their Voyage to
England.

He enjoyed the hospitality of several French Huguenot families who had settled along the river a few years before.
    The river was in flood. Their Sewee Indian guide in a
small canoe

    ferried us in that little Vessel over Santee-River, four
    Miles and eighty-four Miles in the Woods, which the

overflowing of the Freshes, which then came down, had
made a perfect Sea of, there running an incredible Current in the River, which had cast our small Craft and us
away, had we not had this Seewee Indian with us; who
are excellent Artists in managing these small Canoes.
Santee River at this Time, (from the usual Depth of
Water), was risen perpendicular thirty-six foot. . . .

Heading on up river by the Indian path through the
Santee Indian country,

We met in our Way with an Indian Hut, where we were
entertained with a fat boiled Goose, Venison, Raccoon
and ground Nuts. . . . These Santee-Indians are a well
humored and affable people; and living near the English,
are become very tractable. They make themselves cribs
after a very curious Manner, wherein they secure their
Corn from Vermin, which are more frequent in these
warm Climates than Countries more distant from the
Sun. These pretty Fabrics are commonly supported with
eight Feet or Posts about seven Foot high from the
Ground, well daubed within and without upon Laths,
with Loom or Clay, which makes them tight and fit to
keep out the smallest Insect, there being a small Door
at the gable End, which is made of the same composition,
and to be removed at Pleasure, being no bigger than a
slender Man may creep in at, cementing the door up with
the same Earth when they take Corn out of the Crib,
and are going from home, always finding their Granaries
in the same Posture they left them: Theft to each other
being altogether unpracticed. . . . [Next night] we got
to one Scipio's Hutt, a famous Hunter.

(Elsewhere Lawson describes these huts as "miserable
holes," round, shaped like an oven, constructed of woven
sticks covered with cedar bark.)

There was no Body at Home, but . . . we made ourselves welcome to what his cabin afforded, (which is a
thing common) the Indians allowing it practicable to

the English Traders to take out of their Houses what they need in their Absence, in lieu whereof they most commonly leave some small gratuity of Tobacco, Paints, Beads, etc. We found great Store of Indian Peas (very good Pulse) Beans, Oil, Thinkapin Nuts, Corn, barbacued Peaches and Peach Bread. . . . The Wind being at N. W. with cold Weather, made us make a large Fire in the Indian's Cabin; being very intent upon our Cookery, we set the Dwelling on Fire, and with much a do put it out with the Loss of Part of the Roof.

The next Day we traveled on our Way, and about Noon came up with a settlement of Santee Indians, there being Plantations lying scattering here and there, for a great many Miles. They came out to meet us, being acquainted with one of our Company, and made us very welcome, with fat barbacued Venison, which the Woman of the Cabin took and tore in Pieces with her Teeth, so put it into a Mortar, beating it to Rags, afterwards stews it with Water, and other Ingredients, which makes a very savoury Dish. The Santee king . . . is the most absolute Indian Ruler in those Parts, although he is Head of but a small People, in Respect to some other Nations of Indians I have seen. He can put any of his People to Death that hath committed any Fault which he judges worthy of so great a Punishment.

Near to these Cabins are several Tombs made after the manner of these Indians; the largest and chieftest of them was the Sepulchre of the late Indian King of the Santees, a Man of Great Power, not only amongst his own Subjects, but dreaded by the neighboring Nations for his great Valour and Conduct. . . .

(This sepulchre was probably a large mound later known as Fort Watson which was destined to figure importantly in the Revolution.)

Lawson here describes in detail the Santees' manner of interment, in the process of which, with much formality, the flesh is rotted from the bones which are then cleaned, oiled and polished and stored away in wooden boxes, as the precious keepsakes of the descendants of the deceased.

Among the Santees he tried to employ a guide to show them across a large swamp which lay ahead:

He was the tallest Indian I ever saw, being seven Foot high, and a very straight compleat Person, esteemed by the King for his great Art in Hunting, always carrying with him an artificial Head to hunt withal. They are made of the Head of a Buck, the back Part of the Horns being scraped and hollow for Lightness of Carriage. The skin is left to the setting on of the Shoulders, which is lined all around with small Hoops, and flat Sort of Laths, to hold it open for the Arm to go in. They have a Way to preserve the Eyes, as if living. The Hunter puts on a Match-coat made of Deer's Skin, with the Hair on. . . . In these Habiliments an Indian will go as near a Deer as he pleases, the exact Motions and Behaviour of a Deer being so well counterfeited. . . .

About five miles farther they

. . . came to three more Indian Cabins . . . being pleasantly seated on a high Bank, by a Branch of Santee-River. One of our Company that had traded amongst these Indians told us, that one of the Cabins was his Father's-in-law; he called him so by Reason the old Man had given him a young Indian Girl that was his Daughter, to lie with him, make Bread, and to be necessary in what she was capable to assist him in, during his Abode amongst them.

About where the Wateree and Congaree join they were welcomed by

a great many Santees . . . showing a great deal of Joy at our coming, giving us barbacued Turkeys, Bear's Oil and Venison. Here we hired Santee Jack (a good Hunter, and a well humored Fellow) to be our Pilot to the Congaree Indians.

Next day they

> . . . came to the most amazing Prospect I had seen since I had been in Carolina; we traveled by a Swamp-side which Swamp I believe to be no less than twenty miles over, the other side being as far as I could discern, there appearing great Ridges of Mountains [Richland Red Hills]. . . . These Mountains were clothed all over with Trees which seemed very large timbers.

Elsewhere the trees are described as being so lofty that turkeys alighting in their tops could not be shot from the ground.

> Viewing the land here, we found an extraordinary rich black mould, and some of a copper-colour. . . . When we were all asleep in the Beginning of the Night, we were awakened by the dismalist and most hideous Noise that ever pierced my Ears. . . . But our Indian Pilot acquainted us, that it was customary to hear Music along that Swamp side, there being endless Numbers of Panthers, Tygers, Wolves, and other Beasts of prey, which take this Swamp for their Abode in Day, coming in whole Droves to hunt the Deer in the Night, making this frightful Ditty til Day appears, then all is still as in other Places.
>
> The next Day . . . the Indian killed fifteen Turkeys . . . there coming out of the Swamp (about sun-rising), Flocks of these Fowl, containing several hundred in a Gang, who feed upon Acorns, it being most Oak that grow in these Woods.

Next day they passed

> . . . several fair Savannas, very rich and dry. . . . Hard by the Savannas we found the (Congaree) Town, where we halted; there was not above one Man left with the

Women, the rest being gone Hunting for the Feast. The Women were very busily engaged in Gaming. . . . Their Arithmetick was kept with a Heap of Indian Grain. When their Play was ended, the King, or Cheffetta's Wife, invited us to her Cabin. The Indian Kings always entertaining Travelers, either English or Indian; taking it as a great Affront, if they pass by their Cabins and take up their Quarters at any other Indian's House.

These Indians are small People, having lost much of their former Numbers, by intestine Broils, but most by Small-pox, which hath often visited them, sweeping away whole Towns. . . . These Congarees have abundance of Storks and Cranes in their Savannas. They take them before they can fly, and breed them as tame and familiar as a Dung-hill-Fowl. . . . These are very Comely Sort of Indians . . . the Women here being handsome as most I have met withal, being several fine figured Brownettos amongst them. These Lasses stick not upon Hand long, for they marry when very young, as at twelve or fourteen Years of Age. The English Traders are seldom without an Indian Female for his Bed-fellow, alleging these Reasons as sufficient to allow of such Familiarity. First, They being remote from any white People, that it preserves their Friendship with the Heathens, they esteeming a white Man's Child much above one of their getting, the Indian Misses ever securing her white Friend Provisions whilst he stays amongst them. And lastly, This Correspondence makes them learn the Indian Tongue much sooner, they being of the Frenchman's Opinion, how that an English Wife teaches her Husband more English in one Night than a School-Master can in a Week.

A few days more travel and Lawson's party was in the region of the lower Catawba, in what is now Lancaster County, South Carolina. Here he visited the Wateree Chickanee Indians. Thirty years previously the Pennsylvania Dutch explorer, John Lederer, had visited the Waterees and was greatly impressed by the absolute authority of the tribe's cacique. At the time of his visit, this ruler had just sent three of his warriors to a neighboring tribe to kill several young maidens, so that his son, who had recently died, might have these maidens to serve him in the next world.

A century before that it was the Waterees who impressed Juan Pardo above all the people he visited. At that time these people were ruled by two queens. These cacicas with their court of pages and ladies-in-waiting were highly praised by the widely traveled Don. By Lawson's time they seem to have sadly degenerated. He calls them

> . . . lazy, idle People, a Quality incident to most Indians, but none to that Degree as these . . . and great Pilferers, stealing from us any Thing they could lay their Hands on.

Their cabins were

> . . . dark smoky Holes as ever I saw any Indians dwell in.
>
> Bidding our Wateree King adieu, we set forth towards the Waxhaws, going along cleared Ground all the Way. Upon our Arrival, we were led into a very large and lightsome Cabin. . . . They laid Furs and Deer-Skins upon Cane Benches for us to sit or lie upon, bringing (immediately), stewed Peaches, and green Corn, that is preserved in their Cabins before it is ripe. . . .
>
> These Indians are of extraordinary Stature, and called by their Neighbors flat Heads, which seems a very suitable Name for them. In their Infancy, their Nurses lay the Back-part of their Childrens' Heads on a Bag of Sand. They use a Roll which is placed upon the Babe's Forehead, it being laid with its Back on a flat Board, and swaddled hard down thereon, from one End of this Engine to the other. This Method makes the Child's Body and Limbs as straight as an Arrow. . . . [This treatment renders] the Child's Head flat: it makes the Eyes stand

a Prodigious Way asunder, and the Hair hang over the Forehead like the Eves of a House, which seems very frightful. They being asked the Reason why they practiced this method, replied, the Indian's sight was much strengthened and quicker thereby to discern the Game in hunting at a larger Distance. . . .

Lawson then gives us a sort of Kinsey report on the native American women of 1700.

The Girls at twelve or thirteen Years of Age, as Nature prompts them freely bestow their Maidenheads on some Youth about the same Age, continuing her Favors on whom she most affects, changing her Mate very often . . . until she hath tried the Vigor of most of the Nation she belongs to. Multiplicity of Gallants never being a stain to a Female's Reputation, or the least Hindrance to her Advancement. . . . When a Man and Woman have gone their Degrees (there being a certain Graduation amongst them,) and are allowed to be House-Keepers, which is not till they arrive at such an Age, and have passed the Ceremonies practiced by their Nation, almost all Kingdoms differing in the Progress thereof, then it is that the Man makes his Addresses to some one of these thoroughpaced Girls or other, whom he likes best. When she is won the Parents of both Parties (with the Advice of the King) agree about the Matter, making a Promise of their Daughter to the Man that requires her, it often happening that they converse and travel together for several Moons before the Marriage is published openly. After this, at the least Dislike, the Man may turn her away, and take another, or if she disapproves of his Company, a price is set upon her, and if the Man that seeks to get her, will pay the fine to her Husband, she becomes free from him; Likewise some of their War Captains, and great Men, very often will retain three or four Girls at a time for their own use, when at the same time he is so impotent and old, as to be incapable of making Use of one of them, so that he seldom misses of wearing greater Horns than the Game he kills. The Husband is never so enraged as to put his Adultress to Death; if she is caught in the Fact, the Rival becomes Debtor to the cornuted Husband, in a certain quantity of Trifles, valuable amongst them, which he pays as soon as discharged and then all Animosity is laid aside betwixt the Husband and his Wife's Gallant. . . .

They set apart the youngest and prettiest Faces for trading Girls; these are remarkable by their Hair, having a particular Tonsure. . . . They are mercenary, and whoever makes use of them, first hires them, the greatest share of the Gain going to the King's Purse, who is the chief Bawd, exercising his Prerogative over all the Stews of his Nation, and his own Cabin (very often) being the chiefest Brothel-House. . . .

The first day that we came amongst them (the Waxhaws), arrived an Ambassador from the King of Sapona, to treat with these Indians about some important Affairs. He was painted with Vermilion all over his Face, having a very large Cutlass stuck in his Girdle, and a Fusee in his Hand. At Night the Revels began. . . . These Revels are carried on in a House made for that purpose, it being done round with white Benches of fine Canes, joining along the Wall; and a Place for the Door being left, which was so low that a Man must stoop very much to enter therein. This Edifice resembles a large Hay-Rick, its top being Pyramidal, and much bigger than their other Dwellings. . . . All their Dwelling-Houses are covered with Bark, but this differs very much; for it is very artificially thatched with Sedge and Rushes. In these State-Houses is transacted all Public and Private business relating to the Affairs of Government. . . .

The House is as dark as a Dungeon, and as hot as one of the Dutch-Stoves in Holland. They made a circular Fire of split Canes in the Middle of the House. . . . They brought in a great Store of Loblolly and other Medleys, made of Indian Grain, stewed Peaches, Bear-

Venison, etc., everyone bringing some Offering to enlarge the Banquet, according to his Degree and Quality. When all the Viands were brought in, the first Figure began with kicking out of the Dogs, which are seemingly Wolves, made tame with starving and beating; they being the worst Dog-Masters in the World. . . .

After the Dogs had fled the Room, the Company was summoned by Beat of Drum; the Music being made of a dressed Deer's-Skin, tied hard upon an Earthen Porridge-Pot. Presently in came five Men dressed up with Feathers, their Faces being covered with Vizards made of Gourds; round their Ancles and Knees were hung Bells of several sorts; having Wooden Falchions in their Hands, (such as Stage-Fencers commonly use); in this Dress they danced about an Hour, showing many strange Gestures, and brandishing their Wooden Weapons as if they were going to fight each other . . . turning their Bodies, Arms, and Legs, into such frightful Postures, that you would have guessed they had been quite raving mad; At last, they cut two or three high Capers and left the Room. In their stead came in a parcel of Women and Girls, to the Number of Thirty odd . . . with these they made a circular Dance, like a Ring representing the Shape of the Fire they danced about. Many of these had great Horse Bells about their Legs and small Hawk Bells about their Necks. They had Musicians, who were two Old Men, one of whom beat a Drum, while the other rattled with a Gourd that had corn in it to make a Noise withal. To these instruments they both sang a mournful Ditty; the Burthen of their Song was, in Remembrance of their former Greatness. . . .

Their way of dancing is nothing but a sort of stamping Motion, much like the treading upon Founder's Bellows. This Female-Gang held their Dance for above six Hours, being all of them of a white Lather, like a Running Horse, that has just come in from his Race. . . . During this Dancing the Spectators do not neglect their Business in working the Loblolly-Pots, and the other

Meat that was brought thither; more or less of them being continually Eating, whilst the others were Dancing. When the Dancing was ended, every Youth that was so disposed, catched hold of the Girl he liked best, and took her that Night for his Bed-Fellow, making as short Courtship and expeditious Weddings as the Foot-Guards used to do with the Trulls in Salisbury-Court.

After leaving the Waxhaw towns, Lawson passed through the settlements of the Sugarees in the neighborhood of where Charlotte now stands and then visited the populous Catawba towns located along the Catawba River up to its great bend. From there he crossed over into the Yadkin valley and headed eastward to the Coast. There he settled and was eventually appointed surveyor-general.

It was in performing his official duties that he aroused the suspicions of the Tuscaroras, who made him a captive while he was out on a surveying expedition. Venting upon him the wrath they felt towards the colonists' inexorable westward encroachments from their seaside settlements, they condemned him to a horrible death by having a multitude of fat pine splinters driven into all parts of his body and set afire. Thus John Lawson, friend and sympathetic chronicler of the Indians, joined that select group of immortals of history who have died by the violent hands of the people they loved.

❧ ❧ ❧ ❧ ❧ *8. The Carolina*

traders

To the quiet streets of Charles Town the first warm breezes of spring bring an accompaniment of color—color in the elegant gardens of the export merchants and those of the town houses of the planters and even to the modest little side gardens in the humble but artistic small homes of the clerks and artisans. For the better part of the first century of the city's life, to the abundant color of natural beauty was added a vivid accent of a different sort, animate color, mirroring the port city's picturesque economic life.

In the spacious harbor to the east and north of White Point at the foot of East Bay Street, a varied array of masted vessels ride at anchor. Here and there among and beyond them, sails full blown, with swanlike grace glide ships full laden toward the open sea or inward bound with cargoes of manufactured goods and a full listing of hopeful immigrants crowding the deck for those precious first glimpses of their

new home. Among the larger vessels weave the peragios of the merchants and Indian traders, some manned by slave crews of shining ebony, and others poled along by crews of shining copper. The smaller craft, some dragged half up on the muddy banks, fringed with marsh grass, and others navigating seemingly at random in the waters close to shore, for the most part are dugout cypress canoes—Indian designed, and laboriously Indian built, but here serving a variety of uses for a colorful variety of people.

Here and there along East Bay and Broad Streets, tethered in tight semicircles about the hitching posts, stand groups of weary, rough-coated little horses, their galled backs proclaiming them as fresh arrivals from the back country, perhaps from the Waxhaws, or the Cherokees, or the Creeks, or even from the faraway Choctaws or Chickasaws six hundred miles to the west.

Along these dung-littered, sandy streets, among the saddle horses and carts of the town's everyday traffic, tinkle the bridle bells on the lead horse of a trader's pack train, heavy laden with coarse cloth, blankets, axes, hoes, trading guns, bullets, powder, rum, and a miscellany of cheap but fancy merchandise, heading out to the north to the forks of the trading paths, and thence to some faraway, luxury-hungry (and thirsty) Indian nation, where in the months to come these goods will become currency for the trader's purchases of deerskins.

Seen less frequently than the tinkling pack trains, but still common enough to attract little notice are the silent files of Indian burdeners, as their moccasined tread passes along the narrow sidewalks to their employers' warehouses to collect the few yards of bright-colored cloth that would be their pay for carrying those bulky packs weighing a hundred pounds or more along the rough two-hundred-mile trail between the Cherokee Hills and the city.

Grudgingly opening a way for the burdeners to pass are

groups clustered about and thus marking certain doorways here and there along the street as the doors of taverns or of the merchants' offices, or perhaps those of the offices of the Colonial Indian Agent or the Indian Commissioners, from whom the traders' licenses are secured.

Here are buckskin-clad, coonskin-capped traders and drivers, venting at last their store of the tales of their experiences since they were last in town, of the disturbing temper of some French-affected Indian nation, or of a treaty consummated with a remote petty cacique, or perhaps recounting the rumors concerning a fellow trader who has disappeared from the scene. Here are headmen of the Catawbas, the Cherokees and the Creeks, turned out in flamboyant matchcoats saved especially for this occasion, injecting in broken English their own comments on the traders' tales. Here are the slovenly half-breeds in cheap but garish trade garments. And here are the townbound loafers, merchants' clerks and the sailors from the ships in the harbor, drinking their fill of the entertainment offered in the tales of those just in from the back country. Behind the tavern doors many of the traders and drivers are already well on their way to recklessly spending their recklessly earned profits of the past season's operations. In the merchants' shops and warehouses, others are going over their accounts or arranging for the loading of their waiting pack trains. Behind the office doors of the Colonial Indian Agent and the Commissioners, others are arranging for the reissue of their trading licenses. It is the requirement that their licenses be renewed annually at this season that has brought this back-country carnival to the port town.

But more important than any of these are the talks going on behind the more elegant closed doors of the Province House. Here matters of portentous significance to the colony and even to the Empire are being discussed—a new trade treaty with some faraway tribe which the French are wooing; reports on the military garrisons at Mobile and Pensacola, of enemy penetrations into the Carolina trading domain or even of a military deputation for some of the more influential Indian leaders, in order to entice them into the English camp.

To all this add the parading and drilling of the colonial militia resplendent in their scarlet coats—parading to impress the back-country visitors with the English strength and drilling for the war which is ever either in progress or impending.

Those were the spring colors of eighteenth-century Charles Town, fed into the little port town of three or four thousand people down the coast from the North Carolina settlements and the villages of the Tuscaroras and Cape Fears through the Waccamas and Winyahs across the Santee delta and down the Cooper River; from the Virginia Path in the Catawba towns down the Catawba-Wateree River across the sand hills to the Congarees and down the edge of the wide Santee swamps to the great bend of the Santee and thence through the intervening savannas and pine flats to the town; from the magnificent alpine domain of the Cherokees down the Saluda to the Congarees and thence down the great path to the sea; or, from the Choctaws and Chickasaws, across the Georgia red hills of the Creeks, to join another Cherokee Path, near the present Augusta, and thence eastward across the Edisto River to the seaside colonial Mecca. Nowhere else in America was there anything comparable happening in a port city, for nowhere else was there a native-held back country of comparable extent, since from Carolina northward the Appalachians limited the colonial influence to the west.

Appropriately enough it was the colorful Dr. Henry Woodward who planted the first seeds from which this color grew. When the infant colony at Albemarle Point was but a few months old and its grip upon this new land was tenuous indeed, the intrepid Dr. Woodward was already dreaming dreams of empire. And the Doctor was not one of those who stopped with dreaming. Wondering what might lie beyond the setting sun, a contemporary had asked: "If the Porch be so

beautiful, what must the Temple be?" The dauntless Woodward determined to see for himself during that same first summer. Heading inward to the northwest, in a fortnight he was
in "that fruitfull Provence where the Emperour resides . . .
a Country soe delitious, pleasant and fruitfull, that were it
cultivated doubtless it would prove a second Paradize." Students have placed this land he described at about the confluence of the Congaree and Wateree rivers.

Setting the pattern by which the colony was to accomplish its westward expansion in the generations to follow, he
"contracted a league with the Empr. and all those Petty Cas-
sekas betwixt us and them." So excited was the Doctor about
this discovery that he hastened back to the settlement with
the determination to take the news of it back to England, but
the colonial authorities were so dependent upon his intelligence and experience that they prevailed upon him to stay
with the colony until he could be better spared.

During the next quarter century, the trails which Woodward blazed, both across the alien terrain and in the realm of
diplomacy, were to be the great avenues, leading to the rap-
prochement of a great portion of southeastern United States
to the little village on the bay. Hundreds of intrepid—now
mostly nameless—trader-explorers kept pushing farther and
farther into the hinterland, becoming, as they saw the fair
lands they crossed, more and more imbued with the Doctor's
vision of the imperial destiny of the frontier colony, seeing it
as the keystone in the worldwide struggle for power among
the English, Spanish, and French. By 1698, the whole colony
had so embraced his conviction of its manifest destiny that
the people of South Carolina were "greatly alarmed" at the
rumored intentions of the French to settle along the Mississippi. That country belonged to Carolina, and the audacious
handful of Carolinians on the distant coast expected to possess it in fact and hold it against all comers.

Seizing the torch which Woodward had lighted was

Landgrave Joseph Blake, colonial nobleman, a Lord Proprietor, twice provincial governor, aggressive Indian trader himself and, above all, a man of exceptional ability and vision. The fires, storms and pestilences which occurred during his administration, and his untimely death in 1700, prevented him from actually accomplishing much in the direction of physically securing the vast domain he claimed for Carolina, but he permanently imbued the whole colony with the conviction that they were no longer trespassers in Spanish territory but rather, if the Spanish dared settle on the Gulf Coast or the French on the Mississippi, they would be trespassers in Carolina.

Thomas Nairne was a Scotchman. Price Hughes was a Welshman. Both were Carolinians. And it is only owing to the undeserved neglect of the stage upon which they played their thrilling parts that they are not counted as great Carolinians and even placed high among the nation's founders.

While the armies of Prince Eugene of Austria and the Duke of Marlborough were endlessly contending with those of Louis XIV, and mere acres were being bought with blood along a front extending across Europe from Flanders to the Adriatic Sea (all to determine who should be the next king of Spain), the fate of a vast, incredibly rich empire in America hung in balance, and back there in distracted Europe no one seemed to care much which way the balance was tipped. Such moves as were made from abroad during Queen Anne's War, as the War of the Spanish Succession was known in America, were weak and indecisive. The Spanish prepared Saint Augustine and the newly established post at Pensacola against possible attack. The French strengthened their outposts at Biloxi and Mobile and established a new one at New Orleans. The Lords Proprietors of Carolina did nothing.

Even before the beginning of the European phase of the war, the rivalry among the three powers for dominance of the

Southeast had already waxed so warm that the fiction of peace between the mother countries was completely ignored in their North American colonies. Iberville and Bienville on the French Gulf Coast and the Carolina traders were realists. They clearly saw what was at stake. Iberville planned to direct French expansion eastward from Louisiana "au côte de Caroline" and plotted with the Spanish to accomplish this. The Carolinians attempted to forestall the concerted action against them by attacking Saint Augustine in hopes of completely destroying it. By 1704 the European war was on, the Spanish had orders for the "extermination of those enemies and the capture of Carolina," and the French agreed that "the Carolina settlements must be destroyed."

The almost total English neglect of its threatened frontier colony forced upon Carolina an unparalleled self-reliance. With no outside help forthcoming, if the colony was to survive and at the same time hold for England virtually a subcontinent, it would require the skill and devotion of many leaders of extraordinary ability and energy. The rigorous schooling of the Indian trade was unsurpassed as a training medium for such frontier leaders. Thus from among the traders spontaneously sprang the military and diplomatic leaders who were so essential in this crisis. Although bypassed by fame and now all but forgotten, the traders included many a notable figure. By the sum of their efforts and sacrifices an empire was secured for the English. Rarely if ever has any group so small and so obscure exerted such a profound influence on the history of our nation. Outstanding among this colorful group of early frontiersmen are Nairne and Hughes.

Nairne's name begins to appear in the colonial annals about 1698. Soon he is mentioned as a prominent planter and Indian trader. His success in the latter field was based upon his scrupulous honesty, his respect for the Indians' rights, and his quite modern principles of merchandising.

How entwined was the frontier diplomacy with its mercantile life is illustrated by his observation that "the English trade for Cloath alwayes atracts and maintains the obedience and friendship of the Indians, they Effect them most who sell best cheap." Of the colony's customers he observed that "every body knows well wee have the greatest quantity of Indians Subject to this Government of any in all America, and almost as many as all other English Governments put together."

In 1702 and again in 1704 Nairne was with another notable trader-leader, Colonel James Moore, who was leading a large band of friendly Indians against the Spanish-dominated Apalaches near Pensacola. Another three years and his bold imagination and decisive acts had so enhanced the government's confidence in him that he was named sole Colonial Indian Agent. The following year, 1708, he formulated one of the most amazing and brilliant documents of colonial American history. In it he demonstrated his complete understanding of the implications of the then pending struggle of the three great powers for the American interior. He presented detailed plans for the protection of the trade routes between the tidewater capital and the Mississippi and beyond. Moreover, it appears that he clearly realized that, since the Proprietors apparently were going to do little or nothing about these momentous matters, the colony should turn towards the crown and transform Carolina into a royal colony like most of its American neighbors.

In the same year he is found in the realm of action among the French Choctaws in the present state of Mississippi, risking his life in an effort to convert them into English allies. Back again in Charles Town, he is clapped into jail, charged with treason because of his activities against the governor, Sir Nathaniel Johnson, and his unconscionable son-in-law, Thomas Broughton (of Mulberry Castle fame), both of whom were among the less reputable of the Indian traders and persistent violators of the laws prohibiting the enslaving of friendly Indians. By the end of the year his complaints to the Proprietors had brought about the Governor's removal. The next year finds him back in England, trying to build support for his views on the importance of Carolina and its western reaches in the whole American picture. One of those he convinced and recruited for the battle for the great American interior was Price Hughes, a Welsh gentleman of wealth, imagination and boundless daring.

Back in America, Nairne's difficulties with Johnson and his imprisonment had already seriously reacted against the colony's welfare. That clever French diplomat, Bienville, from his seat at Mobile was alienating one after another of the Western tribes. And this was happening just as the North Carolina coastal settlements were calling for help to prevent their extermination by the fierce Tuscaroras under their ruthless King Hancock, in the uprising which had ironically claimed their true friend, John Lawson, as its first victim. The ready response elicited by this plea for help required two campaigns by the South Carolina colonial militia with a large number of recruits from the still friendly neighboring Yamassees and Catawbas.

Even while these campaigns to the north were taxing the strength of the Carolina settlements, such was the vitality of the colony that far to the south and west, in the region of the Gulf and beyond the mountains, the Carolina emissaries and traders were strenuously engaged in rebuilding their damaged diplomatic and trade fences—matching wits and goods with the encroaching French. Here in 1712 we find that adventurous spirit, Price Hughes, following into the setting sun the visions he had imbibed from his friend Nairne. Upon his enthusiasm for the country into which adventure had attracted him, he began to build plans for a new British province in the lower Mississippi valley. The next year found him among the Cherokees, sending down to Governor Craven reports on the French efforts to alienate these mountain people.

A little later he was in the present Kentucky, sending emissaries to Indian nations beyond the Mississippi, seeking to divert the French fur trade, to channel it with the great peltry trade out through Charles Town, and to close the Mississippi to the French to prevent the increasingly tight encirclement which the French were welding around the seaboard English settlements.

Soon he is back in Charles Town, communicating with friends back home in the interest of getting financial support and settlers for the settlements he was planning beyond the mountains. He is trying to reach the Queen through the Duchess of Ormonde, wife of one of the court favorites. He urged immediate "possessing ourselves of those vacant parts of this Province; which they [the French] will otherwise so soon be Masters off." He even foresaw English expansion west of the great river, proposing for this middle region province the "name of Annarea in honour of her Majesty through whose bounty 'twill I hope be settled."

Back in the West again this fabulous "Master You," in the native parlance, was fast gaining both the unbounded admiration and the hostile fear of his French adversaries. With the traders he was establishing new "factories" (trading stations) and making new and firmer treaties with the Indians, even with many of those traditionally under French domination, from the Illinois to the Gulf. New life had been infused into the Carolina expansionists. In the spring of 1714, through his inspiration an army of some two thousand Alabamas, Talapoosas and Chickasaws led by a dozen whites descended on the Choctaws, not to destroy but rather to impose peace and trade with the English. By June he was back in Charles Town with a party of Chickasaw chiefs who had traveled the hundreds of miles to ratify their new treaty. Winter found him back with the Natchez on the Mississippi, still weaving his fantastic web of intrigue and alliances. His successes were driving the French to desperation. His immediate arrest was ordered. But they dared not attempt to seize "my-lord anglais" while he was among his adoring Indian friends. Consequently the arresting party had to bide their time, shadow him for hundreds of miles down the river, and finally capture him by surprise.

Indignant and protesting, he was delivered to Bienville at Mobile. For three days in the stockade there these representatives of rival powers talked. Bienville asked Hughes why he had been going among their Indians with gifts and anti-French talk. Hughes's reply was that all this country belonged to the English, that they had a better claim to it than the French, and that by the next autumn five hundred English families would be settled on the Mississippi.

However, by one of those sudden turns of fate the confident optimism of Hughes was followed by his tragic death. Soon after being released from French custody, on his way back alone to Carolina, Hughes was waylaid and killed by some dissident Tohome Indians, bitter against the English because of slave raids against them in the past.

Suddenly there was trouble on every hand. Nation after nation quickly turned coat. The fierce Yamassees, near neighbors to the English settlements, had for some time been showing signs of discontent with the rum, cheating, and enslavements by unscrupulous traders, which complaints were, no doubt, magnified and encouraged by the Spanish at Saint Augustine. Nairne, who was then the Yamassee Agent, hearing from another trader who had been tipped off by a kindly Yamassee of the plans of his people for a surprise attack on the colony, hastened to the Yamassee chief town to attempt a reconciliation. He was warmly received. A great party was given in his honor. Confidently he accepted the hospitality of the town house for the night. According to a contemporary account

. . . the next day, which was Good Friday, they heard at day break the terrible war cry and at first appearing a great multitude whose faces and other parts of the body were painted in red and black rays, which made them resemble as much as possible, devils coming out of Hell. They jumped at first upon the agents, seized their houses and property, fired upon all sorts of persons without distinction, and killed a great many by torture in the most cruel fashion in the world of those who had escaped being shot.

Among those tortured in such fashion, by lighted splinters driven into the flesh all over the body, was their honest friend Thomas Nairne, another innocent victim of prejudice against a race.

Within a few days it was obvious that the uprising was general. The Creeks from the distant West, the Cherokees from the mountains and the Siouans from along the rivers were on the warpath too. They swept down on the rich Santee plantations, killing or driving out all the whites. From their concert of action it was apparent that at last it had dawned upon the Indians that those who had settled in this land as their welcome guests had in the lapse of half a century become their hated masters. But this realization had come too late. Already the Indians were but a fraction of their former numbers. Already they were too dependent on the whites to be unanimously against them, and already the colony's strength was formidable. So, after dreadful losses both in life and property, and after a year and a half of frightful warfare, the decimated Yamassees pulled up stakes and moved southward to creep in under the protection of the Spanish wing. The Cherokees had switched sides and the Catawbas and their kindred nations had surrendered, never again to go on the warpath against the white men.

With these interruptions finally surmounted, the larger struggle for domination of the Western empire was resumed, the Indians as always being the pitiful pawns. That great struggle was to become even more desperate after it was learned that the relatively unconcerned ambassadors across the ocean had by the Treaty of Utrecht left for later determination the boundary question between the English and the French in the far interior of Carolina, thus stimulating each contender to redouble its efforts to gain the advantage of actual possession of the disputed territory. Partly with the intent to gain more assistance in this international struggle, the colony staged English America's first revolution, replacing the Proprietary government with a royal colonial government. And to get a better grip on the interior, plans were made for the establishment of towns along the great rivers, among them being two on the Santee and one on the Wateree. Only with their settling after 1730, did the English, other than through the far-ranging traders, and the Indians under their influence, actually begin to take possession of the great back country which the influence of the traders had reserved for them for some seventy-five years.

❦ ❦ ❦ ❦ ❦ 9. The challenge of the Jolly Roger

Even before the first settlement at Charles Town, the broad bay with its tricky protecting bars was well known to the notorious Henry Morgan as a safe retreat. Morgan, one of the most notorious pirates in all history, had been so successful in that highly competitive calling that he had in time become admiral of the buccaneers, Governor of Jamaica and, finally, Sir Henry Morgan, in recognition of his genius for ridding the world of a large number of the more enterprising Spaniards at a time when it was a cardinal tenet of English faith to hate a Spaniard as roundly as the devil himself.

The establishment of the settlement there appears to have been no deterrent to him to continue to use it as a place of refuge. Beginning with his eminent example, the harbor and town were freely used in the Morgan tradition for the first quarter century of the colony. Pirate gold proved a far more powerful influence than the government. All too fre-

quently the government itself was deeply involved in the ne-
farious enterprises. If prosecutions were undertaken during
the weak but repeated efforts to rid the colony of pirate stains,
they came to naught through corruption either of the officials
or of the juries themselves with the pirates' ill-gotten gold.
The unsavory reputation which flowed from such shameless
conduct brought a stream of admonitions and reprimands
from the Proprietors and the Crown, all of which had little
effect. Charles Town soon was completely overrun by brigands in bright sashes and bandannas, flocking into town from
every quarter. As their number and power increased, their
confidence of immunity from apprehension and prosecution
in the colony bred an unbearable arrogance. Public indignation finally rose to the boiling point. Happily, this aroused
sense of the infamy of the situation coincided with the admin-
istrations of two honest and capable governors, Joseph Blake
and Quaker John Archdale. The colonists' righteous indignation mounted during the closing years of the seventeenth century, when the advent of rice culture, a staple crop which had
to be exported, made the colony's welfare dependent upon
the safe passage of the ships carrying its economic lifeblood.
The high value of these cargoes made them particularly
tempting to the buccaneers; while the intercepting of their
cargoes by the pirates immediately evoked an ire against
those former friends that no number of outrages against the
shipping of others had been able to inspire.

In 1699 a bumper rice crop, a critical shortage of bottoms for its export, and the seizure of several of these by pirates operating just beyond the harbor bar served as the spark
which exploded the mounting resentment into positive action. The motley rabble of English, French, Portuguese and
Indians that made up the brigand crew became involved in a
quarrel over the spoils, resulting in the English being set
adrift by the others in a long boat. After great hardships the
marooned segment of the crew finally made shore at Sewee

Bay and from there made their way down the coast to Charles Town where they posed as the honest victims of an honest shipwreck. Unfortunately for them, however, the masters of some of the ships they had recently plundered recognized them and gave the lie to their cleverly concocted tales. As soon as their identity was thus revealed, they were apprehended, tried for piracy and condemned. Shortly thereafter, seven of the nine of them were hanging from the gallows which had been deliberately constructed in full view of the entire harbor on the island then known as Shute's Folly (now known as Castle Pinckney), there to dangle for weeks, as grisly warnings to all pirate guests that whatever may have been the past tolerance of Carolinians, it would henceforth be indiscreet indeed to molest Carolina cargoes.

By this time the blood-chilling black flags of the daring buccaneers had become so numerous along all the shipping lanes of the wide Atlantic that nowhere was there safety for peaceful commerce. The pirate hordes had become an unbearable burden to the economic life of the commercial nations. For maritime England the situation threatened disaster. Expediency rather than integrity dominated the steps taken at the turn of the century to remedy the intolerable situation. In March, 1701, King William proclaimed an act of grace, offering pardons for all piracies committed prior to June 4, 1701, if the pirates surrendered and took the oath of allegiance. Not a few old families of the Carolina coast owe their establishment to this act of grace, the region being familiar and attractive to many a buccaneer, including several henchmen of Captain Kidd, who elected to take the absolving oath and settle here in what had been a tolerant clime, redolent with pleasant memories of many a shore leave in the good old days.

The Archdale and Blake period of decent government and these other developments had finally shaken the freebooters' hold on the colony, and the pendulum of sentiment swung far the other way. Apathetic tolerance soon gave way to aggressive pirate hunting. From then on until the strength of the colony was too sorely taxed by the exertions and devastations of the Tuscarora and Yamassee wars, pirates were given short shrift in Carolina. Sometimes with scarcely the formality of a trial, pirate after pirate was silhouetted against the sunrise as it lighted the sky beyond Shute's Folly. A year or two of such receptions and even the boldest buccaneers had taken the morbid hint and were giving wide berth to the colony and its shipping.

This satisfactory state of affairs prevailed until a combination of events suddenly brought a terrible resurgence of the pirate menace. The Treaty of Utrecht in 1712, ending Queen Anne's War, threw numerous privateers out of work. Relatively few of them disbanded their hardy crews and retired from the sea-raiding game. Instead, most of them secured for themselves death's-head pennants and continued in business in a less discriminate way. The Atlantic shipping lanes swarmed with them. Unfortunately, at just this time the Carolina colonies were engaged in a life-and-death struggle, beginning with the Tuscarora rising in the winter of 1712 and continuing on for several years through the Yamassee war. With their defenders away from home on the frontiers in the interior and their resources taxed to exhaustion, the Carolinians lay utterly defenseless from the sea side. The pirates were quick to take advantage of this situation. The almost unsettled inlets of the North Carolina coast became popular buccaneer havens, and from these vantage points they preyed constantly and devastatingly upon the reduced but now even more essential colonial shipping.

Desperately the suffering Carolinians petitioned the Proprietors for help in their distress. The fruit of their petition was the following:

> We, the Proprietors of Carolina, having met on this
> Melancholy occasion, to our great grief, find we are ut-
> terly unable of ourselves to afford our colony suitable
> assistance in this conjuncture, and unless his Majesty will
> graciously please to interpose, we can forsee nothing but
> the utter destruction of his Majesty's faithful subjects in
> those parts.

The House of Commons, on being petitioned, asked the
King to send relief to the colony. The King referred the matter
to the Lords Commissioners of Trade and Plantations. The
Commissioners decided that the government could do nothing unless the Proprietors relinquished the title of the colony
to the Crown. This the Proprietors refused to do. Thus, because of political involvements three thousand miles away,
the highly important, isolated frontier colony, threatened
with destruction from both land and sea, was left to face its
overwhelming odds with its own resources.

Despite these discouragements and the apparent hopelessness of their situation, the Carolinians carried on the fight
with the inspiration and leadership of another able governor,
Robert Johnson. The despoilers of the *Turtle Dove,* the *Pe-
nelope* and the *Virgin Queen* were sent to the gallows.

But still the pirate menace continued. By the end of 1717
the situation had become too critical for the Crown to continue to support inaction. Another act of grace was proclaimed, by George I, promising a general pardon to all who
would surrender. This time, however, there was little response
from the pirates grown too dominant to fear the alternative to
surrender.

The name "Blackbeard" had long chilled the blood of
honest seafarers. That accomplished brigand, whose real
name was Edward Thatch or Teach, had become a terrible
legend even while he lived. In 1717, from his base in Ocra-
coke Inlet, North Carolina, he made himself the special

scourge of the Charles Town shipping. When Governor Johnson reluctantly but dutifully published King George's offer of pardon, Thatch decided to take advantage of it to retire from his lucrative business. Proceeding to his North Carolina retreat and there disbanding his crew, he surrendered at Bath to that high-placed accomplice of the Carolina pirates, Governor Eden, and took the oath of allegiance.

Shore life quickly proved much too dull for Blackbeard, however, and before the arrival of spring, 1718, he was at sea again, harrying shipping southward from his home port all the way to Central America. There, in the Bay of Honduras, while on the lookout for Spanish shipping, he met and made a partnership with one of the most enigmatic of all the buccaneers of history, one Stede Bonnet, who had newly entered the buccaneering business.

Stede Bonnet, until the previous summer, had been a distinguished, highly respected retired army major of Bridgetown in the Barbados. He was well born, well educated and wealthy. As old age approached, he grew bored with the quiet life of the little colonial city. His yearning for excitement finally possessed him and, despite the fact that he had no knowledge of the sea, he purchased a fine ship, which for some inexplicable reason he christened *The Revenge*, equipped it lavishly, employed a crew, and sailed from home to go "a-pirating." After harrying the shipping of the English colonies, including Charles Town, he sailed southward across the Gulf of Mexico, where he ran in with Thatch.

In company the two headed back toward the Carolina retreats. By the time they arrived off Charles Town, they had a fleet of four powerfully armed vessels with a crew of more than four hundred men, the additional ships and crewmen having been recruited from the many captured along the way. They anchored just beyond the bar and, spiderlike, awaited their prey. For several days, every vessel sailing out of the harbor was captured and plundered. By this time the pirate leaders were reckless with success and contemptuous of the strength of the war-torn little colony. In need of medical supplies for his fleet, Thatch boldly determined to secure his needs from the city. Among his prisoners from the captured ships was a particularly distinguished citizen of the province, Samuel Wragg, a member of the Governor's Council—a circumstance highly useful for the pirate's plan. Accordingly a letter was addressed to Governor Johnson, with a requisition for the desired supplies to be delivered over within two days—a demand re-enforced by the threat that any delay in meeting the request or any harm befalling the pirate messenger or crew would be punished by death for the unfortunate Wragg and his fellow prisoners from Charles Town and the delivery of their heads to the Governor. A pirate lieutenant by the name of Richards and a prisoner, Mr. Marks, were provided with a small armed craft for the delivery of Blackbeard's ultimatum.

Among the prisoners in the ship's hold, who had been informed of the plan, anxiety steadily mounted as the allotted two days dragged by with no news from the pirate emissaries. Wragg, summoned by Thatch and told to warn the miserable prisoners to prepare for death, made an impassioned plea for more time and persuaded Thatch to allow a reprieve of one day. One day was enough, for it brought a timely message from Marks that the undue delay was occasioned by an accident in which their boat had been overturned by a squall on its way to the city. As this explanation satisfied the pirate, the prisoners were allowed to come up from the holds to keep their anxious watch upon the western horizon for the craft that might mean their deliverance.

The third day passed with no further news. Losing patience, Thatch swore immediate death for all the prisoners. In a desperate play for time the condemned men proposed a bargain, offering, should proof be received that Richards and his crew had been arrested by the authorities, to pilot the brigand fleet into the harbor and assist in destroying the town. The very possibility of wreaking such a vengeance upon the colony apparently appealed to Blackbeard, for a further stay of the executions was granted.

Meanwhile, back in Charles Town, overwhelming consternation prevailed both in government circles and among the people. The city was so sorely beset by its unhappy quandary that prompt, direct action became impossible. From the beginning it was obvious that the town was completely helpless to defend itself against the might of the fleet of Thatch and Bonnet. There were few fighting men and no fighting ships near enough to be of the slightest assistance. Capitulation to the forces of evil, however, was too foreign to a man of Governor Johnson's integrity for him to yield to grim necessity without the support of his Council, who were called for a further time-consuming conference.

While the authorities were desperately wrestling with their dilemma, Richards and his men were having a glorious time rubbing salt into the city's wounds. They paraded up and down the streets of the town. Their behavior to all they met was grossly insulting. Only through the miraculous restraint of the citizenry was a fatal incident avoided.

Finally, the inevitable decision was faced that the pirate demands must be met. The medicines were prepared without further delay and delivered to Marks for transfer to the pirate fleet beyond the bar. True to his word, as soon as the delivery was made, Blackbeard allowed the prisoners to be put ashore, relieved to be sure of every possession, down to most of the clothing on their backs. Eventually, after many hardships, they made their way back to the city, across the marshes, creeks, and the river, while Blackbeard, Bonnet and company set sail for their North Carolina resort at Topsail Inlet.

At Topsail Inlet, where the company was disbanded, Bonnet was at last able to resume command of his old ship,

The Revenge—for even before the medicine affair in Charlestown Harbor, Blackbeard, in contempt for the nautical ignorance of the gentleman novice, had deposed Bonnet as captain of his own ship and reduced him to a minor post on the
veteran buccaneer's own vessel. Now, free from the grip of
the Pirate King, Bonnet was on his own!

Just at this time war was again officially resumed between England and Spain. This circumstance and the continuing opportunity to obtain a pardon under the Act of Grace
presented Bonnet with a providential opportunity to fulfill his
pirating yen within the cloak of legal sanction. Leaving his
men to refit *The Revenge*, he hastened to Bath, where he formally surrendered to Governor Eden and obtained his legal
absolution and clearance papers for *The Revenge* for Saint
Thomas, ostensibly to obtain a commission to privateer
against the Spanish. Not since Morgan and Kidd had in turn
personally received the royal blessings of Charles and William had a pirate set out under better auspices. Fair stood
the wind, but a tragic fate pursued him. Skilled now in the
ways of the sea and the derring-do of the buccaneer, the lure
of the black flag was too strong for him. Calling himself Captain Thomas, and his ship the *Royal James*, in honor of the
pretender to the British throne, the gentleman pirate returned to plunder, terrorizing the whole coast as far north as
Delaware Bay.

By the summer of 1718 the Indian wars had at last been
brought to a close. Thus when the news reached Charles
Town that Bonnet (or Thomas) was again off the bar in the
Royal James, there was general determination that the time
had arrived to rid the colony forever of the pirate menace.
Adopting the modern conception that attack is the best defense, the colonists decided to go after the pirates rather than
await them. Colonel William Rhett, a colonial official of wealth
and distinction, volunteered to lead the expedition.

Two merchant ships, the *Sea Nymph* and the *Henry,*

then in the harbor, were pressed into service and armed between them with sixteen cannon and 130 men. By the middle of September preparations had been completed and they had sailed out of the harbor on their hazardous mission. The next week was wasted in futile pursuit of pirates Vane and Yeates, who had just previously taken several outbound merchantmen and had been fighting between themselves over the spoils. A few days later, realizing that he was being sought by both pirates and the authorities, Yeates and fifteen of his crew surrendered themselves and a cargo of captured Negro slaves—in return for a certificate of pardon.

Meanwhile Rhett had pursued Bonnet to his lair in the Cape Fear region. There, after a long and bloody battle, he succeeded in capturing him and the survivors of his decimated crew.

Several days later, "to the great joy of the whole Province," over the bar into Charles Town harbor sailed five ships: the *Henry,* followed by the *Sea Nymph,* the *Royal James,* the *Fortune,* and the *Francis,* the latter two being prizes rescued from Bonnet's retreat. As there was no jail in the town then, the thirty-odd survivors of the buccaneer crew were put under military guard and lodged in the public watchhouse. However, for Major Bonnet, a gentleman born, no such indignity was considered. To the aristocratic colonial authorities a man's origin overshadowed his destination. Bonnet was placed under guard in the town marshal's own house, to be joined there two days later by two of his officers who had agreed to give evidence for the Crown.

Three days before the day appointed for the trial, the city was startled by the news that Bonnet and his lieutenant had escaped. The circumstances surrounding their escape gave off a heavy stench of pirate gold. Unquestionably Bonnet had considerable outside help and the whole thing appeared to have been a well-planned and well-oiled plot. Steps were immediately taken to recapture the escapees. "Hue and cry expresses by land and water" were sent throughout the province. Bonnet, joined by friends with a boat, was heading toward his North Carolina haunts, when unfavorable weather forced his party back to seek refuge on Sullivan's Island. There, after ten days of freedom, the pirate was recaptured by Rhett and brought back to closer confinement.

Two days later, after trial and conviction, all but four of Bonnet's crew were hanged at White Point and their bodies buried in the mud below the low tide mark, a spot now well within the city since the landfills of later years.

In another two days gentleman Stede Bonnet himself was arraigned before the learned, austere Judge Nicholas Trott to answer for his many crimes. When the long trial was over and the prisoner, archcriminal though he was, had borne himself with dignity and courtesy, the jury brought in the inevitable verdict and Judge Trott passed sentence in terms characteristic of the tyrannical jurist he was. That the wayward devil might take no comfort in the prospect of the death to which he had been condemned, the Chief Justice painted in frightful detail, well documented by the authorities, the horrors of eternal punishment:

> Consider (said he) that death is not the only punishment due to murderers, for they are threatened to have their part in the lake which burneth with fire and brimstone, which is the second death . . . words which carry that terror with them, that considering your circumstances and your guilt, surely the sound of them must make you tremble, for who can dwell with everlasting burnings?

Perhaps it was this terrifying prospect or perhaps it was a desperate bid for sympathy which might soften his fate that transformed the courageous Bonnet into a miserable figure begging for clemency as the execution date drew near. It is said that he appealed to Colonel Rhett's magnanimity with such success that Rhett offered to take him to England to the

home courts, should the colonial authorities be willing to release him in his custody. To Governor Johnson the old Barbados soldier penned a pleading masterpiece of hypocrisy. In
vain. A few days later he joined his crew.

Many people entertained a fear that the aggressive anti-
pirate policy which the colony had adopted would bring
upon it swift and terrible retaliation. Even while Bonnet was
a prisoner awaiting execution it appeared that these fears
were justified, as the town was thrown into panic by news
that the notorious Moody was off the bar in command of a
ship of fifty guns—a fire power far exceeding any of the town's
defenses.

Again attack appeared to be the only hope of defense.
As a disagreement had arisen between Colonel Rhett and
Governor Johnson, the Governor himself took command of
the proposed expedition. Preparations were made to secure a
fleet with fire power exceeding that of Moody's ship. The
Royal James, which had been renamed the *Revenge*, the *Sea
Nymph* and two others selected from among the score of merchantmen then in the harbor were equipped with guns concealed between decks. A crew was secured, mostly from the
visiting ships, by offering a share of the anticipated booty to
each volunteer.

Early in November, 1718, they sailed out of the harbor,
with crews and guns concealed to give the appearance of a
group of unsuspecting merchantmen. The deception was perfect. The two pirate ships which lay in wait immediately
hoisted anchor and gave chase, raising the black flag as they
got close enough to shout their surrender demands. The reply
of the intended victims was a broadside from the suddenly-
unveiled guns of the masqueraders, as the King's colors were
run up the mastheads. From the hatches poured the heavily
armed crews to add the fire of their small arms. Before the
buccaneers could recover from their surprise and man their

posts, the Carolinians had the upper hand and were soon in hot pursuit, two vessels attacking each pirate craft. After a short but violent battle, as the smaller pirate ship was about to be boarded, most of the crew sought safety below decks, leaving only the captain and a handful of the more stout-hearted to put up a desperate resistance to the boarding party, fighting until all were killed or disabled, while those below deck surrendered.

Meanwhile Governor Johnson with the other two Carolina ships had pursued the larger pirate ship, a pursuit which lasted for several hours as the buccaneers bent every effort toward escape, even throwing overboard their guns to lighten the ship. In vain, for they were finally overtaken and captured.

When the victors boarded the surrendered ship, it was their turn to be surprised, for their opponent of the day had not been Moody, who, forewarned, had discreetly slipped away, but the no less notorious Richard Worley, unsuspectingly anchored in Moody's plunder post. Only this providential substitution of enemies made the masquerade ruse successful. An even greater surprise for the victors lay in the cargo of one of the captured vessels. When the hatches were opened it was discovered that the hold was crowded with women. The ship was the *Eagle,* which, while carrying a cargo of convicts and covenant servants from London to Virginia, had been captured by Worley. Partly from the crew, and partly from the cargo, a pirate crew had been recruited; while the others were held prisoners in the ship's hold.

Before the month was out, all the captured pirates had been duly tried and received death sentences. The spoils of the expedition, including the *Eagle's* human cargo, were sold at public auction, that the proceeds might be divided among the participants in the expedition. As to what became of these miserable white slaves no record remains.

Of tangible reminders of the Carolina pirates there are none. No statues were erected to them. No headstones mark their graves. The ships they sailed and the ships they sank lie, coral-encrusted, under the waves of a concealing sea. Beneath the subtle elegance of some Charleston mansion or its artistic, wall-ensconced garden lie the bones of Bonnet and his hard-bitten crew. An integral part of the earth beneath the half-finished fortifications of Castle Pinckney is the chemical remnant of numerous other brigands who found there the *Ultima Thule* of their sea roving under the skull and crossbones.

Nevertheless, the Carolina pirates, even today, are more than just a glamorous chapter in the story of days long past. Unintentionally, they played their part and made their contribution of permanence to the life stream of Carolina and the nation. There is little doubt that during the "guest period," those early days of the weak colony when Charles Town verged close to being a pirate capital, it was the constant presence of those reckless fighters and their heavily armed ships that kept the Spanish from exterminating the trespassing Carolinians. By way of return: A prayer for your poor souls, brave buccaneers!

Also, thanks is due those desperadoes for the contribution they made to the development of the colony when they became resurgent after the close of Queen Anne's War. As desperate appeals for assistance addressed to the Lords Proprietors brought only excuses and confessions of impotence, colonial sentiment crystallized into a conviction that the colony required royal protection. Royal protection meant farewell to the rule of the Lords Proprietors. Thus, after all it was the pirates who precipitated that first American revolution, immediately after the eventful year of Blackbeard, Bonnet, Moody and Worley.

❦ ❦ ❦ ❦ ❦ *10. The French*
Huguenots

*H*igh on a lonely bluff above
a desolate stretch of river is a granite cross marking the site
of the long-abandoned village of James-town. Here on the
south side of the Santee, north of Hell Hole Swamp, about
thirty miles above the river's mouth, once stood the village
church, the heart of the community and the symbol of the
religious faith—a faith which inspired a courageous band of
French refugees to push their cypress canoes up an unknown
river far into the Indian country and to establish there a
haven of freedom.

To this place they had come as the flotsam of a wave of
merciless persecution which had swept over France for two
hundred years, reaching its crest in the revocation of the
Edict of Nantes in 1685. Many of these homeless French
Huguenots had found temporary shelter in Holland and
England, and it was 1689 before they set foot on the high
banks of the Santee.

THE FRENCH HUGUENOTS

A long trail of time and tears led from the pastoral scenes of the mild rivers of France to the wild and somber beauty of the Santee Swamp, which they dared to choose as their home. A deep and sluggish river flowed between forest walls of oak and cypress, inhabited only by wild animals and widely separated villages of Santee Indians, who claimed this trackless domain. It was only the fact that these people were the heartwood, who had survived the ordeal of fire endured by them and their forebears for generations, which would make possible in a few years the transformation of this remote forest wilderness into a garden spot unequaled in America. It was this tough-fibred heartwood which was to give, down through the years and even to this day, to the life stream of Carolina much of its glory.

As we read over the *Liste Des François* from an old naturalization document, their melodious French names echo like a song down through the history of Carolina: Laurens, Prioleau, Ravenel, and Huger; Horry, St. Julien, Mazyck, Marion and Manigault; Du Bose, Porcher, Gaillard, and Sinkler; Gervais, Guignard, Peyre, and Motte; Myrant, Poinsett, Rembert and Simons; and many, many others.

For a memorable picture of the hardships endured by the French settlers during the early years on the Santee, the best possible description is given by one of them in the following letter translated from the French—a letter written to her brother by Judith Manigault, a twenty-year-old refugee:

Since you desire it, I will give you an account of our quitting France, and of our arrival in Carolina. During eight months, we had suffered from the contributions and the quartering of the soldiers, with many other inconveniences. We therefore resolved on quitting France by night, leaving the soldiers in their beds, and abandoning the house with its furniture. . . . We made the best of our way for Metz, in Lorraine, where we embarked on the river Moselle, in order to go to Treves. . . . We passed on to Holland, to go from thence to England. I do not recollect exactly the year, whether '84 or '85, but it was that in which King Charles of England died [Feb. 1685]. We remained in London three months, waiting for a passage to Carolina. Having embarked, we were sadly off: the spotted fever made its appearance on board our vessel, of which disease many died, and among them our aged mother. Nine months elapsed before our arrival in Carolina. We touched at two ports— one a Portuguese, and the other an island called Bermuda, belonging to the English, to refit our vessel, which had been much injured in a storm. Our Captain having committed some misdemeanor, was put in prison and the vessel seized. Our money was all spent, and it was with great difficulty we procured passage in another vessel. After our arrival in Carolina, we suffered every kind of evil. In about eighteen months our elder brother, unaccustomed to the hard labor we had to undergo, died of a fever. Since leaving France we had experienced every kind of affliction—disease—famine— pestilence—poverty—hard labor. I have been for six months together without tasting bread, working the ground like a slave; and I have even passed three or four years without always having it when I wanted it. God has done great things for us, enabling us to bear up under so many trials. I should never have done, were I to attempt to detail to you all our adventures. Let it suffice that God has had compassion on me, and changed my fate to a more happy one, for which glory be unto him.

In another account she tells how with her husband she grubbed the land, helped fell the trees, and operated the whipsaw. This was the price of conquering the subtropical wilderness. Arduous was the struggle, but firm was the foundation laid in the rich Santee soil. From this soil, the seven-year-old son Judith left at her death in 1711 was, in later years, to reap a golden harvest. This son, Gabriel Manigault, became one of the three richest men in America, and was able to lend the Revolutionary cause $200,000, most of which was never repaid.

Judith's experiences were not too far from typical of the whole French Santee community, for the results of their industry, resourcefulness, and resilience are shown by John Lawson's account of a visit to James-town a bare decade after its founding:

> As we rowed up the River we found the Land towards the Mouth, and for about sixteen Miles up it, scarce any thing but Swamp and Percoarson, affording vast Ciprus-Trees, of which the French make Canoes that will carry fifty or sixty Barrels. After the Tree is moulded and dug they saw them in two pieces and so put a Plank between, and a small Keel, to preserve them from the Oyster-Banks, which are innumerable in the Creeks and Bays betwixt the French Settlement and Charles-Town. They carry two Masts and Bermuda sails, which makes them very handy and fit for their Purpose; for although their River fetches its first Rise from the Mountains and continues a Current some hundreds of Miles ere it disgorges itself, having no sound, bay, or Sand-Banks betwixt the Mouth thereof and the Ocean, Notwithstanding all this, with the vast stream it affords at all Seasons, and the repeated Freshes it so often alarms the Inhabitants with, by laying under Water great Part of their Country, yet the Mouth is barred, affoarding not above four or five Foot Water at the Entrance.

> There being a strong current in Santee-River, caused us to make a small Way with our Oars. With hard Rowing, we got that Night to Mons. Eugee's [Huger] house which stands about fifteen Miles up the River, being the first Christian dwelling we met withal in that Settlement, and were very courteously received by him and his Wife. Many of the French follow a Trade with the Indians, living very conveniently for that Interest. There is about

seventy Families seated on this River, who live as decently and happily as any Planters in these Southward Parts of America. The French being a temperate, industrious People, some of them bringing very little of Effects, yet by their Endeavors and mutual Assistance amongst themselves (which is highly to be commended), have outstripped our English, who brought with them larger Fortunes, though as it seems less endeavor to manage their Talent to the best Advantage.

We lay all that Night at Mons. Eugee's, and the next Morning set out farther, to go the Remainder of our Voyage by Land. . . . At noon we came up with several French Plantations, meeting with several Creeks by the Way, the French were very officious in assisting with their small Dories to pass over these Waters, (whom we met coming from their Church), being all of them clean and decent in their Apparel; their Houses and Plantations suitable in Neatness and Contrivance. They are all of the same Opinion with the Church of Geneva, there being no difference amongst them concerning the Punctilios of their Christian Faith; which Union hath propagated a happy and delightful Concord in all other Matters throughout the whole Neighborhood; living amongst themselves as one Tribe or Kindred, every one making it his Business to be Assistant to the Wants of his Countryman, preserving his Estate and Reputation with the same Exactness and Concern as he does his own; all seeming to share in the Misfortunes, and rejoice at the Advance and Rise, of their Brethren.

Towards the Afternoon we came to Mons. L'Jandro [Gendron], where we got our Dinner; there coming some French Ladies whilst we were there, who were lately come from England, and Mons. L'Grand, a worthy Norman, who hath been a great Sufferer in his Estate by the Persecution in France, against those of the Protestant Religion. This gentleman very kindly invited us to make our Stay with him all Night, but we being intended farther that Day, took our Leaves, returning acknowledgements of their Favors.

About four in the afternoon we passed over a large Ciprus run in a small canoe. The French Doctor sent his Negro to guide us over the Head of a large Swamp, so we got that Night to Mons. Galliar's [Gaillard] the elder, who lives in a very curious contrived house, built of Brick and Stone, which is gotten near that Place. Near here comes in the Road from Charles-Town, and the rest of the English Settlement, it being a very good Way by Land, and not above thirty-six Miles, although more than one hundred by Water; and I think the most difficult Way I ever saw, occasioned by reason of the Multitude of Creeks lying along the Main, keeping their Course through the Marshes, turning and winding like a Labyrinth, having the Tide of Ebb and Flood twenty Times in less than three Leagues' going.

[The river was in flood, causing the] Woods to seem like some great Lake, except here and there was a Knoll of high Land which appeared above the Water.

When we got to the House we found our Comrades [who had been accidentally separated from them] and several of the French Inhabitants, who treated us very courteously, wondering at our indertaking such a Voyage, through a Country inhabited by none but Savages, and them of so different Nations and Tongues.

After we had refreshed ourselves, we parted from a very kind, loving, and affable People, who wished us a safe and prosperous Voyage.

From these beginnings, until the Revolution there flowered up and down the lower Santee a society the grace and elegance of which were perhaps unsurpassed in America. The early farmhouses were replaced with plantation mansions amid fertile fields of indigo and rice. The French planters rapidly amassed fortunes in Negro slaves. In St.

Stephen's Parish alone, which included but a small portion of the Santee swamp, the entire population of five thousand resided in the swamp itself, a region now totally abandoned and given back to the forest. Here a close-knit, cultured aristocracy lived out its day. Their way of life as described in contemporary accounts matches the most idealized and glamorous descriptions of the Old South, replete with lavish entertainments lasting for days, centering around weddings, balls, and race meets, where their blooded horses competed on the plantation race courses.

The golden era of the lower or "French" Santee was brought abruptly to a close by the combined effects of the devastation of the Revolution and a series of unprecedented floods, which soon followed the clearing of the piedmont hills with the great mass migration to them. The termination of the British indigo bounty with American independence and the flood menace sent many of the Huguenot families down the river to cultivate rice on its tidewater reaches, while others moved upstream to "English" Santee, where the floods were less severe. In both these sections there was a post-Revolutionary reflowering of the earlier glory.

When the Revolution broke over the land, their happy condition and their gratitude to England made many of the Huguenots reluctant to join the rebel ranks, and they, for the first time, became a house divided. Even so, from among them came an extraordinary number of outstanding rebel leaders. There was Henry Laurens, President of the first Provincial Congress and President of the Continental Congress, General Benjamin Huger, whose home was the first to receive Lafayette on his arrival in America, General Isaac Huger, colonels John Laurens and Peter Horry, the inimitable General Francis Marion, and a substantial portion of his daring partisan band.

The Huguenot house-divided is illustrated by the tragic

account of the betrayal of Peter Sinkler of Lifeland Plantation. Like so many others of the early Huguenots, he had little opportunity for formal education, but character, industry and outstanding success had made him an influential member of the Santee River planter society. He had commenced life as a penniless orphan and as a young man had gone daily to his fields with his hoecake and ax, but through the years had risen to great prosperity. He was one of the first to join Marion's band and was soon an object of special search by the British. Like others of Marion's Brigade he returned occasionally to his plantation. There he had a place of concealment in the nearby swamp to which he retired when danger threatened. On one of these visits, through the treachery of his brother-in-law who resided with him, when the alarm of an approaching British unit drove him to his usual hiding place he found himself surrounded by the enemy. Taken captive, he was obliged to witness the destruction of almost everything on his rich plantation, even to the furnishings of his home. Among many other things the enemy destroyed twenty thousand pounds of indigo and three thousand bushels of grain; while fifty-five slaves, forty-four blooded horses, 130 head of stock cattle, 150 head of sheep, 200 hogs and $10,000 worth of poultry were carried off. After this ordeal, Peter Sinkler, denied even a farewell interview with his wife and children, was taken to a crowded dungeon cell in Charlestown, where he soon died of typhus. For his services in this treacherous capture the brother-in-law, James Boisseau, was rewarded with a British commission.

Happier was the case of Sinkler's neighbor, Peter Gaillard. First a neutral and later a Tory officer, during which service, in his only engagement, he suffered defeat at the hands of Marion's men at Black Mingo, he later became convinced of the superior virtue of the patriot cause and gave up his British commission and sought membership in Marion's Brigade. Under Marion he proved himself a brave and brilliant partisan officer.

After the war he acquired the Rocks Plantation on the Santee near Eutaw Springs. There he became the first successful large-scale cotton planter, a venture which at first almost ruined him but eventually rewarded him with a sufficient fortune for him to parcel out plantations among his eight children.

The Rocks was destined to become one of the numerous Huguenot plantations of what had been known as "English Santee"—occupying the area now flooded by Lake Marion and that around Eutaw Springs. There, centering about Belvidere, Eutaw, Walworth, Numertia, Pond Bluff, Lawson Pond, Springfield and Mount Pleasant plantations, the French plantation society flowered again with a grace and splendor matching that of its early blossoming farther down the river.

Although the French Huguenots never numbered more than one tenth of the white population of the province, their relative contribution to the development of the entire South is unequaled by that of any other single group. They came to seek religious freedom and to earn their livelihood by producing wine, olive oil and silk; they remained to adopt the religion and language of their English compatriots, and to become founders and leaders in the colonial culture of indigo, rice and cotton, in the raising of fine horses and stock, and in brokerage and moneylending. Their cultural influence further liberalized a colony already the most liberal in America. It has been truly said of them that they were "an aristocracy not of wealth alone but of character and of intellect."

The examples they set on their Santee plantations tremendously affected the agricultural development of the entire South. Their ingenuity and resourcefulness resulted in such trail-blazing inventions as the rice pounding machine of Peter Jacob Guerrard, and later rice manufacturing machines invented by Peter Villeponteux and other French planters. Further stimulation to rice production was given by the revolutionary development of the water culture system by Gideon Du Pont.

When indigo culture was introduced into the Province by Eliza Lucas, its success was in large measure due to her French Protestant assistant, Andrew Deveaux, who became the prime authority on indigo culture and preparation throughout the colony. After him Thomas Mellichamp, a prominent French planter, greatly advanced the manufacture of indigo dye by his inventions.

In the field of printing and journalism the Huguenots were pre-eminent in the colony. Most notable of these was the Timothy (Timothée) family; Lewis Timothy made the *South Carolina Gazette* the first permanent newspaper in the province, and Peter Timothy, his son, carried on to become one of the country's most influential journalists of the Revolutionary period and of the critical years that followed.

Similarly, the Huguenots were leaders in the founding of the first fire insurance company in America: The Friendly Society.

It was also a Huguenot, William Mellichamp, who initiated the first large-scale salt-producing plant in the lower South, a public service of great importance in the economy of the colony.

In addition to their obvious economic significance, the French Protestants made a golden contribution to the spiritual and cultural life of South Carolina in their courageous moral character, their Christian benevolence (they were active in most of the contemporary philanthropic societies, their wills are notable for gifts to the needy, and there was never an uncared-for pauper among their group), and their gift for gracious and abundant living. Long, long ago they left the banks of the Santee and Cooper Rivers, their first home; with a few exceptions, their plantations are no more. Through the region once blossoming with the cherished farms and gardens of the French, the great river flows now by desolate swamp and lonely forest; but the influence of the Huguenots remains a vital presence in the life stream of Carolina and the South.

❀   ❀   ❀   ❀   ❀   *11. Carolina*
golden rice

*I*n sight of the maple-hued
expanse of the lower Santee, a dozen miles from its mouth,
stand the truncated remains of a giant cypress, surrounded
by curiously shaped, rootlike growths, called "breathers" or
"cypress knees." Sixty feet above the knee-studded ground a
few lateral branches, heavily draped with long pendants of
gray moss, still carry their delicate fernlike foliage, bearing
alone the whole burden of providing sun life to the great
mass of their supporting trunk. The old giant owes its survival through the recent timber-hungry centuries to the
fact that its heartwood had rotted away and the timber that
could be got from its hollow shell was not worth the great
task of felling it. And, because most of the time-telling annual rings that once filled the ten feet of its diameter are
gone, its age can only be estimated by comparison with cypresses of similar size, whose soundness invited the loggers'
saw. No doubt it was sometime during the period when Eu-

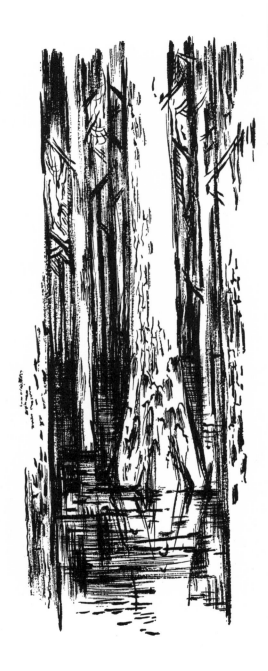

rope was vegetating under the paralyzing dark blanket of the Middle Ages that the tiny seed from which it grew spun to a likely spot and became the one in several million of the seeds of its long-gone parent which sprouted and survived its first dangerous years.

Through all the centuries during which it grew from seedling to sapling and finally to its ultimate equivalent of a ten-story building, had this old riverside dweller had eyes, few humans would it have seen—an occasional canoe, paddled by naked red men, sometimes a group of them passing en route to or from the seacoast for salt, sting ray spines, sharks' teeth and sea shells, now and then being beached in its shadow for an overnight camp on the nearby bluff. Less frequently, men and fire had appeared together, working together to drive and corral the wild creatures of the forest into the natural trap of the boggy swamp in which it stood That was all for half a millennium.

But, still supposing the old tree had eyes, as the seventeenth century waned it would have seen more and more of those canoes fashioned from its more perfect brethren of the Santee swamps; but now they are manned by men of other colors. To the red are added white and black—the propelling being done by the red or the black. As time went on less and less red and more and more black.

They passed and passed, upstream and downstream. Then, one day there were those who didn't pass. They pulled their craft in close by the old tree, carried their meager belongings to the nearby bluff and stayed. During the years that followed, a four-room house of squared logs and several sheds of logs roofed with palmetto leaves came to occupy the small clearing which had been wrested from the forest canopy of the bluff. Behind, away from the river, year by year, to the accompaniment of the ring of the broad axes through the smoke of the clearing fires appeared ever-growing openings, as the settlers' axes pushed the forest farther and farther back on the dryer second level of rich alluvial swamp. In the stump-studded red fields, which had so long been the forest floor, rows of corn, peas, and melons, and lawns of grain appeared.

Hark back a score of years and back to Charles Town Harbor. A New England brigantine, Captain John Thurber, master, on a voyage from faraway Madagascar, on the other side of the world, had just put in to the port for supplies and repairs. While awaiting his ship's readiness to put to sea again, Captain Thurber made the acquaintance of some of the leading citizenry of the town, among them being the extraordinary Dr. Henry Woodward, the mentor of the infant colony. As the captain described for the doctor the wonders of the distant island, he told of the wonderful rice grown there by the native blacks, some of which he had purchased to round out his cargo. The ever-alert Woodward was greatly interested and expressed a desire to make a trial planting here in Carolina. Grateful for the hospitality which had been accorded him, the captain obliged with the offer of a small sack of the unhusked grain. Woodward and several of his friends with whom he divided his gift planted these seeds from Madagascar, and from them grew Carolina golden rice. And from these tiny beginnings, the rice fields spread—up the rivers, over to and up the nearby rivers, and, in later years, up into North Carolina and down into Georgia.

So one day, about the year 1705, the master of the log house on the bluff began to give intent attention to the boggy acres which extended quite a way downstream from where the old tree stood and through which a sluggish stream ran its devious course, from its source in a large elliptical savanna back in the pine flats beyond the river swamp to where it ran into the river some distance below. Then in a little while this saturated swamp area was seething with activity. Uncouth black men speaking in strange tongues, and powerful oxen, both doing the bidding of white taskmakers—hacking, hewing and hauling—building an earthen dam from the bluff, downstream to the next bluff below. It was the fortuitous salvation of the old cypress that, by its being left on the river side of the earthwork, the dam would be shortened; and at the same time the necessity of removing it and ditching through the great roots from which sprang the miniature steeples of its obtruding knees would be avoided.

When the dam was completed all the way down, omitting only the spot where the stream entered the river, the work was concentrated there. Piling and thick heart pine and cypress planks were driven into the soft earth, and upon this embedded foundation a stout wooden sluice was constructed. Either end of the sluice or "trunk" was then equipped with a massive hanging door; the one on the river end would be automatically closed by the pressure of the rising water as the flowing tide ran up the river and would open and let out any accumulated water in the dammed-off area as the counter pressure was reduced when the tide ebbed. The inside gate worked in exactly the reverse manner. Either gate could be made inoperative by raising. Gates so constructed could be used to catch automatically and to hold high tides in the dammed-off area or else, by letting only the outside one function, the low level could be maintained inside, allowing the enclosed area to dry out.

When this ingenious structure was completed, the outside gate was commissioned and in a matter of a few ebb tides the dam-enclosed area was free of all standing water. Soon men and animals could find there earth that would sustain their weight. Then came the incredibly arduous undertaking of removing from the enclosure the subtropical jungle it bore: great trees, stumps and all; underbrush; tough, hard-to-kill grapevines; the deep-bedded giant tubers of the smilax; and the wire-tough network of the native bamboo. The amazing feature of such an undertaking is that anyone without the aid of the most modern machine equipment would dare to try it. But the dauntless spirit that had brought the river settlers from far mellower places to this raw region was not cowed by the prospect. Since daring to try was their greatest hurdle, they succeeded. The jungle was felled, dried and burned. The stumps, roots and tubers were painstakingly grubbed out. At last, behind the dam running between the bluffs the old cypress looked down on a flat, dark-chocolate field of some hundred acres, cleft through its middle by the snakelike channel of the stream.

But the objective of all this effort, a producing rice field, was still far from attained. First the meandering stream through the field must, by backbreaking digging with mattocks and shovels, be converted into a straight ample canal. Around the whole field a lesser canal would have to be dug and the excavated earth spread evenly over the fields. Between these there would then have to be a grid of smaller ditches or "quarter divides," located about fifty feet apart, to round out the aqueduct system necessary for a finished rice field, to provide drainage, irrigation or flooding as needed.

When the last redolent golden tubes of jessamine are falling and the snowy sepals of the flowering dogwood are being suppressed by the sudden unfurling of its fresh green leaves, it is rice planting time. Painstakingly, in shallow drills a few inches apart the selected seeds are dropped and lightly covered. To stimulate sprouting, kill the challenging weeds and protect the seeds from the birds, the field is flooded for a few days as soon as the planting is completed. Growth is stimulated and the crop protected by hoeing and periodic flooding, through the growing season. Finally as the long, hot summer draws to a close, if by the grace of God the region has escaped that scourge of the rice planter, a tropical hurricane, the old cypress will look down on a waving golden sea of ripened grain, forty bushels of heavy grain to the acre.

Singing bands of brightly clad slaves, men and women, swinging shining hooks, cut and stack the harvest. From the field to the threshing shed go the laden carts, carrying in the cut of the previous day. In the shed, through the long hot day, the most powerful of the slaves, with long flails, beat the golden grain from the straw. Through the fall and into the winter in wooden mortars the husks will be pounded from the kernels, the most tedious task of all.

Finally, one winter day, several oversize dugouts will tie up at the little wharf at the rise of the bluff and take aboard their golden cargo—to be poled downstream and through the back waters to Charles Town, fifty miles away. There part will be delivered to the colonial authorities for the quitrents due by the planter to his absentee landlords, the Lords Proprietors, and the rest will be delivered to the warehouse of the planter's factor for shipment to England.

As the years passed, the name Carolina Golden Rice was to prove symbolic indeed of the worth of the crop. The old tree would see rooms added to the planter's house and neat white weatherboarding placed over its hewn log walls. Two long rows of slave quarters facing each other with a "street" between would rise at a respectful distance to the rear. Where another creek entered the river, a substantial mill would be built with a great undershot water wheel supplying its power, whenever the tide was either rising or falling, saving greatly the tedious labor of preparing the grain for market.

Years later a handsome mansion adorned with superbly fashioned woodwork would replace the original home of the master. Extensive stables would be added to the outbuildings behind the great house. Coaches and carriages would come and go as roads released the plantation from its former riverbound existence. To avoid the deadly fevers which were associated with the proximity of rice fields, to flee the oppressive heat of the humid swamps, and to get a taste of urban society, which the isolation of plantation life did not permit, the rice planters would take their families elsewhere for the summer months. From the Santee plantations, many would go to beach homes on Cedar Island at the mouth of the river, for from there the planter could by boat continue to visit and supervise the plantation.

At other seasons, festive occasions would become frequent, while an increasing number of black men toiled their lives away to support the elegant but extravagant society of these river planters.

There were less spectacular but more significant changes occurring on the tawny waters of the great river itself. Almost a century after the first rice dams were being built, there passed downstream a barge heavy-laden with cotton bales and navigated by a stout slave crew wielding long poles. In the years that followed, the passing of such craft became commonplace until they were diverted by the completion of the Santee Canal. It was those cotton barges that proclaimed that a new king was challenging the long rule of rice, and there could be no joint rule. It was one or the other. As the cotton shipments increased, the river grew ever muddier. Freshets increased in frequency and severity, as the forest and grass cover were stripped from more and more of the watershed upriver to prepare the land for the clean-tilled fields of cotton.

The rice planters raised their dams again and again, but the height of the floodwater level rose even faster. More and more frequently crops were lost to August floods, and there was still, even as always, the threat of the September hurricanes.

Yes, old King Rice was already ailing when the challenge of the young king came forcibly to bear. The first generation of free Negroes were far inferior to their forebears as laborers. The wages paid by the booming logging business was attracting the best of them, leaving the less energetic on the plantations. More efficient methods of culture could be used in the extensive new rice areas of Louisiana and so reduce the price that there was little profit left in the crop for the Carolina planters. Consequently it took but the *coup de grace* of the growing freshet menace, coupled with a series of severe tropical storms, to bury the monarch beneath his own rubbish-strewn fields.

As August, 1893, drew to a close, the old cypress surveyed a bountiful crop of yellowing grain waving in the summer breezes that gently swept the field, whose clearing it had witnessed almost two centuries before. High in the air, fluffy clouds sailed across the sky at an uncanny pace, considering the gentleness of the breeze which fanned the tree's delicate foliage. The breeze stiffened and became gusty. The clouds lowered and thickened until they scudded across the sky loosing intermittent showers. In spite of the wind, an oppressive humidity gave a sort of staleness to the air. Through the day the wind rose to a gusty gale as the intermittent showers changed into a slashing downpour, blotting all view of the field below. Through the night and all through the next day, the tempo of the storm mounted. The night of the second day the tide which backed up the river almost topped the protecting dam. And when it was due to ebb, the water level did not drop. The furious east wind driving up the river was building a powerful, even though vaporous, dam across the river's mouth. The next wind-assisted flowing tide met the rain-swollen volume of the river, cluttered with floating logs, uprooted trees and all manner of rubbish. Higher rose the muddy floodwater—over the pitifully inadequate dams, ripping great holes here and there as seething torrents rushed in over the flattened and broken remains of what, but two days before, had been the hope and subsistence of a whole community. And with the crops those brown floodwaters submerged the graceful society which for more than a century and a half had dominated first a colonial province and then a proud state.

As the storm passed and the sun broke through the melting clouds, it shone mercilessly on a scene of awful devastation on every hand. Muddy water, miles of it, extended in all directions, over the fields and under the forests, into the "street" of the now shabby half-abandoned slave quarters, around the foundations of the great house on the bluff, into the stables, halfway up the side of the old ricemill. Great trees by the thousands lay uprooted or cocked at angles against stouter sustaining neighbors. Others, whose roots had held, were broken and torn. And for the giant old cypress, it was the end of glory. No longer would it be a river landmark. Midway its height, the hollow bole had proved too weak to stand the ninety-mile-an-hour gust which struck when the storm reached the height of its fury. With a resounding crack the wind had snatched its upper sixty feet, hurling it a full five hundred yards to the middle of the parklike lawn which stretched from the great house to the riverbank.

Even in the Low Country, where the atmosphere of timelessness is its greatest fascination, time inexorably moves on, ever taking its toll as it flows by. Three decades after the storm that gave the final, mortal blow to rice culture in what had been the principal rice-growing area of the Western Hemisphere, discouragement, retrogression and decay were all-pervading across the entire Low Country. When plantation houses burned, they were rarely, if ever, rebuilt. Instead, the owners either moved into the empty overseer's house, which was now more appropriate to their reduced circumstances, or they gave up the struggle against too much water and a forest too ready to take back to itself the rich domain it had formerly held, and moved away to find a new way of life in the cities or on the more easily tilled but less fertile higher country away from the river. Those places which fire, through the years, had spared, were left to the slower but no less relentless action of decay, where the means of maintenance are absent. The elements soon substituted unkempt ghostliness for beautiful splendor. The battered, sagging outbuildings rapidly diminished in number as they consumed each other, the material from the less essential being torn away to repair the more essential.

The house on the bluff by the remains of the old cypress was among those few which were left to the insidious hand of the elements. There it stood amid the great, somber, moss-draped live oaks, which rose from a weed- and brush-cluttered lawn—in spots even now giving the appearance of a lawn thanks to the herd of goats roaming the place unmolested. There it stood, gray and gaunt, with crooked brow and vacant stare, shutters gone, the once imposing portico sagging and windows all but paneless. It was 1925, when most of the country was fairly drunk with prosperity. As the exuberant waves of plenty rolled, bits of their spray fell even on this now nearly forsaken lower Santee. With money guaranteed from the humming East and North came tycoons, still insatiable, now possessed with a contradictory yearning for the glamorized version of the way of life of the rice tycoons of a day long gone.

Because its boards and mortar gave it a continuity with a proud and romantic past—of which many of the tycoons felt the lack—it was inevitable that to this place a backwash of the prosperity would sweep. And so it did. As the leaves on the few remaining limbs of the old tree yellowed with the first frost, at long last there was once more a hum of activity on the bluff. Architects, restorers, artisans, interior decorators, tree surgeons, and others directed their forces. The grounds were searched for every discarded old brick, the cellars for the cast-off remains of household articles of the long gone planters, that they might be carefully restored or duplicated. Finally, to the rice fields came an assortment of machines, purring and belching, rebuilding the broken dams and gates, that the old rice field might be planted and its crops purposely flooded, unharvested, to entice the mallards, the scaups, and the widgeons into the range of the new "planter's" guns. All in a futile attempt to restore an environment which being dead could never be truly revived, for the essential of that environment was not tangible.

The arduous and hazardous way of life of the rice planters was dead and buried—but here and there magnificent snowy monuments to it were being carefully maintained.

By way of epitaph—which will not be found subscribed in words upon these monuments to their vanished glory—it should be recorded that interred here in this rich brown earth is a civilization which had far more significance than simply being the inspiration for a never-ending stream of romantic novels. To perform the gargantuan tasks of wresting the rice fields from their jungle state, to supply the endless labor in those stifling, insect-ridden, miasmic fields, and to provide servants to wait upon the households of the planters to whom the profits of all this labor flowed, an enormous number of Negro slaves were required on the rice plantations. Consequently, in the last analysis, to the rice plantations can be traced a large part of the race problems which have been the heritage of the South even to this day. And with those black slaves came another heritage which was to curse the South for two centuries. From the Gold Coast, the Ivory Coast, Nigeria, and the Cameroons, in their veins came the germs of the malarias which were indigenous to those faraway lands. Here, through the ubiquitous mosquitoes of the Low Country, those germs were transmitted to the susceptible whites, decimating and chronically disabling the best human stock of the region.

Finally, yet another fact might have been added to that epitaph. The vast supply of cheap Negro labor with which the exigencies of rice growing endowed the Low Country has even to this day so discouraged the immigration of other labor into the area, that, except for such as are based on local resources, industry has avoided the whole so-called "Black Belt," to the end that that balance of industry and agriculture essential for economic good health is still lacking there.

❧   ❧   ❧   ❧   ❧ *12. Red clay and freedom*

*B*y 1755 the children of the fifth generation to call Carolina their home were playing in the streets and parks of Charlestown or beneath the spreading branches of the live oaks of the plantation seats or along the canals and dykes of the rice fields. In North Carolina the old towns of New Bern, Edenton and Bath were no longer raw settlements. They had become planter capitals. The planters and merchants, particularly those of Charlestown, completely dominated Carolina from Beaufort to Elizabeth City. The society they had built was a rich and gracious one, a delightful way of life—for them. But however glamorous that society may appear in retrospect, from the standpoint of the development of the colonies the planter-merchant society had become an evil force. The mid-seventeenth-century Carolina coastal society had become literally exclusive, effectively excluding growth by immigration. While the slave population multiplied, the white population showed little increase.

Here artisans and laborers would face the competition of slave labor. Few chose to face that competition. Along the Southern coast from the Chesapeake Bay to Florida an intangible wall against immigration had been built. And the society that had erected that wall showed little inclination to push it back very far from the tidewaters. Life was pleasant as it was, and rice, the staple crop of the slave-operated plantations, was not adaptable to the interior terrain.

As late as two decades before the Revolution there was scarcely any inland community in South Carolina which could be called a town, and in North Carolina the Low Country villages of Halifax and Fayetteville were on the frontier. Only a few frail fingers of some semblance of civilization reached up the Indian trading paths, and here and there along them trading posts had attracted primitive satellite settlements which would be the nuclei of Orangeburg, Ninety-Six, Camden, Charlotte, Salisbury and Hillsboro. With exceptions such as these, the interior was still wild and unowned. But that is not to say that there was not already a substantial white population in this vast back country. However, they probably numbered less than the former Indian population of the area, and, after settling in the wilds, they largely foreswore civilization and adopted the way of life of their Indian neighbors. Typical of the accounts of Piedmont Carolina during this period is that given by the Moravian bishop, Augustus Spangenberg, who visited the region of the upper Catawba River in 1752:

> The next settlement from here is that of Jonathon Weiss, more familiarly known as Jonathan Perrot. This man is a hunter and lives 20 miles from here. There are many hunters about here who live like Indians: they kill many deer, selling their hides, and thus live without much work. . . . There were no roads save those made by buffaloes. The wolves, which are not like those in Germany, Poland and Lapland (because they fear men and

do not easily come near) give us such music of six different cornets, the like of which I have never heard in my life. Several brethren, skilled in hunting will be required to exterminate panthers, wolves, etc.

The bishop then went on to describe with great admiration the open prairies which then covered much of the North Carolina piedmont, calling them "buffalo fields," abounding in "tame grass" and "wild peas" so thick that they prevented crossing; and in the valleys he found extensive abandoned Indian fields of "rich and fertile" soil.

These red hills and all the red hills of Carolina were to witness during the next two decades what was perhaps relatively the greatest mass migration and land rush of American history.

In 1755 the stage was set for this great land rush. Already the region was the most popular resort for those who, for one reason or another, were fugitives from the law of the more settled provinces to the North, and for many hardy adventurers whose daring spirits sought a frontier which could not be found east of the mountains in the Northern colonies; and already there was a trickle of impoverished new settlers seeking good land for no cost in money. To this slowly swelling flow of southward migration, Braddock's disastrous defeat added a great wave rolling southward from western Pennsylvania and Virginia to escape an expected French-encouraged Indian attack in those parts.

To these migrations was added a lesser wave of settlers flowing in through Charlestown, and from there passing through the coastal settlements to the back country. This latter wave of migration was the culmination of the efforts of the South Carolina planter-merchant aristocracy to supply an incentive to settle the hinterland, which their society had failed to develop, with the idea of counterbalancing the colonies' already terrifying numerical preponderance of slaves.

As the population of their so-called "internal enemy" approached triple that of the whites, the danger of their situation became apparent. Since they themselves lacked the incentive to move inland and abandon all they found so to their liking in the Low Country, they devised measures to attract others to settle the interior in order that those settlers would be on hand to protect their way of life should a slave uprising threaten it. To this end, beginning in 1751, heavy taxes were imposed on the importation of slaves and the proceeds of these taxes were allocated for bounties for new settlers for the interior. This artificially stimulated wave of immigration from abroad met the waves pouring southward. And these waves kept pouring into the red hills of Carolina until checked by the terrible devastation which was visited upon the region during the Revolution.

First it was thousands, then it was tens of thousands who had come in their heavy wagons down the Catawba Path from Pennsylvania, from Maryland, from Virginia, fording the rivers, straining up the slippery hills through the deep-cut ruts, down past the log courthouse at Hillsboro, through the raw village of Salisbury, on through the abandoned Catawba village sites into the wide untamed wilderness of western Carolina. From the well-worn but unworked trail, they turned left and right along the old buffalo paths and minor Indian paths—always seeking land which was unoccupied. Settlements repelled them, for there land had a price. The wilderness attracted them, for there land could be had for the taking. So towns and even villages were slow to develop.

Driving his team down the rough way from Pennsylvania was rugged Andrew Jackson, a Presbyterian Scot from County Antrim, Ireland, with his young wife and their small boys, headed for the red clay hills of Waxhaw where he would soon die in the struggle to wrest fields from their forest cover, after siring another Andrew he was never to see but who was

destined to become the idol of these freedom-loving people
and to be honored by them with the name of the toughest
fiber in these hills, "Old Hickory."

Also along the same path from Pennsylvania to the Waxhaws came another Andrew and his son, Scotch-Irish Presbyterians, the Pickens. The southward wave of settlement in
later years was to push the young Andrew Pickens across
South Carolina to its southernmost red hills where he would
gain fame as a dashing partisan general in the Revolution.

Also from Pennsylvania to the region between the Yadkin and Catawba came Squire Boone with his small son, Dan,
who in later years would lead the way to other new lands to
the west. Nearby was the shack of Lindsay Carson, father of
the famous frontiersman, Kit Carson.

Down from Virginia, first to the Waxhaws and then to
the neighborhood of Pickens's new home in the Ninety-Six
district, came a fiery Scot, Patrick Calhoun, of Donegal, Ireland, to become a militant spokesman for democratic government, a leader in the Cherokee war, and later, in the near
war between his folk and the coastal aristocracy. The rough
old Pat passed his fighting spirit and many of his principles
on to the delicate-timbered son of his old age, John C. Calhoun, born to become, a half-century later, the idol and
spokesman of the planter aristocracy the father so roundly
despised.

A neighbor of Pat's who also came down from Virginia
was Frederick Tillman. But his posterity would stay truer to
the ancestral mold. A grandson of his, Benjamin R. (Pitchfork
Ben) Tillman, was to become the prototype of the clever,
rabble-rousing demagogues who were to curse the South for
more than a half century, until mass education showed them
the door.

In the Tyger River region between the present Spartanburg and Greenville, Anthony Hampton had staked out his
claim and built a cabin for his numerous family which he had

wagoned down from Virginia. There, a few years later, he and most of his family would surrender their scalps to raiding Cherokees. But a son, Wade, was to survive to become illustrious as a Revolutionary officer and to hand his name down to one who was successively a great planter-sportsman-aristocrat, dashing Confederate cavalry general, postwar governor, and senator.

Another boy from the Virginia backwoods who came to settle on the Santee near Eutaw Springs was Thomas Sumter, who had left his native state on an adventurous trip as escort to England for a party of Cherokee headmen and who, as an energetic and contentious partisan general, was to lead his rebel militia all over these Carolina hills in countless hit-and-run campaigns.

Lured south by red clay and freedom were all the Carolina leaders who made their names immortal at the brilliant victory at Kings Mountain. From Pennsylvania had come Colonel Edward Lacy and the German-born Colonel Frederick Hambright. Colonel Benjamin Cleveland, Colonel James Williams, Colonel John Sevier, Major Joseph McDowell, and Major Joseph Winston, among others, had come to Carolina from Virginia. Colonel Isaac Shelby had immigrated from Maryland. Also active in the victorious resurgence of the South, after the rebels had been all but conquered there by the British and Tories, were Generals William Davie, the father of the University of North Carolina, William Lenoir and William Davidson. Davie came to the Carolina red hills from England, Lenoir and Davidson from Virginia.

Of all the notable military figures of the Revolution in the Carolinas, where proportionately more men were engaged and more battles were fought than in any other area, only generals Francis Marion and William Moultrie were native sons. All the others were of the aggressive newcomers in search of freedom and red clay.

Along with those remembered through the written page or marble tablets came the multitude of the forgotten ones. Here and there across the region, creek names come down to us as verbal monuments to those who built their first rude huts along those waters so long ago. But time has rendered those personal names impersonal. What sort of men were those McDows, McMullens, Kirkpatricks, Gilkeys and Duncans? And their neighbors, the Dutchmen? Individually, time has obliterated all but their names. Severally, they were land-hungry poor men, adventurers, horse thieves, oppressed men seeking freedom, fugitives from justice, land speculators, ambitious younger sons, and bond servants, some still serving their temporary slavery, some in flight. They were German Lutherans and Quakers, French Huguenots, English and Swiss, but mostly they were Scots, transplanted from Scotland to an oppressive existence in northern Ireland. In character and background they were a varied lot. But one characteristic they overwhelmingly had in common—a stiff-necked resistance to law and government and a powerful aversion to being organized and regulated. To this day those traits have colored their Piedmont hills, and the mountains and states to the west which their children settled.

Though the sands of time have covered the memory of all but a few of those who dared the dangers of that great migration, the river itself, through its creek names and the place names of the valley, tell much of what the migrants found when they came and gave names to the nameless geography they found. Commemorative of the wild life they met are the half-dozen Buffalo Creeks that feed into the Santee tributaries, the dozen Beaver and Beaverdam creeks, Elk Creek and Elk Shoals, Bear Creek and Wolf Creek. The several Dutchman and Frenchman creeks proclaim the nativity of some of them. The hardships they met are memorialized in Terrible, Pinch Gut, Hard-bargain, Puzzle, Hungry and

Hurricane Creeks. But, along them they staked out their claims and built their first crude huts. Along them and along Indian, Skull, Canoe, and Granny's Quarter creeks, and by the rushing waters of the Swannanoa, the Tyger, the Pacolet, the Enoree, and the Waxhaw, around Buffalo Lick and All Healing Springs, in Quaker Gardens and Pleasant Gardens, and along Fairforest Creek, they possessively grabbed their hold, until soon this new population was "crowded together as thick as in England." But they kept on coming, pushing up into narrow mountain valleys where some would settle and thereby condemn their posterity for generations to a continuance of their isolated frontier existence; while others, their land hunger unsatisfied by their tardy arrival in Carolina, dared their all and pushed on over into the Watauga and Holston River valleys of the Cherokees, there to purchase with blood the sites of those first settlements from which Tennessee and Kentucky would grow.

Although the land that this horde of land-hungry immigrants had taken unto themselves was rich and bountiful and the climate of the hills was healthful, for years to come the lives of the mass of them were incredibly hard. Isolated as they were by the almost total absence of roads or navigable streams, practically everything they required had to be produced painstakingly from such materials as the region held. Iron was smelted from the poor ores of the region, with only wood fuel to heat the furnaces. The settlers' huts were the only factories to fashion everything needed, from their clothing to their wooden dishes and spoons. Contemporary accounts paint somber pictures of their struggles.

On a trip to the back country to treat with a delegation of Cherokees, the Governor of South Carolina talked to an old man who had preceded the great immigration and by him was told that "he had never seen a shirt, been in a fair, heard a sermon, or seen a minister in all his life." Writing of the South Carolina Piedmont in 1753, Governor Glen said that most of them had good crops and large herds of cattle, hogs, and children, "equally as naked and fully as nasty. The parents in the back woods come together without previous ceremony."

An Englishman who some years later traveled through the region described the appearance of these Carolina backwoodsmen:

> Their whole dress is very singular, and not very materially different from that of the Indians; being a hunting shirt, somewhat resembling a waggoner's frock, ornamented with a great many fringes, tied round the middle with a broad belt, much decorated also, in which is fastened a tomahawk. . . . being a hammer at one side and a sharp hatchet at the other; the shot bag and powder horn. . . . and on their heads flapped a hat of reddish hue. . . .
>
> Sometimes they wear leather breeches, made of Indian dressed elk, or deer skins, but more frequently, thin trowsers.
>
> On their legs they have Indian boots or leggings. . . . On their feet they sometimes wear pumps of their own manufacture, but generally Indian moccasins, of their own construction also. . . .
>
> The women wore linsey petticoats and "bed gowns" and went without shoes in summer. . . . Their hair was commonly clubbed.

Especially pride-dispelling are the accounts of the region that appear in the journal of the Reverend Charles Woodmason, an educated Anglican priest who came to Pine Tree Hill (the present Camden) in 1766, and for several years preached, married and baptized mostly up and down the Wateree-Catawba region, but also up in Anson and Mecklenburg districts of North Carolina and southward to the Congaree-Saluda area. Upon his arrival at Pine Tree he found:

The People around, of abandon'd Morals, and Profligate Principles—Rude—Ignorant—Void of Manners, Education or Good Breeding. . . . Not a house to be hir'd—Nor even a single Room on all this River to be rented, fit to put my Head or Goods in. . . . The People all new Settlers, extremely poor. . . . Live in Logg Cabbins like Hogs. . . . and their Living and Behaviour as rude or more so than the Savages. Extremely embarrassed how to subsist. Took up my Quarters in a Tavern. . . . and exposed to the Rudeness of the Mobb. People continually drunk. . . . Found the School Room that was intended for me turn'd by the Taven Keeper into a stable. Only 3 Boys offer'd, out of 2 or 300 that run wild here like Indians. . . . But as their Parents are Irish Presbyterians, they rather chuse to let them run thus wild, than to have them instructed in the Principles of Religion by a Minister of the Church of England.

In some neighborhoods he found things better, as at Rocky Mount, up the Catawba on the west side:

The land is good, and plowed to the Summit, being Wheat Rye Indian Corn and all kind of Grain and Fruit Trees. . . . I gave service to about 400 people among whom a great number of Baptists and Presbyterians. . . . The Women sing as well or better than the Girls at the Magdalen Chapel, London. . . . They all come from Virginia and Pennsylvania. . . . Not an English person or Carolinian among them.

And over near the Broad on Sandy River, he

met with many serious and Religious persons. . . . the Service perform'd this day (to about 500) with as much pomp as if at St. Paul's.

But his task was arduous and he complains that there is

no other Clergyman of the Church of England from the
Sea to the Mountains, on the North Side of Santee River
to the Province Line. Number of miles rode this year (All
perform'd by one Horse) 3185.

And mostly he was horrified by what he found:

> Preached at Granny Quarter Creek to a mix'd multi-
> tude of People from various Quarters. . . . But no bring-
> ing of this Tribe to Order. They are the lowest Pack of
> Wretches my Eyes ever saw, or that I have met with in
> these Woods. . . . And wild as the very Deer. . . . No
> making them sit still during Service. . . . but they will
> be in and out . . . forward and backward the whole
> Time (Women especially) as Bees to and fro in their
> Hives. . . . How would the Polite People of London
> stare, to see the Females (many very pretty) come to
> Service in their Shifts and a short petticoat only, bare-
> footed and Bare legged—dressed only in their Hair,
> Quite in a State of Nature for Nakedness is counted as
> Nothing. . . . as they sleep altogether in Common in
> one Room. . . . The Indians are better Cloathed and
> Lodged.

It was no better on Flat Creek in Lancaster County,
where he preached to a "mixed Multitude":

> I baptised about 20 Children and Married 4 Couple.
> . . . most of these People had never before seen a
> Minister, or heard the Lord's Prayer, Service or Sermon
> in their Days. I was a Great Curiosity to them—and they
> were as great Oddities to me. After Service they went to
> Revelling—Drinking—Singing—Dancing—and Whoring.
> . . . and most of the Company were drunk before I
> quitted the Spot. . . . This Country contains ten times
> the Number of Persons beyond my Apprehension.
> Now will come the Season of Festivity and Drunken-
> ness. . . . The Stills will be soon at work for to make

Whisky and Peach Brandy—In this Article, both Presbyterians and Episcopals very charitably agree (Viz.) That of getting Drunk.

Certainly the hard-pressed minister was strongly prejudiced against the Presbyterians and Baptists, and that is what most of these folk nominally were, and perhaps he was biased by their poverty and lack of education, but his actions prove that he loved them in spite of their shortcomings for before he left the province, broken in health, he was to become the voice of those very people in the bitter struggle for some measure of government for the Upcountry which they militantly waged against the rule of the "overgrown Planters, who wallow in Luxury, Ease, and Plenty." And he was hopeful of a better future for his benighted charges as he concluded the journal of his first two years in the hills:

. . . . have rode near Six thousand Miles, almost on one horse. Wore myself to a Skeleton and endured all the Extremites of Hunger, Thirst, Cold, and Heat. Have baptised near 1200 Children—Given 200 or more Discourses—Rais'd almost 30 Congregations—Set on foot the building of sundry Chapels Distributed Books, Medicines, Garden Seed, Turnip, Clover, Timothy, Burnet, and other Grass Seeds—with Fish Hooks—Small Working Tools and variety of Implements to set the Poor at Work, and promote Industry to the amount of at least One hundred Pounds Sterling: Roads are making—boats building—Bridges framing, and other useful Works begun thro' my Means, as will not only be of public Utility, but make the Country side wear a New face, and the People become New Creatures.

❧ ❧ ❧ ❧ *13. The regulators*

*O*ne morning in March, 1769, those who arrived early at the Exchange in Charlestown were shocked, distressed, infuriated or amused according to their personalities or politics, but mostly according to their station in life in the aristocratic city state, to read this advertisement which was posted there (until torn from the board by one of the irate gentry against whom it was aimed):

ADVERTISEMENT

TO BE DISPOSED OFF

ON THE CONGAREE, SALUDY, SAVANAH, WATEREE, AND BROAD RIVERS

A CARGO OF

FIFTY THOUSAND PRIME SLAVES

(*Remarkably healthy, and free from Small Pox*)

LATELY IMPORTED FROM GREAT BRITAIN, IRELAND, AND THE NORTHERN COLONIES

IN THE GOOD SHIP

CAROLINA

GEORGE REX, MASTER

In a short Passage of Ten Years——The Sale will begin on Monday the 17th day of April next——Credit will be Given till——Public Good be preferr'd to Private Interest——

N. B. The above Slaves are sold for no fault——But their being stript of their Property by Theives and Vagabonds—Plunder'd of their Effects *according to Law,* by Mercenary Demagogues——and given up as Prey to Vagrants and Outlaws, for to have their Throats cut——their Estates rifled their families ruin'd——Wives insulted——Daughters deflowered, and their Properties sacrific'd and dispers'd——And not having any Courts of Justice where to lodge Complaints——Or proper Magistrates to whom to seek for Redress of Injuries—— Or Rulers to notice their Greivances——Nor any Places for Public Worship wherein to implore the Divine Protection against, and Deliverance from these and other Evils, renders it absolutely necessary for the above Sale taking Place——

Public Spirit——Love of Country——Religion—— Humanity——Charity Patriotism, and such Old-Coin will be taken in Payment

Its greatly to be hop'd, That the Gentlemen of the Long Robe, will attend, and buy away at said Sale.

The posting of this mock advertisement was but another effort on the part of the mostly new, but already numerous, back-country citizenry to dramatize their grievances against the planter-merchant-dominated colonial governments of both the Carolina provinces. In both provinces the struggle between the back country and the colonial authorities had been growing in intensity and bitterness for more than ten years when this advertisement was written by the Reverend Charles Woodmason. Born of that long struggle were the organizations known as the Regulators. In 1769 Woodmason was one of the leading spokesmen of the South Carolina Regulators.

The very conditions the Regulators were organized to alleviate, the lack of any real government in the newly settled hill regions of the Carolinas, has, through the resulting deficiency of contemporary records, shrouded the origin of the Regulators in mystery. Various historians ascribe to various times and places the beginnings of these early "vigilante" or phantom governments of the backwoods. Anson County, Hillsboro, the upper Yadkin and the upper Catawba in North Carolina, and the Wateree-Congaree forks and the Middle Peedee region of South Carolina have all been claimed as the birthplace of the Regulators. This much is certain: The day after Christmas, 1755, a party of settlers organized under the name of Regulators, and with Daniel Boone as one of the leaders, set out from the Moravian settlements of the upper Yadkin to attack the mountain hide-out of a band of bold robbers who had long been the scourge of the Piedmont settlers and who had recently kidnaped the daughter of one of them. During the next dozen years the organization is found almost everywhere throughout the Carolina back country, serving as a sort of informal military government in the struggle of the settlers to hold in check the numerous lawless bands which roamed the region, much as did the more publicized vigilantes of a later American West. Not only were the Regulators the progenitors of the vigilantes, but they no doubt directly spawned a much less reputable progeny in the lynch mobs which were to curse the South with their self-ordained "justice" for the century and a half to follow.

As the inevitable conflict arose between the entrenched coastal aristocracy and the colonial governments they controlled on the one hand, and the numerous neglected, disproportionately represented and liberty-loving folk of the back-country hills on the other hand, the local Regulator organizations became the vehicles of protest, the representatives of their several communities; and finally from them evolved the almost province-wide political organizations of the same name. Upon the Regulators devolved the duty of speaking and acting for the emigrees in their efforts to obtain what they conceived to be their rights as citizens.

In North Carolina their principal grievance was the corruption of the back-country representatives of the colonial government. But there was also bitter opposition to an unfair tax system and the disproportionately small representation permitted the back country in the colonial Assembly. From 1765 on, petitions, resolutions and formal protests addressed to the General Assembly begging for the needed reforms poured in from all over the western part of the province, from the residents beyond the Haw River, from those along Rocky River, from Anson County, Orange County and Rowan. There were Regulator activities along the Catawba, in Mecklenburg and in Cabarrus County, but their activity was greatest in the Orange, Randolph and Chatham County region for there resided the foremost leader of the Regulators, a Quaker, Harmon Husband, who had come to the Carolina Piedmont from Pennsylvania; and there also resided the outstanding object of Regulator ire, Colonel Edmund Fanning. Fanning was the clerk of the court at Hillsboro, and both personally and in the administration of his office he represented everything the Regulators found obnoxious in the government. Fanning was haughty, overbearing and avaricious and was unconscionable in the overcharges he required for his official acts.

When finally in the spring of 1770 the tumultuous denunciations of Fanning forced indictments against him for extortions, and in case after case he was found guilty by the jury only to receive a fine of one penny in each case, the fury of the Regulators knew no bounds. Some of them proceeded to Fanning's home, where they destroyed his property and burned his house. Others took charge of the court, after driving out the presiding judge and other officials, and in semi-comic judicial proceedings began to dispense justice according to their liking.

With these overt acts on the part of the stiff-necked Regulators, the fat was in the fire. No self-respecting government (and about the only respect accorded Governor William Tryon's government was self-respect) could fail to act in the face of such open defiance. Accordingly, Tryon proceeded with plans to force the submission of the Regulators. By the spring of 1771, the vainglorious Governor, who by profession was a soldier, was with the hated Colonel Fanning west from New Bern at the head of some twelve hundred well equipped troops. May fifteenth found Tryon's troops in the neighborhood of Alamance, near the present city of Burlington, where about two thousand Regulators were gathered, about half of whom were armed. Overtures on the part of the Regulators seeking to bargain for a hearing on their complaints were met with a demand for complete submission, with no promise of even a consideration of their complaints. The next morning the colonial troops proceeded to the Alamance campground of the Regulators. In response to another petition for arbitration of their grievances, the Regulators were sent an ultimatum requiring

> you who are now assembled as Regulators, to quietly lay down your arms, to surrender up your leaders, to the laws of your country and rest on the leniency of the government. By accepting these terms within one hour from the delivery of this dispatch, you will prevent an effusion of blood, as you are at this time in a state of *Rebellion* against your King, your country, and your Laws.

Less than an hour later the arbitrary Governor himself opened the battle by firing the first shot, killing, it is said, an unarmed negotiator, who was there seeking to avoid the conflict. After the first exchange of fire, the battle took on the pattern which was to become familiar in the Revolutionary battles soon to follow, the King's troops proudly doing battle from formation while their opponents found individual fortresses in the tree trunks of the neighborhood. Even so, the half-armed, virtually leaderless Regulators were no match for Tryon's troops and after two hours of the battle, their leader slain, the woods in which they had taken refuge aflame, and their ammunition exhausted, the Regulators fled the field leaving a dozen dead and some thirty prisoners in the hands of the uncompromising Governor. One of the prisoners was summarily hanged on the field. The others Tryon paraded through the western part of the colony for a month-long march of pillage and terror amongst the settlements of the Regulators. Upon return to Hillsboro in June, the prisoners were tried; twelve were condemned to death, and of these six were hanged, paying the price of a criminal's death for having started the American Revolution four years too soon. Harmon Husband, the Quaker-pacifist Regulator, had fled back to Pennsylvania when the firing at Alamance began, but his brother-in-law, James Pugh, was among those hanged. Before Fanning choked off the last words of this stouthearted rebel by kicking the barrel from under him, James Pugh is said to have made the prophetic remark to the assembled audience that his blood would be as good seed sown on good ground, which would produce an hundredfold.

What happened during these tension-filled years in North Carolina was closely paralleled by events in South Carolina. In the latter province, however, the principal complaint of the Regulators was not maladministration but rather the almost total lack of the protection and privileges of government in the back country and the almost total lack of representation of that suddenly populous section in the Assembly. In North Carolina most of the Regulators' animosity was directed against the royal governor and in consequence the popularity of the Crown suffered severely. In South Carolina the *bête noire* of the Regulators was the Assembly and, since it was controlled by the planter-merchant group of the coastal region, the hatred of the South Carolina Regulators was largely directed against that aristocracy and its capital—and the Crown was generally regarded as their ultimate source of assistance should all else fail. So the prime object of hate of the South Carolina Upcountry was Charlestown and the class which dominated it, while the hate of the North Carolina back countrymen was directed against the Governor and the source of his power—the English throne.

In the decade to follow, these prejudices would become significant indeed in the fate of the nation.

Along with the great influx of worthy and honest settlers who moved into the Carolina back country during the decade preceding 1767, there also came many of less virtuous character—robbers, unscrupulous adventurers, outcasts and fugitives from justice. The relative freedom from the restraint of any law in the area and the possibilities for plunder no doubt attracted an unduly large number of these vagabonds. By 1766 they had organized themselves into numerous marauding bands, so powerful that the whole region lay, helpless and terrified, at their mercy—and the chronicles of the day show that they possessed little of that quality. Appealing to Charletown for some measure of protection for the honest settlers, Woodmason complained:

> Our large Stocks of Cattel are either stollen and destroy'd. . . . Our Cow Pens are broke up. . . . and All our valuable Horses are carried off. . . . Houses have been burn'd by these Rogues, and families stripp'd and turn'd naked into the Woods. . . . Stores have been broken open and rifled by them (wherefrom several Traders are absolutely ruin'd) Private Houses have been plunder'd; and the Inhabitants wantonly tortured in the Indian Manner for to be made to confess where they secreted their Effects from Plunder. Married Women have been Ravished. . . . Virgins deflowered, and other unheard of Cruelties committed by the barbarous Ruffians.

Appeal after appeal to Charlestown produced a few promises but no help. To the coastal gentry, those poor crude inhabitants of the hinterland constituted a comforting barrier between their sumptuous plantations and the Indians; and there was ever and always the even more terrifying possibility of a slave revolt, in which these backcountrymen might well mean their salvation. For these considerations they were welcome to their remote red hills, but beyond that their interest in their less fortunate fellow Carolinians did not extend.

In default of any real assistance from the indifferent seaside capital, the backcountrymen were forced to seek protection among themselves. Spontaneously, in neighborhoods all over the region, armed bands of settlers organized themselves for mutual protection. To their organizations they applied the already familiar backwoods name of Regulators. During the spring of 1767 the Regulators undertook an aggressive clean-up campaign and soon brought some semblance of order to the harassed area. However, back in Charlestown the colonial authorities were casting dark frowns of disapproval upon the Regulators' assumption of authority.

Stimulated by their successes in breaking the dominance of the brigands over their homes and with the lesson learned of the potency of united numbers, the Regulators soon transformed themselves into a militant pressure organization seeking to force from the coastal aristocracy the benefits and privileges of government for those living in the Upcountry. This rank boldness in such trash evoked disdainful disapproval in the capital, and on November 5, 1767, the Governor, Lord Greville Montagu, appeared before Colonial Council and Assembly to recommend action for the suppression of

> those licentious Spirits that have so lately appeared . . .
> and assuming the name of Regulators, have in Defiance
> of the Government, and to the Subversion of good Order,
> illegally tried, Condemned and Punished many Persons.

In the face of this plea His Excellency must have been considerably embarrassed by the events which transpired during the next few days. Four Wateree planters had arrived in the city bearing an eloquent "Remonstrance" prepared by the ever vehement Woodmason, but signed by the four planters, according to their accounts, for four thousand of their fellow Upcountrymen, who were prepared to invade Charlestown personally unless steps were taken to remedy their grievances. Two days later this Remonstrance was read before the Assembly. After forcefully pointing out the numerous injustices being suffered by the Upcountry settlers, including their lack of protection, their lack of representation in the Assembly, the necessity of going to faraway Charlestown for any legal business, even for land titles and marriage licenses, the necessity for going to Charlestown for court relief; the lack of churches, schools and roads, of laws for the care of poor orphans, of courthouses and jails; the lack of regulations for taverns, limitations upon unrestrained hunting, the failure to publish the laws of the province; the need for the creation of additional parishes in the Upcountry, for ministers, for public schools, for restraints upon the fees of lawyers, for laws requiring that trials be held where the offense occurred, for measures to encourage manufacturing and agriculture, and finally for the distribution of a

Quantity of Bibles, Common Prayers, and Devotional Tracts, to be distributed by the Ministers among the Poor, which will be of far greater Utility to the Province, than erecting the Statue of Mr. Pitt.

Woodmason reported the reception of this document:

Great was the Uproar and Noise in the House on Reading of this Petition. . . . The Lawyers storm'd. . . . Would vote it a Libel and, Insult on the House. Moved, that the Deputies should be taken into Custody of the Black Rod Sent to Gaol. . . . That the Paper should be burnt by the Hangman, and the Like.

The reference in the Remonstrance to the "Statue of Mr. Pitt" was to a marble statue, costing one thousand pounds sterling, which was soon to be delivered for erection at the intersection of Broad and Meeting Streets, by way of recognition of that statesman's efforts to secure the repeal of the Stamp Act. When the Assemblymen ridiculed the suggestion that the money could have been better spent for Bibles there was posted on the State House:

Inscription for the Statue of Mr. Pitt:

What Love to their adopted Sons
is by our Fathers shown?

We ask'd to taste the *Bread of Life*
And Lo!—they give—A Stone!

There is no telling whether it came through a sincere
recognition of justice past due or whether it was simply because of the fear of the threatened invasion of the city by the
militant backcountrymen that within a few days the government completely reversed its attitude. Quickly, favorable action was taken on many of the Regulator complaints. For the
Wateree deputies hospitable entertainment replaced the
threats of jail. Regulators were named magistrates, replacing
the bandit-allied magistrates of the interior, and Regulators
were commissioned in the military companies which were
planned to police their country. With what appeared to be
an overwhelming victory to their credit the deputies returned
to their people to the accompaniment of "Bonfires and Fir-
ings, and every Demonstration of Joy."

Soon, however, it became apparent that these celebra-
tions were premature indeed. The crisis was far from over. It
developed that most of what they had thought were accomplishments had been little more than empty promises. The
law providing for courts for the back country was vetoed by
the Crown, and the news leaked out that the reason for the
veto was the inclusion in the bill of a clause which was put
there by some smart Charlestown lawyers for the very purpose of assuring the veto. The promised troops to keep order
in the Upcountry did not come, and yet, when the Regulators
continued to regulate, warrants for their arrest were
promptly issued at the behest of the bandit leaders. So, after
but a brief subsidence, the Regulators reorganized with increased numbers, greater determination, shorter patience,
and a magnified hate for the Charlestown government. A vast
number of delegates met at the Congarees and adopted a
"Plan of Regulation." This plan amounted to a declaration
of revolution. Up to this point the Regulators had been per-

forming governmental functions without the sanction of government. But now the plan was to openly flout and defy the government. The authority of the Charlestown court was denied in the back country since, as the Regulators saw it, that region "ought to be by right out of it." Only those writs and warrants that the Regulators thought proper might be served in the region. Soon the plan included the refusal to pay any taxes on the argument that there is no right of taxation without representation.

A bloody crisis arose when the constable bearing warrants for the arrest of Regulators between the Santee and the Peedee summoned a band to aid him. A skirmish between the warrant bearers and the Regulators occurred near Mars Bluff, and several of the constable's party were killed. An attempt to arrest those who had taken part in the Mars Bluff incident was frustrated by a great show of force on the part of the Regulators. Relations between the government and the Regulators deteriorated from bad to worse. Soon the province was on the brink of an active civil war, averted only by the fear entertained by the coastal planters of a slave uprising should they leave their plantations to attempt to quell the Regulator revolution. The Charlestown government, in a foolhardy attempt to counter the power of the Regulators and at the same time permit the slaveowners to stay with their property, began commissioning the bandit leaders of the back country as its deputies to serve its writs and warrants. Most disgraceful of all was the naming of the region's most notorious robber leader, one Joseph Scoffel, as a colonel in the provincial militia. In March, 1769, Scoffel's troops had arrested several Regulator leaders and were attempting to deliver their prisoners to the jail in Charlestown, all the while plundering the homes of the settlers along the Saluda. In response to a summons to arms, Regulators from all over the province were gathering to oppose him. After some preliminary skirmishes in which several lives were lost, just as the two forces were facing each other for battle, three gentlemen from Charlestown arrived with messages from the government disowning Scoffel's acts.

It was following these events that the satirical advertisement of a "Cargo of Fifty Thousand Prime Slaves" appeared on the Exchange bulletin board. To head off the impending conflict—with a speed resembling panic—the Governor and the Assembly began taking more sincere and effective steps to remedy the Regulators' grievances. As these reforms were put in operation, the Regulator movement began to subside, but the spirit lingered on, and the prejudices born of their conflicts with the colonial authorities were to have serious consequences for years to come.

These prejudices made Tories of most of the South Carolina backcountrymen until they themselves felt the restraining heel of the British forces in their own red hills. At the same time it was prejudices carried over from the Regulator movement that made Rebels of most of the North Carolina back country, because of their hate for Governor Tryon, the King's representative. When the Revolution started, Scoffel elected to fight as a Tory. That the Regulator spirit still pervaded the region is shown by this excerpt from a newspaper story of February, 1776:

> The young ladies of the best families of Mecklenburg County, N. C., have entered into a voluntary association that they will not receive the addresses of any young gentlemen of that place, except the brave volunteers who served in the expedition to S. C. & assisted in subduing the Scovilite insurgents. The ladies being of opinion that such persons as stay loitering at home, when the important calls of the country demand their military services abroad must certainly be destitute of that nobleness of sentiment, that brave manly spirit which would qualify them to be the defenders and guardians of the fair sex.

And it was the old Regulator spirit, excited by the news of the Battle of Lexington, manifesting itself in the menfolk of Mecklenburg and culminated months before, on May 20, 1775, leading them to

> dissolve the political bands which have connected us to the Mother Country,

and to go on and resolve that:

> we do hereby declare ourselves a free and independent People, are and of right ought to be, a sovereign and self-governing Association, under the control of no power other than that of our God and the General Government of the Congress; to the maintenance of which independence, we solemnly pledge to each other our mutual cooperation, our lives, our fortunes, and our most sacred honor.

And it was the same freedom-loving, oppression-hating Regulator spirit which moved the North Carolina Assembly to become the first colonial assembly to authorize its delegates to the Continental Congress to declare independence from Britain.

And it was the revolutionary spirit of the Regulators with their advocacy of free schools, disestablishment of the church, state-supported orphan homes, regulated lawyers' fees, and, yes, even income taxes, which joined forces with the merchants and artisans of New England to transform the American Revolution from a war fought simply for independence to a revolution in fact.

Of all the interesting aspects of the Carolina Regulator movement, none can surpass the enigma of its neglect by most American historians. That they have almost completely ignored such a dynamic revolutionary spirit with profound effects upon the stream of American history, and that the

Battle of Alamance is little known beyond the Carolinas, can only be explained by confessing a far superior "press agency" for those events which occurred in the East. One suspects that the shot at Concord was "heard" round the world mainly because of the publicity Emerson gave it. Alamance had no Emerson. Agreeable to this argument is the observation that every school child in America knows of the *Mayflower*, but almost none have ever even heard of its unadvertised predecessor, the *Sarah Constant*, which had landed the first permanent English settlers in America more than a dozen years before the *Mayflower*'s famous voyage.

🌷 🌷 🌷 🌷 🌷 *14. Christopher Gadsden's Liberty Boys*

*P*eace and quiet were not in the cards for Charlestown. For a long time past and for a long time to come, crisis was endemic in the city. As the tension which had gripped the colonial capital as a result of the demands of the back-country folk was eased somewhat by grudgingly granted partial reforms, the ever-growing tension between the colonies and England mounted apace. The joy and relief that had swept the town when the news arrived that the Stamp Act had been repealed had been soon dispelled by the news of the unreasonable Townshend Acts, of which the tax on tea was the longest lived and the most resented.

By 1775 there were already disillusioned citizens seriously advocating the removal of the statue of Mr. Pitt from its place of high honor in the intersection of Broad and Meeting Streets, partly because it was proving a serious traffic obstruction of the town's busiest corner, but, principally, because of the bitter memories it evoked of past high hopes now fast becoming disillusionment. It had been a happy day in the troubled history of the town when the ship bearing the statue had been welcomed with wild enthusiasm, crowds cheering, ships decorated for the occasion, bells pealing. And then there had been the day of pomp and ceremony several weeks later on July 5, 1770, when, to the accompaniment of a twenty-six-gun salute and much grand oratory, the statue was placed upon its pedestal. That day it seemed that the colonists' struggle to gain the full traditional rights of Englishmen was bearing fruit and that happier days lay ahead.

Pitt's success in securing the repeal of the Stamp Act had taken much of the wind from the very wide sails of the eloquent Christopher Gadsden, who had for years been whipping into violent enthusiasm a militant minority, mostly composed of the artisans of the city. Nightly, except Sundays, beneath the Liberty Tree, a giant oak in Isaac Mazyck's pasture near where the present Calhoun Street met the marsh of the wide Cooper River estuary, the erudite merchant harangued his Liberty Boys on the iniquities of Parliament and the King across the sea, on the one hand—and, curiously enough, the equally militant and even more liberty-loving Regulators, in the interior, to the west. For a while, what with the Regulators mollified by the steps which had been taken to establish courts and schools and a degree of representation in the Assembly for the interior, and with the Stamp Act repealed, the conservative gentry of the city entertained high hopes for the eclipse of their radical member, of whom they disapproved as heartily as they did of his New England counterpart, Samuel Adams.

But a stupid and blundering government and a headstrong King, determined not to be pushed around by a bunch of insolent colonials, dashed the hopes of that brilliant group of moderates who controlled the colony, among whom were

Henry Laurens, the Rutledges, John and Edward, and William Henry Drayton.

Just when the crisis atmosphere was being measurably dissipated, in 1771, three pistol shots from two dueling pistols opened anew the dying agitation and spread repercussions the whole length of the colonies. Ordinarily, duels were private affairs and, however tragic their consequences, were accepted by society as a part of the social order of the day. But this one was different. One of these shots had taken the life of the son of the Huguenot Chief Justice De Lancey, of New York, a prominent Tory. The shot was fired by Dr. John Haley, whose political sympathies lay with Gadsden's Liberty Boys. Rendered indiscreet by too much to drink in a public tavern in St. Michael's Alley, the two men became involved in a political discussion. Dr. Haley had remarked that the Tories in Boston and New York were influenced in their political opinions solely by money reasons, which was proven by the fact that the northern Whigs were all poor men; while in South Carolina, he said, neither Whigs nor Tories were influenced by property interests, as evidenced by the fact that some of the wealthiest citizens were Whigs. De Lancey shouted that this was a lie, and necessarily a challenge followed. Ordinarily, no charges of murder were brought after a killing in a duel, but in this instance both parties ignored the niceties of the dueling code and simply retired to an upstairs room to shoot it out by candlelight without seconds and the other requisite formalities. The moderate John Rutledge defended Dr. Haley before a Royalist court and secured an acquittal on the grounds of self-defense. The case became a *cause célèbre* and the justice of the verdict was widely disputed. And always the disputants' views were political rather than legal. The Liberty Boys celebrated with bonfires at the Liberty Tree, and had a great dinner in honor of the acquitted doctor.

To these rekindled fires the blundering administration

of Lord North added fuel in the form of a determination as a matter of principle to enforce the duty on tea. Not only in New England but also in the ports of North Carolina and in Charlestown harbor, this imperial determination was met by an equally determined colonial resistance. With each successive cargo of tea arriving in the harbor, resentment increased. During 1773 resistance to the tea tax became violent. At first the shipments were forcibly impounded and stored. Incident piled upon incident until, in the fall of 1774, shipments were consigned to the harbor waters of both Charlestown and Georgetown.

As feeling mounted, Gadsden's artisans were joined by many of the more prominent citizenry. Finally a "General Meeting" of protest was called and nonuse pledges were generally circulated. From this General Meeting by direct, uninterrupted descent grew the representative government which would henceforth control first the colony, later the independent republic, and finally the State of South Carolina. Through the rostrum of the General Meeting, the political thinking of the colonial leadership quickly moved from the specific to the general, from the tea tax to the fundamental rights of Englishmen and on to the doctrine of the sovereignty of the people. By the summer of 1774, Gadsden's militant minority was powerful enough to name three of the five delegates to the First Continental Congress in Philadelphia. With Gadsden, sharing his left-wing views, were the elder Thomas Lynch and Edward Rutledge. The conservatives were Henry Middleton and John Rutledge.

In spite of the fact that during much of this period the King's colonial representative was the beloved William Bull, the Lieutenant-Governor, as the months passed relations between the colony and the mother country rapidly deteriorated, the rift widening to a chasm. Many were already convinced that the chasm could not be bridged—that armed conflict was inevitable. Concrete preparatory steps for that conflict were well under way early in 1775.

When in April the General Assembly dutifully met in response to summons from His Excellency for the purpose of receiving a message of very grave import, the members must all have worn the expression of the proverbial cat that swallowed the canary. Solemnly they listened to the reading of the message informing the Assembly that from the third story of the State House in which they were meeting a great quantity of arms and ammunition were missing. Included in this "very extraordinary and alarming disappearance" were some eight hundred guns, two hundred cutlasses, and sixteen hundred pounds of powder. All enquiry into the matter had failed to reveal the identity of the guilty parties. With ostentatious formality the Assembly appointed a committee to investigate the matter. After a plausible interval the committee reported that it had made all possible inquiry but had been unable to get any information relative to the removal of the arms. To keep His Excellency informed as to the temper of the times the pure conjecture was made that

> there is reason to suppose that some of the inhabitants of this colony may have been induced to take so uncommon and extraordinary a step in consequence of the late alarming reports received from Great Britain.

So was played a little comedy which was to prove to be but the prelude to the great tragedy to follow. For everyone in the Assembly knew that the arms affair was the work of the "Secret Committee," most of whom were sitting right there in the Assembly chamber. That committee, headed by William Henry Drayton, had been appointed by the Provincial Congress (the direct descendant of the General Meeting) "to see that the State take no harm." The gentlemen of the Assembly knew, the Lieutenant-Governor knew, and they both knew that the other knew, all about the whole thing. A crowd, including such notables as Henry Laurens, Thomas Lynch, Colonel Charles Pinckney, the President of the Congress, Benjamin Huger and William Bull, the Governor's own nephew, had witnessed the robbery from the guarded building. And the thieves wore no masks or disguises. Yet not a witness could be found who could identify any one of the culprits! This was very suggestive of a later day when the public was deaf and blind to the very public activities of unorthodox justice by the "invisible empire" of the Ku-Klux.

Thus the stage was set for the awful tragedy which was to be the lot of this region in the years to come. The duel psychology had gripped those in control. With reckless disregard of their own best interests, throwing discretion to the winds, the Charlestown leaders, radicals and conservatives alike, who together led but a minority of the Carolinians, made ready for war.

They made ready for a war which at first was no more a revolution than was the Confederate War that would again crush the country eight decades later. They were marching into a war of independence from a central government whose acts they resented in principle—even in the face of what must have been obvious to them, that this war meant ruin to their colony, which at the time was the flower of colonial America.

Henry Laurens, William Henry Drayton, the Rutledges, Charles Pinckney, Arthur Middleton, Rawlins Loundes and Christopher Gadsden were brilliant men. They must have known that the lifeblood of the Carolina economy was export—export to England. Economically, England had been partial to the colony. Its indigo bounties had stimulated this principal crop of the region to an annual 1,170,000 pounds of the precious dyestuff. War would and did mean the utter ruin of this crop. Exports from South Carolina (and

North Carolina was in the same boat to a lesser degree) to Great Britain for the years just before the war far exceeded those of all the colonies north of Maryland and were greater than those of Virginia and Maryland combined. There were such items as an annual average export of 125,000 barrels of rice, 250,000 pounds of hemp, 200,000 barrels of tobacco, 100,000 pounds of raw silk, 15,000 pounds of beeswax, and 184,000 deerskins. For a few thousand producers these were rich exports indeed, all of which would cease with war. Visiting in Charlestown on the eve of the Revolution, Josiah Quincy of Masschusetts described the harbor of the capital as crowded with more ships than any other in America. He told of the grand music at the St. Cecelia concerts, listened to by the elegantly dressed ladies and men, attired in great finery, most of the men with beautiful dress swords; of the horse races, in which extravagantly priced horses were matched; and of the grand mansions of the gentry such as that of Miles Brewton—"a most superb house said to have cost eight thousand pounds sterling."

Knowing full well that war with their best customer would destroy the economic base upon which this cultivated society rested, these brilliant men prepared, nevertheless, for the sake of their honor and the fundamental principles involved, to fight the duel, regardless of the odds, in defense of the principle that the Assembly which they had long dominated was the governing power of their land; and that the Stamp Act, the tea duty, the shipping laws and other such acts of the Parliament, the central government, were in violation of "Provincial Rights," a principle from which in the years to come would stem that of "States' Rights."

Moreover these men must have known that the course they were following was reckless as that of any duel ever fought, however great the odds. They must surely have known that they had back of them a very small minority of the people. In their own city most families were themselves divided, Tory and Whig. In the back country the large settlements of Germans in the Orangeburg District and in the forks of the Saluda and Broad were loyal to the German King George and would remain staunchly Tory throughout the conflict. The numerous Scotch-Irish were Presbyterians and Baptists, hating with religious fervor the Established Church to which belonged most of the Charlestown leaders. The sentiments of the Regulators were still very much alive. Most of the grievances that inspired that movement still remained, and those grievances emanated from the coastal aristocracy, not from Great Britain. Stamp taxes and tea taxes were of little concern to those people. They had little dealings with paper of any kind, and tea was rarely found in their cabins. And it was Charlestown that had been governing them and taxing them without representation of their section in the Assembly. So these back-country people were overwhelmingly Tory with a radical revolutionary bent directed against the provincial government.

Only among those who had been swept into the North Carolina Regulator movement was there to be found any large body of Whigs in the back country. The people of Mecklenburg, Anson, Orange and Rowan had been so incensed against the army of Governor Tryon, who to them represented the King in America, that they were ready recruits against the mother country. From these regions would come much of the fighting strength of the Rebel militia that would eventually turn the tide of the war in its later years.

Of more serious import than the disaffection of so much of the back country to the cause was the disinterest of the overwhelming preponderance of those people. And it is probable that even the brilliant leaders in Charlestown and in the other colonial centers of government did not anticipate this apathy on the part of the great majority of the people living out of touch with the sea. The truth is that up and down the whole length of the American colonies only a small proportion of the people were sufficiently interested in the issues to fight on either side, and of those who did fight many more fought as Tories than as Rebels. Washington's army never exceeded twenty-two thousand men, and not more than eighteen thousand on the American side were ever involved in any battle during the war. An estimated fifty thousand Americans served in the British army. Had the Americans been as united in their cause and as fervently patriotic as were the African Dutch in the Boer War, the American army should have had three hundred thousand men. Even with the eventual help of the French, and the invaluable assistance of the semiorganized bands of militia, especially in Carolina, where so much of the burden of the war was borne by them during the latter years of the conflict, the ultimate victory stands out as a most remarkable achievement of an inspired minority. The disinterest of most Americans during the Revolution was much less prevalent in the Carolinas than in any other section. For here, mostly in the valleys of the Santee tributaries, most of the battles were fought during the last three years of the war. Here as nowhere else for three long years the war was carried on in the populous interior. Under such conditions it was well-nigh impossible for individuals to avoid involvement. Here it was largely a civil war, Americans against Americans. That is why relatively far more Carolinians fought in the American Revolution (on one side or the other) than was the case in any other section.

So as the gentry of the coast were preparing to face a trial by bullets for the sake of honor and principles, they must have had a fearful realization of how alone they stood —Tories in their midst, Tories in the interior, beyond that in the hills a little-interested multitude. Finally, there were large numbers of Negro slaves, comprising a substantial majority of the entire population of the region, who were regarded as a potential, dangerous "internal enemy" which must always be watched. As the leaders prepared to risk their all for liberty, and, later, as they read the immortal words of Jefferson that "all men are created free and equal," a delicate sophistry must have been required when they thought of these black men who were the numerical majority of all Carolinians. The irony of the double standard under which the Carolinians then lived is pointed up by an incident during the tension-filled days of 1775. Some slaves, many of whom could speak few words of English, had heard shouts of "Liberty" on every hand and began parroting the word during times of gaiety. Hearing the "sacred word" from the lips of the blacks suddenly brought terror to the heart of the city. Rumors of an impending slave uprising swept the town and the plantations, calling for special vigilance on every hand until the fright passed. The liberty for which a war was about to be fought was emphatically exclusively for the white minority.

May 8, 1775, news of Lexington and Concord reached the city—the awaited signal to fire for those who stood ready on the field of honor.

❧ ❧ ❧ ❧ ❧ *15. Stout hearts and tough logs*

*I*t was early in the morning of June 28, 1776, the day on which a red-haired young genius from Virginia, Thomas Jefferson, would rise before the worry-worn congregation of bewigged gentlemen of the Continental Congress in Philadelphia and read the elegant flowing words in which had been couched the principles of Locke and Paine for popular consumption in his Declaration of Independence. The nation's umbilical cord was cut.

Six hundred miles to the south, on Sullivan's Island, a sandy sea island, which forms the upper lip of the mouth of Charleston harbor, a heavy-set, middle-aged officer in a scarlet-trimmed blue coat and white breeches and with a black feather in his cap was leisurely riding along a sandy path which snaked its way among the wind-clipped clumps of myrtle, cassina and scrubby live oaks on his way to the northeast end of the island, where ran the shallow inlet separating this island from the next island beach to the north, which now is known as the Isle of Palms but then was called Long Island. This officer was Colonel William Moultrie of the South Carolina regulars, who was taking advantage of the freshness of the early morning of a day which promised to be exceedingly warm, to inspect Colonel William Thompson's motley aggregation of two hundred North Carolina Provincials, two hundred South Carolina Provincials, a small group of local militia, fifty coonskin-capped riflemen from the back country, known as the Raccoon Company, and a band of Catawba warriors. These troops had entrenched themselves behind low barricades of palmetto logs in hopes of preventing nearly three thousand British regulars, under Major General Lord Cornwallis and Sir Henry Clinton, from crossing the shallow waters of the narrow inlet from Long Island where they had landed several days before. As the path approached Colonel Thompson's post, it emerged from the brush-covered dunes to an open area, permitting a view of the whole expanse of the Charlestown harbor entrance. Reining his horse to a stop, he turned his stern, hard-bitten face across the water to Five Fathom Hole, where now, for almost a month, a formidable British fleet of some fifty vessels had ominously lain in wait for the right time to storm the colonial metropolis of the South. What Moultrie saw as his eyes surveyed that now-familiar sight caused him instantly to wheel and gallop with all haste back along the sandy path he had just traveled.

By ten o'clock he was back at the odd-looking, half-built log-and-sand structure locally known as the Fort on Sullivan's Island. As he entered the great timbered gate in the partially built back wall, he snapped immediate orders for the long roll to beat summoning the garrison to their posts. Hurriedly, but painfully, for the Colonel suffered from gout, he made his way up the ladder to the vantage of the gun platform where before that day was done, by dint of bravery, fortitude and quite a liberal bounty of good luck, he would emblazon his name in the top echelon of American Revolutionary heroes. Tense and alert, the gun crews waited. With billowing sails shining in the sunlight, with fair wind and tide, eleven fighting ships of His Majesty's navy were just coming within range, as they bore down on the miserable looking structure, which was absurdly daring to challenge their power and majesty.

Leading up to this shining hour had been more than a year of hectic preparation since the armed clashes in New England had turned this long extended conflict from a state of quasi war into a shooting war throughout the land.

Realizing that they could rely on the assistance of but a small portion of the entire population, the Carolina revolutionists' first moves were directed towards increasing their own numbers. To this end every device was soon being employed—oratory, dulcet talk, boycotts, threats, and even rail riding and tarring and feathering those who were slow to appreciate the advantages of liberty. The Provincial Congress had created an association which pledged its members to "go forth and be ready to sacrifice our lives and fortunes to secure her [South Carolina's] freedom and safety," and to "hold all those persons inimical to the liberties of the colonies who refuse to subscribe to this association." As such pressures were being exerted against the conservatives in the capital, Drayton and the Reverend William Tennent set out for a tour of the back country to enlist Association members among the people back there who were now for the first time very much desired by their former enemies of the coast. Their tour was a complete failure. The people in the hills were not "interested in the issues or the conflict." A few recruits to the Whig camp were gained through the indignation aroused by false rumors of a British plot to bring the Cherokees down on the frontier. Local rivalries recruited a few more for the Rebels, as Tory detachments under local officers began roaming the back country and organizing the countryside for the King. By the fall this ferment had exploded into armed conflict and the civil war which was to last in the hills for seven bloody years of almost ceaseless struggle was begun.

Back in the capital the authorities were bending every effort to prepare the city for the inevitable attack. In September all semblance of royal government disappeared when the new Governor, Lord William Campbell, was forced to take refuge on a man-of-war in the harbor, proudly taking with him the Great Seal of the colony. This development was soon followed by a formal declaration of war by the Provincial Congress on November nineteenth.

Several weeks previously Colonel Moultrie's provincial troops had seized the city batteries, and a detachment under Captain Charles Cotesworth Pinckney had crossed the harbor and seized Fort Johnson (which would in the years to come loom large in history when its batteries would fire the first shots of the Confederate War), the principal defense work of the harbor, guarding its southern shore. But attacking ships might easily run by this fort by hugging the north shore of the bay so, if the city was to be successfully defended, some fortification of the northern shore was imperative. Accordingly, in January, Mr. Dewees, who owned the sea island above Long Island, was instructed

> to furnish palmetto logs until further orders, not less than ten inches diameter in the middle. One third are to be eighteen feet long, the other two-thirds twenty feet long.

He was to

> be allowed one shilling per foot for all such logs as delivered in which delivery the utmost expedition must be used.

Of these logs and the sand of the island, with the help of a few other timbers and some iron bolts, the fort on Sullivan's Island was built. The site chosen for the structure was the narrow southwest end of the island, where a wide shallow cove separated the island from the mainland behind which in turn lay the expanse of the lower Cooper River, isolating it further from the city the fort was to defend. The design of the fort was simple indeed, a plain rectangular structure, large enough to accommodate a thousand troops, with bastions at each corner. The strength of the work was to lie in the double walls, sixteen feet apart, built of Dewees's palmetto logs securely bolted together, with the space between filled with sand. Inside, ten feet from the top, the gun platforms were to be built of heavy oak timber.

Day after day, through the spring, volunteer artisans from the city and large gangs of Negro slaves hired from the neighborhood planters sweated and strained at the job. Even so, by June only the southeast and southwest walls were finished. And the day of reckoning was prematurely at hand. On June 1, 1776, to the despair of the worn workers at the fort and to the consternation of the people back in town, a terrifying armada of fifty sails loomed on the horizon and dropped anchor just beyond the harbor bar. Work on the main structure was immediately abandoned and all hands were detailed to protect as far as possible the two missing sides with low breastworks of earth and heavy timbered fences. But discouraging work this must have been. They must have felt that they had lost their race against time, for what chance had a two-sided log fort with its little garrison of four hundred green troops and but sixty-two guns in place against the broadsides of ships of the line by sea, and at the same time an attack by land by the formidable army which all those transports must be carrying?

This discouraging outlook was made even more gloomy

by the arrival on the scene a few days later of Major General Charles Lee. Soon after his arrival, he crossed the river from the city to inspect the half-finished fort. In disgust he called it no better than a slaughter pen. The General was particularly shocked by Moultrie's failure to provide a retreat bridge from the fort across the waters of the cove to the mainland. Colonel Moultrie, accompanying the General around the works, was little impressed by this objection. To him a retreat bridge was entirely superfluous since the possibility of a retreat was nowhere in his plans. Retreat would mean the sacrifice of Colonel Thompson and his men, and this Moultrie would not consider. He and his devoted men expected to stay on the island, come what may.

To command the Southern area in the spreading conflict, General Washington had selected General Lee and ordered him to Charlestown to direct its defense. His brilliant reputation gained in wars all over Europe had preceded him, so when he arrived in the city on June fourth, the crisis-bound town welcomed him jubilantly. Giving vent to a vast store of wishful thinking, they regarded him as their delivering genius. But the brusquely military, intensely energetic, ill-mannered, bad-tempered and unprincipled officer was either an empty barrel undeserving of his high reputation or he was already the traitor he was to prove himself at Monmouth two years later when he robbed Washington of his full victory by inexcusably permitting Clinton's trapped army to escape, and Washington to his face called him a "damned poltroon."

But in June, 1776, with the enemy fleet lying in wait at the harbor entrance, his reputation and energy did inspire hope and activity in the populace of the frightened city. The whole town, freemen and slaves alike, were set frantically to work preparing the defense. Down came the wharf houses along the East Bay water front, that the defending guns might have free play for any target afloat. Breastworks were hastily thrown up along that water-front street and in many other places where attacks might be made. Hundreds of women and children were evacuated to the already crowded plantation houses. Peter Timothy's presses were hidden in the country and the *Gazette* suspended. Lead for bullets was taken from the windows of houses and even from the churches. Fort Johnson was strengthened. Day after day the General was frenetically dashing about the port, personally directing all these activities. And almost every day a personal visit was made or a courier was dispatched by canoe across the bay to the confident Colonel in the log fort on Sullivan's Island, continuing to urge the construction of a retreat bridge and instructing him on what steps he was to take when his powder became exhausted. But for the interference of John Rutledge, who had great confidence in Moultrie and little confidence in Lee, the General would surely have ordered the fort evacuated without a shot's being fired.

Such was the American prelude to those sails which could be seen bearing down on the log fort on the morning of June 28, 1776.

From the standpoint of the British command, happenstance had brought them there. During the previous December, Lord Dartmouth, who was directing the American war, had equipped a naval expedition under Sir Peter Parker, to attack the Southern colonies. It was to co-operate with Major General Sir Henry Clinton, who would add part of the troops being evacuated from Boston to the nine regiments which accompanied the naval force. On Clinton's staff was young Lord Cornwallis who on this expedition would receive his first introduction to the region he would for so long struggle in vain to subjugate for his king. Dartmouth had given Sir Peter the option of striking at Virginia, Cape Fear or Charlestown. The deposed royal governors, Martin of North Carolina and Campbell of South Carolina, had joined the expedition and each urged attack on his erstwhile bailiwick by representations of the Tory strength that would welcome

the invaders. Governor Martin won out, and plans were laid
to direct the attack up the mouth of the Cape Fear River.
But when they reached North Carolina, these plans were
jolted by news of the decisive defeat the North Carolina
Tories had suffered at the hands of General Richard Caswell's Whigs in the battle of Moore's Creek Bridge. This
development called for a council of war on the *Bristol,* Sir
Peter's flagship, where the plans for attack were reviewed,
and Charlestown received the nod. So it came to pass that, on
June first, the fleet dropped anchor there beyond the protecting bar. Ten days later soundings had revealed the entrance channel and the fleet had entered the calmer waters of
Five Fathom Hole. In the days that followed, between two
thousand and three thousand men were ferried from the
transports to Long Island, there to suffer from the heat
and "Moschetoes, than which no torment can be greater,"
while they awaited the attack in which their part was to be
an attack across the shallow water of the inlet to gain the
north end of Sullivan's Island, where Colonel Thompson's
command awaited them, hoping thereby to flank the log fort
and attack its unfinished rear.

With the dawn of June twenty-eighth, word was passed
among the ships of the fleet and on to the troops on Long
Island that their long wait was over. The tide was right,
the wind was right. This was the appointed day. On the
Bristol and the *Experiment,* fifty-gun ships of the line, on the
bombship *Thunder* and on the twenty-eight-gun frigates *Acteon, Solebay, Sphynx, Syren* and *Active* and on the twenty-
six-gun *Friendship* could be heard the varied sounds of preparation. Nine o'clock and sails were aloft and the leaders
under way towards the contemptible pile of logs on the sand-
spit to the northwest. They could easily have sailed safely by
on the other side out of range of the guns of the fort—and in
another day they would no doubt have done just that—but

in the eighteenth century the book didn't include by-passing and leaving strong points isolated to the rear. The fort was there to challenge their might and it must be attacked.

Back in the fort, behind the palmetto logs, Colonel Moultrie, Colonel Isaac Motte, and Major Francis Marion were giving last-minute instructions to their untrained gun crews who would this day become seasoned veterans. In the tense moments as they waited before the first bomb burst among the palmetto-leaf shelters which had been built in the enclosure for the garrison, they must have looked with pride on their new blue flag with the white crescent in its corner as it fluttered in the breeze above the southeast bastion.

Puffs of black smoke rolled from the mortars on the *Thunder,* which had anchored a mile and a half away. A tense moment—blood-chilling whines—a series of earth-shaking explosions, as the thirteen-inch bombs fell and exploded in and around the fort—and the battle was on. It later developed that these first shots from the *Thunder* very nearly put it out of commission without doing any appreciable damage to the Americans. In an effort to stretch their range the gunners had overcharged the mortar seats and nearly broken up the ship itself, all to little avail, for most of the bombs buried themselves either in the soft sand or in marshy spots, so that even when they exploded they did but slight damage.

Eight other ships sailed on towards the fort and anchored before it in a double line, some of them less than five hundred yards away. Soon, amid clouds of black smoke they were all pouring furious broadsides from their 238 guns. All who were supposed to know about such things had predicted that under such pounding the fort would be leveled in less than an hour. But these authorities were not familiar with palmetto logs. They did not split, splinter, or break. With dull thuds the cannon balls simply sank themselves into the soft fibrous logs. Nor did the grapeshot ricochet, so only the balls that passed through the gun embrasures could do damage.

With methodical coolness the fort began to reply with deadly accuracy of aim. But there were long intervals between shots, for Colonel Moultrie had but a scanty supply of powder, barely twenty-eight rounds for the twenty-six guns which could be aimed at the enemy ships in the position in which they had anchored. The broadsides from the fleet did little more than shake the fort while its infrequent but telling replies were wreaking havoc on the ships, especially on the flagship and on the *Experiment*, for throughout the day these two had been the special targets of the Americans, Moultrie's orders being to "Mind the Admiral! Mind the fifty-gun ships!"

Seeing that they were getting nowhere by the frontal assault, Sir Peter sent the *Acteon*, *Sphynx*, and *Syren* to round the point that they might direct their fire across the unfinished rear wall directly at the defending gunners. Here good luck played a trump card for the Rebels: ignorant of the channels, the ships ran aground and two of them suffered serious damage by collision as they came about after escaping from the shoal. But the *Acteon* was stuck hard and fast in the sand of the shoal, the same shoal which would again loom large in history as the site of Fort Sumter. By this time the bomb ship had so injured itself that it had to drop out of the battle. The decks of the fifty-gun ships were strewn with wreckage and running with blood. But still the attack was stoutly pursued and the heavy cannonade continued.

As the afternoon wore on the supply of powder in the fort was becoming perilously low, and so for long intervals the fort remained silent in the face of the unrelenting pounding it was receiving. A powder reserve had to be saved for the rifles in case Colonel Thompson should be forced back into the fort by Clinton's men, who were attacking across the inlet from Long Island.

It was during one of these periods of impatient waiting for the next shot that was permitted that an enemy shell severed the staff carrying the blue banner which, through the day, as it waved above the bastion, had become the pride of the garrison; and the flag had fallen to the ground in front of the fort. When he heard the cheer which rose from the British ships as the flag went down, Sergeant Jasper, an untaught boy from Georgia, called to Colonel Moultrie:

"Colonel, don't let us fight without our colour!"

"How can you help it, the staff is gone?"

By way of response, Jasper climbed to the parapet and down the log wall which was then being raked with fire. A moment later he was back on the bastion with the rescued flag, fixing it to a sponge staff. This accomplished, he stayed to give three huzzas before leaping back to the safety of the gun platform. Later in the war, at Savannah, Jasper lost his life as he attempted to duplicate this heroic feat.

Meanwhile, at the other end of the island where Thompson's five hundred faced Clinton's overwhelming numbers across the shallow inlet, fate had again fortuitously evened the odds. A spring tide augmented by a stiff sea breeze had made the inlet much deeper than usual. With this assist, Thompson's riflemen and three small cannons had repulsed every effort of the British to make the crossing to Sullivan's Island.

As night fell, a violent thunderstorm descended on the harbor. Thus nature provided an appropriate finale to the day. The guns on the ships fell silent. As the storm lifted, the battered vessels dropped back to Five Fathom Hole, leaving the *Acteon* on the bar. Next day her crew set fire to her and rowed away. When the fire reached the magazine she blew up with a tremendous explosion, which mounted into a high column of smoke capped with a great ball atop the column, outlining a gigantic palmetto tree.

By way of epilogue: President Rutledge presented his own sword to Sergeant Jasper. The Continental Congress voted its thanks to General Lee! The fort on Sullivan's Island was named Fort Moultrie, in honor of its gallant defender and he was made a brigadier. A palmetto tree was put in the center of the blue flag with the crescent in its corner. The British sailed away, not to return, except for halfhearted offshore blockades, for three more years.

❧ ❧ ❧ ❧ ❧ *16. The seeds of wrath are planted*

*I*n the winter of 1779, for the American cause there was no basis for optimism and even little occasion for hope. It had been nearly three years since the victory of Fort Moultrie and more than a year since that at Saratoga—the only two significant victories of the war thus far. The encouragement which they and a few minor successes offered were far from sufficient to offset the discouragement engendered by what otherwise appeared to be an endless series of defeats. The fortuitous victory at Saratoga, in October, 1777, was soon followed by the horrors of Valley Forge, where Washington's ill-clad, half-starved army dwindled to a discouraged three thousand—half-starved, not because food in the neighborhood was scarce, but rather because the farmers of the region preferred the good hard cash of the British customers to the continental currency with its very dubious future. The long-sought alliance with the French in February had brought little in the way of tangible

help and there had been no more victories to lift the patriots'
waning spirit before another hard winter was upon the Continental Army, and it again shrank to a bare three thousand
men. During this ebb tide of fortune, the whole American
government, civil and military, was riven clear to its failing
heart by the notorious Conway Cabal, having for its objective
the removal of Washington from his position as supreme
commander. Amid the mounting disasters it was difficult for
even the more astute to see, as we now see, that merely by
keeping his army intact in the field Washington's persever-
ance was slowly beginning to win the war by attrition of the
enemy. Certainly, in the winter of 1779, the British did not
realize that. To them it seemed obvious that now only the
coup de grace was necessary to end the war. But that in itself was extremely difficult. Experience had already clearly
demonstrated that Washington was a genius of the maneuver
and had proved impossible to capture. For four years he had
eluded every trap set for him. So another trap, on a continental scale, was planned.

This plan called for an attack up through the Southern
colonies. Except in capturing Charlestown, little difficulty
was anticipated in accomplishing the first phase of this plan
—the conquest of the Southern colonies—for Georgia was
largely unsettled then and South Carolina was overwhelmingly Tory in its inclinations, at least beyond the coastal
fringe. With these initial conquests accomplished, Washington would be caught in a great pincers movement between
Clinton's forces operating out of New York and the army
moving up from the South. The problem of supplying the latter force would not be great, for as it moved up through the
South it would be traversing a rich, well-settled area and
could easily live off the conquered land.

The primary objective of the first phase of this master
plan was the Santee valley, stretching as it does all the way
across South Carolina and extending more than halfway

across North Carolina towards Virginia, through rich country where supplies could be easily obtained; and at the same time difficult terrain, fevers, and disaffection of the low-lying coastal country could be avoided. The only major difficulty in the execution of this plan would be the capture of a convenient port of entry into that valley. All roads of the region led to Charlestown. It was the traditional sea outlet of the whole valley and even beyond, to the borders of Virginia. So it was decided that another attempt would have to be made to seize the town. But the lesson of 1776 was too well remembered to permit another attempt at a frontal attack. Plans were laid to take the city by land.

To this end Savannah had been seized, without much difficulty, in December, 1778. After consolidating his position around that port by the following spring, General Prevost was moving up the coast to attack Charlestown, pillaging and burning as he went, unless the owners redeemed their property from the torch by an oath of allegiance to the King, which a great many did. In early May, he crossed the Ashley River, moved down the narrow neck between the Ashley and the Cooper, and laid siege to the town with about twenty-four hundred men, mostly British regulars; but the authorities in the city thought he had a much larger force and so had little confidence in any attempt to defend the town with their three thousand troops, most of whom were green militia. In the face of what he thought were overwhelming odds, John Rutledge, whose title had recently been changed from President to Governor, concluded that the city's best hope lay in a play for time in the hope of relief in the form of the Southern Continental Army under General Benjamin Lincoln, a New Englander of respectable mediocrity whom Washington had recently sent down to take command of the Southern Department. While Prevost was knocking at the gates of Charlestown, Lincoln, with five thousand men, was dawdling in the neighborhood of Augusta, considering an attack on Prevost in Savannah. Couriers from the Governor, telling of the capital's plight, brought him painfully slowly to the rescue. While the besieged city fearfully awaited the expected attack, the Governor studiedly kept alive negotiations for surrender. Next came a costly blunder. Stupidly, Lincoln dispatched a messenger through the enemy lines with a note to the Governor, telling him of his approach. The message captured, Prevost, in the nick of time, slipped by night back across the Ashley and soon was safe behind the protection of the marshes separating the sea islands to the south of the city from the mainland.

With a sigh of relief from what it had thought was a mortal threat, the city resumed for another year the more or less peaceful way of life it had enjoyed for the three years past. And for that year, as during the previous three years, the main feature of that life was a hectic wartime prosperity. During most of that time the other principal American ports were in British hands. Consequently, a large part of the outside supplies for the Americans had to enter the country through Charlestown and from there be sent northward by wagons as far as New Jersey. In the divided back country an informal armed truce prevailed. And even there the outlook for the cause had measurably improved.

Soon after the "Battle of Fort Moultrie" there had been a burst of fearful Cherokee raids against the frontier settlements. The conviction was widespread that these attacks had been inspired by British agents. This conviction served to convert many Tories and an even larger group of the undecided into the Whig camp. These raids promptly brought against the Indians fearful punitive expeditions from both the Carolinas—designed and executed to effect a devastation of the Cherokee villages so complete that the border would be safe while the war with Britain lasted. A footnote to this Indian war, significant in the history of the region, was the massacre of the family of Wade Hampton on Fairforest Creek in the Spartanburg district. Fortunately four of the Hampton boys, Edward, Richard, Henry and Wade, were absent from home at the time and so lived to serve well in the later years of the Revolution and to leave descendants whose lives would loom large in the history of the region.

Moore's Creek Bridge, Fort Moultrie, the Cherokee affair and Prevost's attack had none of them been costly engagements. So, by the time the sixth war year arrived, the Carolinas had been little more than singed by the fire that had raged so long. However, Prevost's attack was but a dress rehearsal for the first scene of the climax act on the far-flung stage of the war—an act which would concentrate the remainder of the war almost entirely in the Carolinas, especially in the Santee and Cooper valleys, turning them into the bloodiest and eventually the most devastated region of America; while the outcome of the whole war was being determined along the swamps of the Cooper and the Santee and amid the hills and valleys of the Santee tributaries all the way up to the distant mountains.

When Prevost reported his easy progress from Savannah to the gates of Charlestown, Clinton was inspired to stake the whole war on his plan to strike up through the Santee valley in force, to trap the elusive Washington. Being determined to run no risk of another failure in his attack on the key port city, he dispatched one of the largest forces employed in any battle of the war, about eleven thousand men, and a strong fleet to move co-operatively against the city by land and sea. Part of this army moved up from Savannah along the road Prevost had taken, but most of it was landed from the ships onto the sea islands down the coast from the town. By the end of March, 1780, Clinton had moved up from the south, crossed the Ashley and was setting siege to the city, into which Lincoln had unwisely retreated. Between the wide estuaries of the Ashley and the Cooper, with Sir Henry's army stretched from river to river on the north, Lincoln and his five thousand were effectually "treed." It was now only a question of how long it would take for the kill.

What with Fort Johnson on the south side of the harbor already in the enemy's hands, with the siege line across the neck and the sea blockade, the city was quickly shut off from all communication with the outside world, except for a not very helpful breathing tube across the Cooper estuary to Haddrell's Point and from there up the east side of the Cooper River to the lower Santee region. To close this gap and effect a complete encirclement, Clinton sent his dashing but ruthless cavalry officer, Colonel Banastre Tarleton, up the Cooper River against Colonel Isaac Huger at Monck's Corner. With almost no losses to his forces, Tarleton cut to pieces and completely routed the Americans in a surprise attack.

This opened the way for Cornwallis to cross the Cooper with three thousand troops and to move down to Haddrell's Point; and from there, the site of the present-day Mount Pleasant, he was able, without great difficulty, to accomplish what he had failed to accomplish in 1776—to take Fort Moultrie from its weak back side. The encirclement was now complete, but before this last avenue of escape was closed, to avoid the entire government falling into the hands of the enemy when the city fell, Governor Rutledge and two of his Council, Daniel Huger and John L. Gervais, left the city and headed up the Santee for the back country.

In the weeks that followed, broadsides from up to two hundred cannon hammered away at the tabby wall of lime and oyster shells which had been constructed all the way across the neck and at its abatis of embedded sharpened logs buried in the ground before the wall. And almost continually shells were falling among the buildings of the city, causing terrible damage. Fires raged, as fire shells ignited the wooden shingles of the housetops. A shell from Fort Johnson across the harbor carried away an arm from the statue of

Mr. Pitt, which had now become an ironic reminder of a more optimistic day when it was thought that the good efforts of that statesman had avoided just what the country was now suffering. Amid the turmoil of these horrors, acting Governor Christopher Gadsden and the other bearers of the torch of the Liberty Boys wrangled with General Lincoln and his military staff. They would not see the inevitability of defeat. They would not consider surrender. But, after forty days of siege, as the destruction mounted and it became increasingly clear that there would now be no help from outside, and with the enemy laterals dug to within twenty-five yards of the tabby wall, even Gadsden consented to terms when a petition for surrender, signed by a majority of both the residents and the militia, was handed to him.

Clinton's terms were irresistibly generous. While the Continentals were to be kept under guard as prisoners until exchanged, the citizens, including government officials, were to be considered as prisoners free on parole and the militia were to be

> allowed to go to their respective homes, and should be regarded as prisoners of war upon parole, which parole, so long as they observed it, should secure them from being molested in their property by the British troops.

Sir Henry moved into the Miles Brewton house, which, since its owner was lost at sea fleeing the city during the early days of the war, had become the town house of his sister Rebecca Motte. Comfortably ensconced there in the house which Josiah Quincy had so extravagantly admired, the general "requested" Mrs. Motte to attend to the housekeeping for him and his staff, which assignment she undertook until she obtained permission to move to her hill plantation overlooking the lower Congaree. As long as she stayed in Charlestown, she carefully kept her three pretty daughters under lock and key on the third floor of the mansion.

Within a week after the fall of Charlestown, Clinton dispatched columns to the interior to put the finishing touches on the conquest of the state which was already almost complete, simply through the fall of its capital. The largest of these, an army of about twenty-five hundred men under General Lord Cornwallis, was to proceed to Camden. He had ferried his army across the Santee and was proceeding up the east edge of the great swamp when he learned that hereabouts, a few days before, a regiment of infantry and a company of artillery under Colonel Abraham Buford had turned tail on hearing of the fall of Charlestown and were heading back towards Virginia whence they had come. Colonel Tarleton with 130 of his hard-riding cavalrymen, a hundred of whom had infantrymen mounted behind, set out in pursuit of Buford. His route lay through the High Hills of Santee where stood the summer home of Colonel Thomas Sumter, who in 1776 had been an officer under Colonel Thompson when Cornwallis and Tarleton had made their unsuccessful attempt to flank Fort Moultrie by crossing to Sullivan's Island from Long Island. Although he could hear the siege cannon in Charlestown during the second phase of the war, Sumter had this time stayed at home. But still he was considered an enemy. To even the score, Tarleton stopped here long enough to plunder and burn Sumter's home and thereby "roused the spirit of the lion."

Shortly before daylight, on May twenty-ninth, Tarleton's file of weary horsemen clinked and clattered along the steep and narrow road through the hills in the neighborhood of Colonel Henry Rugeley's plantation and mill. In the forty-odd hours since they had left the army by the Santee, they had already come 130 miles. They had left Camden at two that morning after resting a scant two hours. A man had already been sent ahead to notify Colonel Rugeley, a substantial Tory of the neighborhood, of their approach, that he might be getting ready for them, and now the Colonel was, without doubt, busily preparing for their arrival.

When the messenger arrived informing the Colonel of Tarleton's approach, the gentleman of the house was faced with a most difficult dilemma. At that very moment, asleep under his roof and recipients of his hospitality, were the fleeing Governor Rutledge and his Councillors—all that remained now of the civil government of South Carolina. Under the circumstances, where lay the host's "superior obligation?" His decision gave to history one of the very few chivalrous incidents in a war which was soon to become too bitter for chivalry to find a subject among its war-hardened hearts. With much difficulty, the Colonel awakened his travel-worn guests and sent them on their way northward towards Charlotte just in time to avoid his arriving guests.

Ten hours later, thirty miles farther up the road, Tarleton caught up with Buford's infantry and immediately attacked with overwhelming ferocity. While Buford's men were facing Tarleton's infantry troop, in the open woods, the British cavalry rode around Buford's flanks and began attacking from the rear. In a few moments they were being literally cut to pieces and Buford ordered a surrender flag. The officer displaying the flag was cut down by Tarleton's sword. No quarter was permitted and the slaughter continued. The Americans lost 264 killed and wounded too severely to leave the ground—more than two thirds of those involved in the battle. The British lost but five killed and a dozen wounded. It was a small battle, but it had a lasting significance, in that it immediately became known as Buford's Massacre, and the term "Buford's Quarter," with the irony it expressed, became a battle cry of the Rebels. It was a costly battle for the British, for Tarleton that day planted, in the red soil of that minor battlefield, the first seed from which would grow American victory in the South, the defeat of Clinton's great plan, and the ultimate achievement of independence.

At this point South Carolina was completely conquered. Beyond was North Carolina, all but defenseless. The conquest route to Virginia lay open. To all but the most optimistic the situation spelt only early and complete defeat of the American cause. Except in enemy prisons, in all South Carolina there was not left a single continental officer or even an organized band of Whig militia. Civil government was nonexistent. The only vestige of what had been the state's civil government was Governor Rutledge, who with his two Councillors was holed up back in northern North Carolina. For a long time this semblance of civil government would have its seat wherever hung the Governor's hat. The dynamic Drayton was dead. Henry Laurens, former president of the Continental Congress, had begun his long imprisonment in the Tower of London, which was to last until he was exchanged for Lord Cornwallis after Yorktown. Of the State's four signers of the Declaration of Independence, Thomas Lynch had been lost at sea and Arthur Middleton, Edward Rutledge and Thomas Heyward were on their way to spend the remainder of the war in Saint Augustine as British prisoners. A cell in the dark, roach-infested dungeon in the old Spanish fort in that town was chosen by the liberty-loving die-hard, Christopher Gadsden, rather than a bargain with the hated enemy for even the limited parole that would have meant for him the relatively comfortable existence which his fellow prisoners chose. Tough old Moultrie was a prisoner awaiting his exchange for Burgoyne. Colonels William Washington and Francis Marion had escaped capture at Charlestown but had been forced to flee to North Carolina, practically devoid of their commands, their men having melted away in the face of disaster. Colonels Isaac Hayne, Andrew Pickens and Joseph Kershaw had surrendered and taken protection. And beside the slow-flowing Cooper the Liberty Tree lay prostrated by British axes.

Meanwhile, during the few weeks which had elapsed since the fall of Charlestown, the leaderless Carolinians throughout the area were giving overwhelming co-operation to the conquerors. The surrender terms which Clinton had prescribed seemed liberal enough for a hopelessly conquered people. So, as soon as contingents from Charlestown established posts at Georgetown, Camden, Ninety-Six and Augusta, the people flocked into these places by the thousands to take the oath of allegiance and to receive protection certificates which they supposed guaranteed protection of their persons and property so long as they did not engage in armed opposition to the victors. The Tories came with hearts glad for the opportunity, the apathetic sought the security of the winning side with relief that the issues were being settled, and the Rebels sought protection from revenge because their cause seemed utterly lost.

A few days later, back in Charlestown, however, Clinton made a stupid and momentous blunder. During the few days prior to his departure for New York, Sir Henry largely devoted himself to his paper work. Reporting home to the Secretary of State, he wrote: "I may venture to assert that there are few men in South Carolina who are not either our prisoners or in arms with us." A long letter of instructions went to Cornwallis at Camden, outlining the steps he was to take in carrying the campaign up through the Carolina Piedmont to Virginia—obviously confident that this contemplated campaign was already all but won. Then came the great mistake—for some reason, he appears to have thought that an additional measure of firmness would serve to insure a larger measure of tranquillity during his absence. So a proclamation was published notifying the prisoners of war, who had "taken protection" and been released on parole, that their status as paroled prisoners might be revoked unless they actively supported the King even to the point of taking up arms against the Rebels. In effect, this was an order to turn traitor to the cause for which they had fought.

In the prostrate and conquered province the seeds of wrath were planted.

❦ ❦ ❦ ❦ ❦ *17. Brother against brother*

As Carolina was being wrapped in her oppressive blanket of summer, other seeds of wrath were added to those already planted by Tarleton and Clinton. The British victory had been the signal for a revoltingly ruthless group of Tory leaders to start "campaigning" all over the prostrate land, pillaging, burning and hanging. With the arrival of this period of Tory ascendancy, Colonel "Bloody Bill" Cuningham and Colonel Thomas Browne commenced paying back tenfold the indignities they had suffered during the years of Whig ascendancy. The accounts of Captain Christion Huck's barbarities are almost beyond belief. Major James Wemyss burned Presbyterian churches wherever he came upon them, calling them "sedition shops," thereby inflaming the numerous Scotch-Irish of the back country, especially in the country lying on both sides of the Catawba River near the present city of Charlotte. And to a people little accustomed to restraint, the not very gentle heel of the occupying military forces brought indignant reaction when they undertook to requisition the crops and livestock of the neighboring farmers.

Watered by tears of grief and disappointment, tears of frustrated anger and despair, the seeds of hate planted by the British and Tory leaders swelled and burst. The conquered province began to bristle.

In the wide path of utter destruction cut by Major Wemyss across the Williamsburgh region north of the Santee rose a tiny but desperate resistance band under Major John James. This band would soon be the nucleus of "Marion's Men." Huck's atrocities along the Catawba River inspired the organization of Colonel "Billy" Hill's regiment, to form the backbone of Sumter's partisans. The hangings of "Bloody Bill" Cuningham, in the Broad River region, recruited Colonel James Williams's regiment from the less cowed Rebels of the Laurens area. The unmerciful vengeance of Colonel Thomas Browne for a tar and feathering he had received at the hands of the Whigs led Colonel Andrew Pickens of the Ninety-Six District formally and officially to renounce his parole and take to the field again.

Rather than submit to the requisite oath to obtain parole, a goodly number of die-hard Rebels had fled before Cornwallis's advance and taken refuge in North Carolina in the "hornets' nest" of the Rebels, the region of the upper Catawba. Here many of them joined up with Sumter who was then organizing his forces. Meanwhile, North Carolina was also being given a taste of Tory pillage by "Colonel" James Moore, a notorious Tory of the Catawba region, inspiring there the same responses as were being given such conduct in South Carolina. Quickly, by the grapevine telegraph of the backwoods, General Griffith Rutherford, Colonel Francis Locke and Major Joseph McDowell called together their partisan bands and set out after Moore. At Ramsour's Mill, Moore's eleven hundred Tories were routed by a Whig force a quarter the size. News of the expected advance of Cornwallis into the state put militia commanders Colonel William Davidson and Major William R. Davie in the field, the latter to become one of the outstanding partisan leaders of the war and a peacetime leader of even greater stature. Early in July, his partisans successfully attacked the strong British post at Hanging Rock, a dozen miles east of where the Catawba becomes the Wateree. The same day Davidson attacked an outpost on the Peedee. The hornets were beginning to sting.

News of a Continental army moving down from the North further stirred the hornets' nest. Huck's hanging career was soon put to an end by his death when his post on Fishing Creek was attacked by a detachment of Sumter's men under colonels Edward Lacy, Hill, and Andrew Neel. A few days later Sumter marched down the west bank of the Catawba and laid siege to a fortified British post at Rocky Mount, overlooking the river near the mouth of Rocky Creek. Here the British were saved by a providential thunderstorm which extinguished the fires that volunteers, in the face of a rain of enemy bullets, had started by throwing pitch balls on the roof of their fortified house. Crossing to the east side of the river —a feat in itself for the swift wide stream was then in flood —he was joined by a group of North Carolinians under Colonel Robert Irwin and Major Davie. The objective of this rendezvous of the partisans was to pay a return visit to the crack Prince of Wales Regiment, which then occupied a challenging position on the north bank of Hanging Rock Creek.

Guided by the sound of the horse bells of the enemy, early Sunday morning, August sixth, the American line stealthily moved down into the ravine, on the opposite crest of which about fourteen hundred unsuspecting British were camped. With but five rounds of ammunition for each of their six hundred men, the partisan leaders with inspiring dauntlessness led their men across the boulder-strewn creek and up the almost precipitous slope to the British camp. In half an hour the Tory militia which was camped with the British regulars were in flight. Then the battle took on a traditional complexion, the British regulars massed in formation, bravely standing their ground as the partisans from protected positions behind trees and boulders poured their deadly fire into the mass. Ammunition from the bodies of the fallen enemy served to replenish the partisans' exhausted supply, permitting the battle to rage for three violent hours, until the men were so blackened by smoke that they looked like Negroes. But even as the battle raged, looting and drinking began. This distraction and the near exhaustion of their ammunition caused Sumter to call off the fighting and retire northward towards Charlotte Town. The partisans had lost seventy men, the British several hundred.

A thirteen-year-old boy with a tousled shock of red hair, bursting with pride in his recent appointment as an orderly and armed with a pistol given him by Major Davie, received that day his battle baptism. Andrew Jackson (even then unable to resist the lure of a scrap) had followed his sixteen-year-old brother, Robert, of Davie's band, from his nearby Waxhaw cabin.

Meanwhile, over in central North Carolina, heading southward from the slowly approaching Continental army, rode a score of ragged, half-starved horsemen, some white, some colored, having in common only their black leather caps embellished with a silver crescent and the words "Liberty or Death." At the head of the motley little column rode an unimposing, small, wiry, hook-nosed, middle-aged man, attired in a close, round-bodied, crimson jacket of a coarse texture. This man was Francis Marion, riding towards the wide swamps of the Santee—Francis Marion, riding into fame. A few days more and he, at the head of James's diehards, would be harassing the British supply lines extending from Charlestown to the interior along both sides of the Santee swamp.

As Marion was getting acquainted with the mere hand-ful of patriots of his new command and was directing them to affix white cockades in their hats that they might be dis-tinguished from the Tories in the raid he was already plan-ning, the Continental army crossed the Peedee, headed for Camden, where, under the command of Lord Rawdon, lay the bulk of the British forces in the interior.

For the background of this expedition it is necessary to turn back a bit and view the war on its larger national stage.

At the time Charlestown was under siege, the fortunes of the American cause had fallen to their lowest ebb. Washing-ton reported to Congress "there never has been a stage of the war in which the dissatisfaction has been so general or alarm-ing." He was sustained and inspired to carry on in the face of defeat only by the hope that Lafayette would soon return from France with sufficient aid to save the cause.

To add to the apparent hopelessness of his situation came General Lincoln's message informing Washington of his desperate situation in Charlestown and appealing for an expedition for his relief. Although Washington entertained little hope that any expedition he might send would be able to reach Charlestown before it would be forced to capitulate, and although he could ill spare any of the ten thousand men he then had under arms in the North, he knew that he must send assistance or the South would soon be entirely lost. Many people down there already entertained the conviction, and with the assistance of the enemy it was becoming widespread, that Congress was little interested in the Southern states and that it would make no great sacrifice to save them. So, if resist-ance was to continue in the predominantly Tory South, a relief expedition would have to go forward, even if it had al-most no hope of getting to Charlestown soon enough to help Lincoln. Accordingly, early in April, the Maryland line and the Delaware regiment, some two thousand men under Major General Baron de Kalb, moved southward. Encountering terrific difficulties in obtaining sufficient supplies, and constantly delayed by the lack of food, but picking up along the way some two thousand Virginia and North Carolina militia, he pushed slowly forward through a region poor in supplies and disaffected in sentiment. Heat, insects and violent thunderstorms added to his army's miseries. De Kalb, who had had wide experience in campaigning in Europe, wrote a friend that they there did not know what warfare was, that they "know not what it is to contend against obstacles." In Virginia and North Carolina, the governments lent no assistance, being only interested in their own militia, and in South Carolina there was no government. July was drawing to a close and Charlestown had long since fallen, and still the relief army had got no farther than central North Carolina. Here, to de Kalb's great relief, General Horatio Gates arrived and supplanted him in his command. Under pressure from the Congress, Washington had sent the "Hero of Saratoga" to command the Southern Department, although Washington himself realized that Gates was not a top-flight officer and far from deserving of the adulation he was then receiving.

Gates was shocked and discouraged by the conditions he found in his new command and industriously set about trying to remedy them. He became peremptory with the North Carolina militia which had been demonstrating little respect for de Kalb's orders. He made a valiant effort to rid the army of its enormous impedimenta of hundreds of camp followers with whom were being shared the meager rations and inadequate transport. This effort met with but partial success, and the army moved on into South Carolina with hundreds of women riding in the overburdened supply wagons.

Having crossed from the Peedee to the Catawba region on August fifteenth, Gates's army was encamped at Tory Colonel Rugeley's plantation, "Cleremont" on Granny's Quarter Creek, fifteen miles above the British station at Camden. That afternoon in Rugeley's big log barn, General Gates laid before his general officers the plans he had made. That night under the cover of darkness they would move down the road leading to Camden to where it crossed Sanders Creek. There, astride the road, they would take their positions along the north side of the three-hundred-yard-wide, muck-filled swamp through which the creek flows. Since, except where the road crosses it, the swamp was as good as any fort against Tarleton's cavalry, this position would be very strong. There, with the seven thousand men he thought he was commanding even though the majority of them were militia, Gates was confident of the outcome if he were attacked. To force upon the enemy a choice of attack or withdrawal back to Charlestown, he had sent Colonel Sumter and Colonel Christian Senf, his Swedish department engineer, across the Wateree, to proceed down its west bank and destroy the ferry across which came the British supplies from Charlestown. Marion was already making the supply road on the other side of the river too hazardous for regular dependence. The plan was excellent—unfortunately nothing else was.

As the officers left the log barn to prepare their commands for the night march an officer handed Gates a report of an actual count of his strength. It showed 3,052 rank and file fit for duty! And of these most were weakened by dysentery induced by their recent diet of green peaches. Not a very auspicious beginning for an all-night march and the battle to follow.

Meanwhile, down in Camden, which was then but an agglomeration of log cabins, taverns and frame barter stores, by sheer coincidence, closely parallel events were transpiring. In the town's only big house, the newly completed residence of the prosperous merchant, Joseph Kershaw, now a British prisoner, Lord Rawdon, Colonel Tarleton and the other British general officers were receiving from Lord Cornwallis orders of a surprise night attack on Gates's position at Rugeley's. On hearing of Gates's approach, Lord Cornwallis had rushed up from Charlestown to take personal command of Lord Rawdon's army of twenty-two hundred men, of which some six hundred were North and South Carolina Tory militia.

With strictest orders from their respective commanders that they move forward through the night in complete silence, the two armies marched along the crude road following the old Catawba Indian path which but a few years before had been widened enough to permit carts to pass. Each had commenced its march at exactly ten o'clock. Through the unbroken forest which still bordered this section of the road the two armies crept forward to surprise the enemy. Suddenly, above the muffled sounds of the march came a sharp challenge, quickly followed by shots—then confusion and consternation spreading and running back both ways along the road. In a moment Tarleton was demonstrating the value of experience, when, to the accompaniment of loud huzzas, he threw his intrepid cavalry into the American column. Before their terrifying onslaught, the forward units of the American forces were sent reeling back into the rear units, creating a general confusion which persisted even after Tarleton had called his men back to their own lines and the firing subsided.

Two hours later, as day dawned, the two armies lay facing each other, nervously awaiting some overt act that would renew the battle. Meanwhile each had deployed its contingents all the way across the low sandy ridge to the edge of branch swamps which flanked the ridge on either side. On the American right were the Delaware and Maryland Continentals. In the center were General Caswell's North Carolina militia, while the Virginia militia had the left flank.

Being fearful of the stamina of the militia under fire, the Americans sent fifty volunteers out among the trees between the lines, to distract the initial fire from the militia lines; but the ruse only served to trigger the resumption of the fighting. An initial volley from the British riflemen and artillery filled the dead-still morning air with such a dense cloud of smoke that the steady advance of the Redcoats which immediately followed was almost hidden in the haze. The resulting eeriness of the moment and the huzzas of the advancing enemy was too much for the weary, illness-weakened militia. In the words of one of their officers, it

> threw the whole body of the militia into such a panic, that they generally threw down their loaded arms and fled, in utmost consternation. The unworthy example of the Virginians was almost instantly followed by the North Carolinians; only a small part of a single brigade made a short pause.

Discussing this turn of affairs an officer on Gates's staff later wrote:

> He who has never seen the effect of panic upon a multitude can have but an imperfect idea of such a thing. The best disciplined troops have been enervated and made cowards by it. Armies have been routed by it, even where no enemy appeared to furnish an excuse; like electricity, it operates instantly; like sympathy, it is irresistible where it touches.

So, stricken by contagious panic, in a matter of minutes the American army was without the left half of its line. The rear of those standing firm, the Continentals and a regiment of North Carolina militia, was wide open to attack across the missing flank. Although but a few minutes old, the battle was already lost; however for an hour more, even in the face of the obvious hopelessness of their situation, the thousand Continentals held the field in the face of as violent fighting as a whole war had known. Commanding this desperate stand was Baron de Kalb. After his horse was shot from under him, he fought on with his sword, until he was finally brought to earth pierced by eight bayonet wounds and three musket shots. Even so sorely stricken, he still commanded while his devoted aide, Le Chevalier du Buysson, stood over him to shield him with his own body from further injury.

The final outcome was calamitous for the Americans— their worst defeat of the entire war. So complete was the rout that only one group of one hundred men left the field in a body. All the rest were killed, captured or scattered. In the days that followed, less than one thousand survivors reassembled in North Carolina. Gates was in the vanguard of the wild flight which ensued. He spent that night in Charlotte Town, seventy miles from the bloody field where he had so suddenly ceased to be the "Idol of Congress."

Idle speculation: What a different story history might have told of the Battle of Camden had green peaches not been so plentiful in the neighborhood of Rugeley's place. Had Gates marched ten minutes earlier or Cornwallis ten minutes later, the armies would have met at the narrow way across Gum Swamp. With the tree-studded mire of the swamp serving as an abatis against Tarleton's terrifying cavalry onslaughts, would the militia have held their ground?

Before leaving the Battle of Camden, a footnote should be added on Baron de Kalb, the noble German who crossed the sea to an alien land, there to give his life in sacrifice for his ideal of liberty. Forty-five years later, the Marquis de Lafayette would come again from France to a quiet churchyard in Camden and bow his head in a final farewell to his old friend as a monument was there being erected to the memory of the brave baron, thus placing a period to the chapter of the American adventure which they had begun together nearly a half century before when they landed on these shores at Georgetown, a hundred miles down river to the east.

The destruction of Gates's army left the Carolinas again without a Continental force. South Carolina was once again a conquered province with no semblance of government except the military of the conqueror; and it appeared only too obvious that there was no preventing North Carolina from soon sharing that unhappy condition. Regardless of their earlier sentiments, all but a few of the more impractical visionaries now bowed to the inevitable, resigning themselves to the role of loyal British subjects. So apparent was it that their bread was now buttered on the British side that when Lord Cornwallis triumphantly returned to Charlestown after his Camden victory he was publicly congratulated by the "loyal inhabitants of Charlestown" who execrated "the contemptible remains of that expiring faction" opposing "that government under which they formerly enjoyed the highest degree of civil and political liberty." Among the discreet who were so gracefully throwing in the sponge were Colonel Charles Pinckney, Gabriel Manigault, Wade Hampton and even Daniel Huger, a Council member who had fled the state with Governor Rutledge. But those men down in the capital had never understood the back country and they still didn't. With that blind spot they misjudged the course of the future. From Charlestown they couldn't see the hornets swarming about their disturbed nests—already relentlessly stinging to death the clumsy invader.

Even on the day of the disaster at Camden, Sumter's partisans had met with brilliant success in the execution of their part of the over-all plan—the raid down the western side of the Wateree to the Camden ferry. And after the battle Marion's men saw to it that the British had even more difficulty in getting many of the prisoners back to Charlestown than they had encountered in capturing them from Gates in the first place.

The gloom caused by the catastrophe at Camden was somewhat lessened by the news of a small but brilliant victory of the backcountrymen over the British at Musgrove's Mill on the Enoree. Aroused by the ruthless depredations of the Tory bands ranging through the Piedmont country, Colonel Joseph McDowell in July had left his picturesque fields along the upper Catawba, gathered his followers and headed south. On his way, he was joined by his friend Colonel Isaac Shelby and his followers. Entering South Carolina, they had captured Thicketty Fort and a Tory band commanded by the notorious Captain Patrick Moore. Pushing on south across the Pacolet, Fair Forest and Tyger rivers, Shelby's command was joined by colonels James Williams and Elijah Clarke. Together they dared an attack on a strong British post at Musgrove's Mill (the same spot made famous by John P. Kennedy in his classic historical novel, *Horseshoe Robinson*). After an all-night ride they arrived on the bank of the Enoree opposite the mill. To their dismay they learned that the post had just received reinforcements and far outnumbered their force. Since their presence had been observed they had no alternative but to fight in spite of the odds against them. Flight was impossible, for on their worn mounts they would be quickly overtaken and cut to pieces. To save the situation a ruse was devised. While the bulk of the American force concealed themselves behind fallen trees and other cover on the gentle hill sloping up from the river, Captain Shadrack Inman and some twenty-five volunteers moved towards the river and opened fire on the enemy on the other side. As the British started across the river in gleeful pursuit, Inman's band fled up the hill leading their pursuers into the deadly ambush that there awaited them. The results of the battle were: American losses, thirteen, including Inman himself; British, 223, being more than the total number of Americans participating in the affair.

Just as the last of the enemy were being chased back

across the river, a messenger arrived telling Shelby of what
had happened three days before at Camden. South Carolina had suddenly become again a very unhealthy place for
a Whig to tarry, especially an armed Whig. There was nothing to do but to seek the safety of the hornets' nest itself,
back in North Carolina. Hesitating only long enough to feed
their tired horses and eat raw corn from the fields, they rode
northward. When the little army broke up and scattered to
their homes, they had fought a battle and ridden for forty-
eight hours without a moment's sleep.

Meanwhile Sumter, most energetic in attack and careless in repose of any of the partisan leaders, was slowly making his way northward to the same Rebel haven, impeded
by the enormous amount of booty he had seized in his raid
down the west bank of the Wateree River. While his men
were seeking relief from the August midday heat a little
above where Fishing Creek enters the Catawba, and he himself was napping half-clothed beneath a wagon, Tarleton led
his brigade across the wide Catawba shoals below and
moved up unobserved to the creek. Many of his men were
exhausted by their long ride from Camden in the heat and
consequently Colonel Tarleton selected but 160 to ac-
company him in the surprise attack on Sumter's camp. This
number proved quite sufficient for his purpose. With a wild
dash and resounding yells they charged. The surprise and
the ensuing rout were complete. With a loss of but sixteen
men, Tarleton killed 150 Americans, captured 310, together with 800 horses and all the booty Sumter had taken a
few days before. Partly clothed and riding an unsaddled
horse, Sumter succeeded in making his getaway to Charlotte
Town.

This left South Carolina for the second time in three
months a conquered province. Not only was there now no
Continental force in the state; a few days later there wasn't

even an organized partisan band, for in late August even
Marion had been forced from his swamps to the more remote
refuge of the North State. With the fleeing partisans, however, went an increased store of bitterness in their hearts, for
again the Tories were burning and pillaging in the unde-
fended lower regions. While militarily the late summer conquest was even more complete than that of the early summer,
it was in nowise a repetition of it. This time, although the
armies were vanquished, the people weren't conquered. A
powerful spiritual resistance had grown through the summer
from the seeds of wrath so widely sown by the enemy. If the
defeats of the summer momentarily cut away the growth,
they only served to stimulate a new and more widespread
growth.

The remote and academic questions of liberty involved
in the issues of taxation without representation and trade
restrictions had little appeal to the backcountrymen, in
whose land the war was now being fought. But personal liberty was something they could understand—and it was something they dearly prized. That sort of liberty they would pay
any price to secure. The hard boot of the British military and
the unbridled cruelties and ruthless destruction wrought by
the Tory bands had transformed the issue of the war into one
of personal liberty, involving men's homes, property and individual lives.

Men devoted to personal liberty could not submit to
Cornwallis's order after the Battle of Camden that all who
signed paroles and afterwards resisted "should be punished
with the greatest rigour" and all who refused to bear arms
for the King "be imprisoned and their whole property taken
from them or destroyed." It was "ordered in the most positive
manner that every militiaman who has borne arms with us
and afterwards joined the enemy shall be immediately
hanged." The grisly stories emanating from Camden consti-

tuted now a continuing call to arms. From there it was reported that it was no longer a question of who, but rather of
how many, would be hanged today.

Stupidly and recklessly the hornets' nest was being
stirred.

❧ ❧ ❧ ❧ 18. "The sword of the Lord and of Gideon"

From the picturesque, grassy, rolling hills of the region between the Catawba and Broad rivers a few miles southwest of Gastonia, North Carolina, rises an astonishing, geologically improbable, loose chain of low but rugged mountains. With descending magnificence, from the cliff-walled Pinnacle, in southwest Gaston County, these freakish mountains extend southwestwardly across a corner of Cleveland County into South Carolina, ending there with a relatively inconspicuous long, narrow-crested hill about a mile and a half south of the state line. Giving the silhouette of this lowly member of the chain its only mark of distinction is a tall stone imitation of the Washington needle. Because of the event this obelisk commemorates, because of what happened on that quiet, forest-covered hill, during a single hour in the long history of its existence, a single hour during the afternoon of October 7, 1780, this relatively insignificant mountain has all but taken for itself alone the name it shared until that day with its more rugged brethren, and King's Mountain has become familiar to every American school child from that day to this. And deservedly so, for here was fought a battle which for sheer drama is perhaps without a rival in all American history—and which has few rivals in historical import.

On either side of the path running along the mountain's narrow crest, stone markers attempt to reconstruct for the interested what transpired there during that violent hour when this peaceful mountain smoked like an active volcano. At the foot of a path running partly down the steep slope near the northeast end of the mountain, in a small, comparatively level, tree-shaded glade is an unkempt pile of rough field stones shaped as a high grave mound. A rude headstone is inscribed: "Here Col. Ferguson is buried." Thus is commemorated the vital, red-haired young Scot who, as the almost loved villain, played the lead in the drama which had its climax during that momentous hour.

Soon after the fall of Charlestown, Sir Henry Clinton made plans to carry forward his expressed determination to conquer the Americans with Americans. So, in addition to the army he was sending to Camden under Cornwallis, he planned for the interior several small contingents to wage a war of persuasion and conversion among the already largely receptive folk of the back country. Most of these expeditions were to serve as garrisons for posts at various interior points, but one of them was to roam the region organizing the Tory militia and taking paroles from Whigs ready to quit the Rebel cause. Such a mission would require an exceptionally capable leader. Among his younger officers, Clinton had just the right man for this assignment—able, energetic, ambitious Major Patrick Ferguson. Although still only thirty-six, Ferguson had had campaign experience in Flanders, and in the West Indies, before the Revolution. During the Northern campaign he had shown outstanding skill at Monmouth and at Brandywine where he had been severely wounded, losing permanently the use of his right arm. His fame as a marksman was known throughout the army. He had invented the first successful breech-loading rifle which was just then being introduced into the service. More important for this mission was his unusually magnetic personality. His only liability, from the standpoint of the English commander, was that he was from north of the border, a product of Aberdeen; but this should prove his greatest asset in talking with all the Scotch-Irish back in the hills. So Major Ferguson was elevated in rank, given the additional title of Inspector-General of Militia, and sent on his way up the Saluda River to Ninety-Six, with Captain F. de Peyster, of New York, as his second in command, and with about two hundred Provincial regulars recruited in and around New York.

All summer long he moved from camp to camp across the high red ridges running up towards the mountains between the Saluda, the Enoree, the Tyger, the Pacolet and the Broad, meeting with great success everywhere he went. By the end of summer he had organized and trained a Tory militia of four thousand men and had taken countless paroles from the discouraged Whigs of the region. Then his very success began to spell out his ultimate doom.

Reveling in their new-found safety of movement, the ruthless Tory bands re-emerged with vengeance in their hearts and beset the whole region, visiting unrestrained pillaging, burning and torture upon all suspected of Whig inclinations. Blackened ruins dotted the landscape. Destitute families, homeless and frequently fatherless, were everywhere. As a wider and wider area was stripped, the Tory marauders kept extending their field of activity. Soon they were operating north of the Broad in North Carolina. This was the region into which the South Carolina partisans had fled, to add the remnants of their commands to those of Davie, Davidson, Rutherford, and the McDowells. These forays to the north breathed a new hate-inspired life into the partisans. Obviously, unless the enemy were checked, it would soon be their turn to feel the Tory rope.

In view of Ferguson's success in the back country, by September Cornwallis was convinced that he could proceed with the grand plan to trap Washington without concern as to the security of his rear. He moved his army north from Camden to Charlotte Town, hampered only by the annoyingly persistent stings of Davie's elusive partisans. The only organized Rebel resistance remaining south of the North Carolina line was Colonel Elijah Clarke's small band in the Savannah River region, and ten days later this last remnant was in flight northward through the mountain foothills after an unsuccessful attack on the British post at Augusta. When news of this reached the post at Ninety-Six, orders were immediately dispatched to Ferguson for him to try to intercept Clarke before he could join the other partisans to the north. This order found Ferguson at Gilbert Town, near the present Rutherfordton, since by that time he had extended his mission into North Carolina. From the moment Ferguson received that order, the events in the drama which culminated on King's Mountain two weeks later moved inexorably, as if preordained by a majestic script writer.

Aware of the uncompromising Whig views of the unreconstructed Regulators who had settled over the mountains when the Regulators met with their defeat at Alamance, Ferguson, before leaving Gilbert Town in pursuit of Clarke, sent a message to the "Back water Men" couched in terms they could understand. He told the paroled prisoner he sent over the mountains to tell the men there:

> that if they did not desist from their opposition to the British arms he would march his army over the mountains, hang their leaders, and lay their country waste with fire and sword.

The message was duly delivered to that unflagging patriot partisan, Colonel Isaac Shelby, who had but recently fled to cover in those remote parts after his exploit at Musgrove's Mill. Shelby relished neither its tone nor its content. And, what is more important, from what he had seen on his forays into South Carolina he was convinced that Ferguson would make good these dire threats unless he were forestalled by concerted aggressive action. Shelby was well aware that, although the frontiersmen thereabouts were warmly sympathetic to the Rebel cause, they felt that the war was already lost and they had accepted that fact with a disinterest bred of a feeling of security for themselves, as long as the high mountains stood as a fortress against the enemy. Nevertheless he determined to attempt to arouse in them a sense of imminent danger for their cherished love of liberty. After all, it had been their zeal in that sentiment which had caused them a few years before to challenge the hold of the Cherokees on this beautiful country, and to seize it as a refuge from a colonial government they resented.

Ferguson's threat had arrived at an opportune time. Just then many of the men from the Holston, Watauga and Nolichucky settlements would be gathered at the races being held near the present Jonesboro, Tennessee. Colonel John ("Nolichucky Jack") Sevier would surely be there, and if Shelby hoped to organize a reply to Ferguson's threat, he would have to have the support of that seasoned Indian fighter (whose dramatic career rivals that of his friend, Daniel Boone), and his mountain boys of the Washington militia. So Shelby traveled the forty miles of mountain trail to the races, where Sevier enthusiastically fell in with the plan to organize a concerted action by all the hill and mountain militia for an attack on Ferguson before his force joined the main British army. A message was immediately dispatched to Colonel William Campbell, urging him to bring his upper Holston Virginia mountaineer regiment and join in the proposed expedition. At the same time letters were sent to the McDowells on the upper Catawba and other leaders of the Piedmont militia, telling them of the plan that they might join them as they moved toward Ferguson. Sycamore Flats on the Watauga had been named as the place where all the "back-water" men were to gather, on September twenty-fifth, that they might go over the mountains together. Equally informal arrangements were made to finance the expedition. About the only money there was on the other side of the mountains was the fund in the hands of John Adair, the collector for public lands. When Sevier laid Shelby's plan before Adair, he gave him, without hesitation, the $12,000 he had on hand, trusting that the outcome of events would justify his action.

September 25, 1780, was a memorable day for the Watauga folk. Never before had such a multitude gathered in that wild, sparsely settled country. For days quite a group of Colonel Joseph McDowell's men, fugitives from their homes since Ferguson had moved north, had hung around and caroused with the local boys. Then came the Nolichucky crowd, who were soon followed by bands from the lower Holston. Finally, amid the cheers of the earlier arrivals, red-haired Colonel Campbell rode into the narrow valley followed by some four hundred Virginians from the upper Holston. The "Back-Water Army" was complete and ready to move—except for the orations and blessings. The orations to the assembly concluded with an exhortation and blessing from the Reverend Samuel Doak, an eloquent backwoods preacher. Men have never provided any minister with a more magnificent pulpit than the Reverend Mr. Doak had that evening, as he stood on a rocky eminence beside the liquid crystal of the rapids of the river while the light of the declining sun struck the towering heights of nearby Yellow Mountain, enhancing its autumn glory. Beyond, the escarpment of the unbroken mountain wall added a melody of blended color. His congregation was equally extraordinary. In a semicircle, kneeling before him were a thousand rough and rawboned backwoodsmen, uniform only in their moccasined feet and in the coonskin caps they respectfully held. Behind them in groups made bright by linsey, calico and brightly dyed homespun were the womenfolk and children of the neighborhood. Tethered and hobbled beyond, in an outer semicircle, waited the mounted infantry's thousand shaggy horses. As he concluded his exhortation with the words, "the sword of the Lord and of Gideon," the men responded in kind and "The Sword of Gideon" became the rallying cry and inspiration of the expedition.

Winter strikes early in those mountains. Before their long file started down from Gillespie Gap, the narrow, rocky path through the rhododendron tangles was made even more difficult by snow. The high spirits with which they had set out were further dampened by the suspicion that two of their number had already deserted—to the eastward, probably to carry Ferguson warning of their advance. But the sun shone again by the time they had traveled down the Catawba to the plentiful provisions of Quaker Meadows, the fertile plantation of Colonel McDowell, three miles west of the present Morganton. Here they were soon joined by 350 Yadkin boys under ponderous, uncouth Colonel Benjamin Cleveland, who had already gained a lurid reputation for summary hangings of Tories. Nevertheless, "They made the welkin ring with their glad acclaim."

Meanwhile, the two who had deserted the mountineers found Ferguson at Gilbert Town and informed him of the conspiracy which was hatching against him, causing him immediately to dispatch a message to Cornwallis in Charlotte Town, telling the general of his peril and strongly hinting that Tarleton's dragoons be sent to his aid. This message was entrusted to two Tories of the neighborhood. Along the way they aroused the suspicion of a staunch Whig at whose place they had stopped to rest and feed their horses. Shortly after they set out again their host sent his two young sons after them. When the messengers discovered that they were being pursued, they hid in the woods by day and only ventured forth under the cover of darkness. They were thereby so delayed that Ferguson's request for help did not reach Cornwallis for almost a week—until the very day Ferguson was trapped atop King's Mountain. The next day after his message to Cornwallis, Ferguson started his thousand men moving towards the safety of Cornwallis's army, but not by the most direct route, as he hoped to deceive his pursuers into thinking he was headed towards Ninety-Six instead of Charlotte Town. His line of march was down the north side of the Broad River as far as David's Ford. From his camp there, to gain more Tory recruits, he issued a proclamation to the people of North and South Carolina.

> The Back Water men have crossed the mountains; McDowell, Hampton, Shelby and Cleveland are at their head, so that you know what you have to depend upon. If you choose to be degraded forever and ever by a set of mongrels, say so at once, and let your women turn their backs upon you, and look out for real men to protect them.

By the sixth, having crossed the Broad River twice in his southward march, he was camped on its east bank, a few miles west of King's Mountain. Now very much the pursued, as exaggerated reports reached him of the partisans' numbers, he sent the following urgent message to Cornwallis:

> My Lord:—A doubt does not remain with regard to the intelligence I sent your Lordship. They are since joined by Clarke and Sumter—of course are become an object of some consequence. Happily their leaders are obliged to feed their followers with such hopes, and so

to flatter them with accounts of our weakness and fear, that, if necessary, I should hope for success against them myself; but numbers compared that must be doubtful.

I am on my march towards you, by a road leading from Cherokee Ford, north of King's Mountain. Three or four hundred good soldiers, part dragoons, would finish the business. *Something must be done soon.* This is their last push in this quarter.

Except for errors of detail, Ferguson's information as to his peril was substantially true. He was justified in his fear that he might be attacked at any moment. As the patriot force consisted of all mounted troops, unimpeded by wagons or other supply trains, and almost free of the necessity of stopping to cook, living as they did upon the parched corn meal each carried in his saddlebag (except when Tory cattle were conveniently available at an overnight camp), the Rebels were able to move rapidly. Guided by the neighbor-to-neighbor backwoods intelligence, they were now hot on Ferguson's trail. But he greatly overestimated their numbers. What with having to leave a substantial force to guard against an attack on their frontier settlements by the Cherokees, which was just then threatened, and the steady erosion of their numbers by the hardships of the march, acting upon both men and mounts, the Whig force never exceeded sixteen hundred. The fact that there were nine colonels among the pursuing forces was deceptive. These officers had simply been elected to that title by their men, so sometimes only a handful of men was under the command of a colonel. On the march southward, the need for a single supreme commander of the force became obvious and, because he was the only senior officer who was not a Carolinian and also because he commanded the largest force, Colonel Campbell was elected commander of the expedition until a Continental officer could be sent them. To secure such an officer, Colonel

Joseph McDowell set out for Gates at Hillsboro, leaving his brother Charles to command his Catawba boys.

Ferguson was in error in thinking that the mountaineers had been joined by Sumter and Clarke. However, more than two hundred of Sumter's men, under colonels Edward Lacy, Frederick Hambright and William Graham, had joined forces with them at Cowpens, some twenty miles west of King's Mountain, while Sumter, himself, was cooling his heels, awaiting a decision from Governor Rutledge on the priority of his brigadier's commission. Colonel James Williams, a brave but self-seeking veteran, with a small group

he had enlisted east of the Catawba on promises of good plundering, also joined at Cowpens in time to participate in the feast which was being prepared at the expense of the herd of the prominent Tory upon whose plantation the Whigs were camped. Here Colonel Graham received a message that his wife was having a baby and needed him, so he turned homeward, leaving Hambright in command of his South Carolinians.

While the men were enjoying their first substantial meal in days, two spies, one a cripple who successfully passed as a Tory, and the other an accomplished actor who could convincingly feign idiocy, brought word that Ferguson had planted his eleven hundred men, 150 Provincial regulars and 950 Tories, on the narrow flat top of King's Mountain, and that, from that position he defied "all the Rebels outside of Hell" to drive him.

With the long-sought quarry treed so near at hand, and with the fear that at any time Tarleton's brigade might come to the rescue, the partisan leaders decided to move without delay, in spite of the hard march the men had already endured that day and the cold rain that had begun to fall. Such an untrammeled army as this could be on the march in a matter of minutes. So, by nine o'clock, the same evening, a selected 910 whose horses and whose persons were still relatively sound, set out along the slippery wet clay road leading towards the mountain, while the rest trailed behind on foot. Carefully protecting their slim supplies of powder and their precious rifles with their blankets, they sloshed all night, and all next morning, through the penetrating cold drizzle. About noon, the rain stopped and the sun came out, just as they reached the foot of the steep rise of the mountain.

Campbell dismounted his men and divided them into two single files, one headed by himself, the other by Shelby and his mountaineers; Campbell's column going around and posting themselves along the southeast side of the ridgelike hill while Shelby's column spread along the northwest base. All this was accomplished by the moccasin-clad frontiersmen with Indian stealth. By three o'clock they had almost all gained their posts around the base of the mountain, when rifle reports were heard from Shelby's sector, and the battle was prematurely triggered.

With a spine-chilling whoop, descendant of the Indian war whoop and ancestor of the "Rebel Yell," rising all around the mountain base, the backwoodsmen started their attack, scrambling and crawling from tree to tree up the steep, wooded slopes. Piercing the whoops of the attackers and the shouts of encouragement from their officers, came the shrill scream of Ferguson's famous silver whistle, attracting the attention of his men to his orders, as he prepared them for bayonet charges against any Rebels who might gain the ridge. When the Holston men neared the crest they were met by charging bayonets before which they gave way, as they were without any such accessories for their hunting rifles. By sucking many of the defenders from the ridge, the retreat enabled their friends on the opposite side of the mountain to gain the crest. Then a bayonet charge directed against them in turn relieved Campbell's men so they could again attack the top. All the while the carnage being wrought in the British lines by the deadly accuracy of the frontiersmen's rifle fire from both slopes was quickly reducing the numbers of the enemy who could participate in the repeated bayonet attacks. As the crest became more and more cluttered with the British dead and wounded and the battle had raged with blazing fury for almost an hour, white flags began to appear among the Tory troops, only to be cut down by the indomitable Ferguson, himself.

He knew what those unauthorized white flags in his ranks meant. They were clearly telling him that the battle was hopelessly lost. But his pride would never permit him to surrender to those "mongrels." To avoid such humiliation he and a group of his more determined mounted troops made a dash down the northeast slope, in the vain hope of breaking through the tightening cordon of riflemen, to the Charlotte Town road. But that plan failed when Ferguson toppled from his gray horse—rescued from surrender by six Rebel bullets, one through his head.

With the valiant leader fallen, white flags quickly appeared all through the shattered ranks, but were little heeded by the Tory-hating Whigs. A hundred or more died amid vengeful cries of "Buford's Quarter" before Campbell's orders to desist were heeded. By then, of the eleven hundred defenders of the King's Mountain, nearly four hundred lay dead and wounded—a better fate than awaited many of the seven hundred others who were captured. The partisan losses (including the controversial Colonel Williams) were less than a hundred. Tradition had it that the first person to fall in the enemy camp was Ferguson's mistress, Virginia Sal (and she also lies buried beneath the pile of stones that mark his grave), but that Virginia Paul, also with him, survived the battle and returned to Cornwallis's camp after she was released by the victors.

News of this sweeping victory served as a new call to arms for the Whig forces in the South, who, before that battle, had all but lost the civil war into which the Revolution in that region had deteriorated. So it developed that the incredible series of events climaxing on King's Mountain played a major role in determining the final outcome of the war for American independence. But most of all it was the spirit demonstrated there that made King's Mountain great; the liberty-loving spirit that impelled those men beyond the mountain wall, without pay or promise of material reward, to face together a major challenge with but the meager resources of men and materials they themselves had; the spirit that led them without orders or direction from any governing body, state or national, without even a unified command, to unite spontaneously into an effective army, to march for two weeks without supplies other than those in their own saddlebags, finally to face a larger, well-trained, unified force on a battlefield of its own choosing—and win. The fact that every man of the vanquished enemy, except Ferguson himself, was also an American, proves rather than disproves that statement. It was the inspiration of the victors which made them the victors.

Unfortunately the final chapter of the King's Mountain story sadly tarnishes the luster of the achievement.

"THE SWORD OF THE LORD AND OF GIDEON"

The morning after the battle, thinking they were fleeing the vengeance of Tarleton's dreaded dragoons, the victors started the long trek homeward, using the hated Tory prisoners as burden bearers for the captured equipment and for their wounded comrades. For four days they marched with little rest and even less food, for two days with none. The fare of the prisoners was mostly raw corn on the cob and green pumpkins thrown into their pens at the campsites. On the marches the prisoners who could not keep the pace were slaughtered. And still the animosity against them mounted. On the fourth day after the battle, when they were camped near the present Rutherfordton, the decision was made to organize a war crimes tribunal and try the prisoners. A hastily organized court found thirty-six of them guilty of plundering and other offenses, and these were accordingly condemned to be hanged. While the executions which immediately followed were in progress and nine had already been hanged, a small boy with a flair for dramatics effected the escape of his condemned older brother. The interruption caused by his successful dash for freedom broke the mob seizure of the band. A short conference among the officers was followed by a pardon of the twenty-six, who but a few minutes before were saying their final prayers.

The next day, still driven by the conviction that they were being pursued by Tarleton, the Whigs and their miserable prisoners pushed on northward. It would have been comforting to them had they known that just then, not only Tarleton, but Cornwallis's entire army was fleeing southward to Winnsborough, thinking that the "Back Water men" were after them.

19. "The captains and the kings depart"

King's Mountain emphatically revealed the clay feet of the British lion. Emboldened by the sweeping success of their fellow partisans, Sumter and Marion were soon back in South Carolina, snapping at its flanks and hindquarters. A few days later Andrew Pickens publicly renounced his parole, a step provoked by a Tory raid on his plantation, the protection of which his parole was supposed to guarantee.

Proceeding southward down the Broad during November, Sumter captured the notorious Tory house-burner, Major James Wemyss, at the Fishdam Ford of the Broad and defeated the heretofore invincible Tarleton at Blackstocks on the Tyger, at the cost to himself, however, of a severe wound. (He was carried away to North Carolina cradled in a raw oxhide suspended between two horses, and was out of action for several months while he recuperated there beyond the war arena.) Down the river Marion was using the same unconventional hit-and-run tactics so tantalizing to the more conventional British leaders. During the last six months of 1780, engagements of this type occurred in the Santee system area on the average of one every five days—a rate which would be stepped up in the coming year.

King's Mountain and the numerous smaller engagements also brought major changes in the enemy plans— changes indicative of a rising desperation. Energetic Tarleton and his select brigade were sent out with orders to track Marion down in his swamp retreat and annihilate him. From this frustrating assignment he was recalled to stop Sumter's foray down the Broad River. Cornwallis needed more men if he was to defend his flanks and rear successfully and at the same time move on with his grand march northward. In anticipation of that northward march, Clinton had sent General Alexander Leslie, with twenty-three hundred men to meet him in Virginia. The need in Carolina being now more pressing, Leslie re-embarked for Charlestown to reinforce Cornwallis. Awaiting Leslie's arrival, his army lay at Winnsborough while all around him the evidence mounted that Carolina, although beaten, was no longer conquered.

While Cornwallis waited, General Nathaniel Greene arrived in Charlotte Town to take command of the miserable, half-clad, half-starved remains of Gates's shattered Continentals. He set energetically to work to attempt to rebuild a fighting force, wisely selecting capable Colonel Davie as his commissary. That part of North Carolina having been plundered to the bone, he decided to move his troops to the less stripped Peedee country near Cheraw. Being a master of retreat, Greene planned a strategy to entice the enemy farther and farther afield, requiring an ever longer supply line through a less friendly region. He sent General Daniel Morgan westward to maneuver in the Broad River region, hoping both to encourage the partisans operating in that region and to lure Cornwallis northward from his station so that an opportunity might present itself for Greene to move in behind him and attack his posts in his rear.

With Morgan was Colonel William Washington and his cavalry brigade. When they came to the Camden-Charlotte Town road, Washington made a hurried detour southward along that road and thereby provided a little comic relief from the all-pervading gloom which possessed the suffering country. Down at Cleremont, the plantation of Colonel Henry Rugeley, where Governor Rutledge had so narrowly escaped capture and where the unfortunate Gates had rested his army on the eve of his disaster near Camden, the Colonel had fortified his large, heavy, log barn and garrisoned it with a hundred-odd neighborhood Tories. When Washington came in sight of the barn and saw its strong protective abatis, he dared not attack it without the aid of artillery, and he had none. Withdrawing a way, he proceeded to remedy this lack by the simple expedient of a convenient log of the proper size and a pair of wagon wheels. When the garrison saw him approaching down the road, trundling this formidable piece, they hurriedly showed a white flag. The incident cost Rugeley his brigadier's commission which was just then being prepared.

Morgan and Washington moved on westward to the Broad River region where they were joined by several hundred Whig militia, including Colonel Pickens and his newly recruited band. As soon as Cornwallis learned of Morgan's moving south down the river he sent Tarleton and his green-coated dragoons to drive him back. The prospect of attack by that dreaded cavalry officer with the face of a girl and the heart of a tiger called for a hurried retreat. But Tarleton was too fast to be avoided by flight. When, on January 17, 1781, Morgan raided Cowpens in Cherokee County a few miles south of the North Carolina line, he realized he had to fight or face inevitable disaster in an attempt to cross the then swollen Broad River, which lay both north and west of the position into which Tarleton had outmaneuvered him. In the battle which followed, the Carolina and Virginia militia, which composed the majority of Morgan's force of 940, redeemed the reputations they had lost in their rout at Camden. Supported by Washington's veteran cavalry, they gave the star field commander of the British forces and his thousand regulars, including his hand-picked dragoons, one of the most overwhelming defeats of the war: Tarleton lost 784 men at a cost of but 62 Whigs killed and wounded.

Stung by this disaster, so close on the heels of the catastrophe at nearby King's Mountain, and reinforced now by Leslie's troops, Cornwallis determined to pursue Morgan with his whole army. King's Mountain had ended his first northward push. Cowpens precipitated his second. By a skillful retreat, and the good fortune of the Catawba's suddenly rising just after he crossed to its east bank, Morgan successfully rejoined Greene, who meanwhile had moved far up into North Carolina to Guilford Courthouse. By persisting in his pursuit of Morgan, the British general let himself be enticed through the dead of winter along a road which lead farther and farther from his Carolina bases and on to his ultimate ruin, twenty months later, at Yorktown— and the loss of the war itself.

Greene, being still too weak to chance a battle with the main British force of the South, as Cornwallis approached, continued his retreat on into Virginia. With the partisans continually preying upon the long and vulnerable supply line, reaching now more than three hundred miles back to Charlestown, the British army soon found itself little better off than the American forces. Its attractiveness to recruits reached the vanishing point and it slowly began to diminish. On the other hand, Greene's masterful retreat brought wide acclaim and recruits came flocking in. By March, he was ready to risk open combat. He moved back down to Guilford Courthouse and there battle was joined. When the militia reverted to form and fled, in many instances without firing even a single shot, the battle was given over to the Continentals, who put up a magnificent fight but were eventually forced to give up the field. For all but the militia who had so quickly sought the relative safety of their nearby homes, the battle was a bloody affair. But, diminished and isolated and facing a growing American force, Cornwallis realized that unless he returned to the coast and supplies he would soon be in desperate straits. His nearest port was Wilmington, so towards the safety it offered he directed his crippled army.

While the cat was away in North Carolina, the mice were freely playing all over the country he had left behind him. Sumter, having recovered from his wounds, led his militia down the Broad and Congaree, crossed the Santee, and moved back up the Wateree, attacking post after post along the way, sometimes successfully. But even the unsuccessful attacks helped the cause, wearing down the enemy by the losses they incurred and by the necessity of constant vigilance. Across the wide Low Country there was no rest for the British posts and no security for their supply routes as Marion kept up a relentless series of forays from his hiding place in the Santee and Peedee swamps. Marion's force, by this time, had become truly formidable as he now had the benefit of a select brigade of cavalry, led by the dashing Colonel Henry (Light Horse Harry) Lee, father of the Confederate leader.

Hoping thereby to check this unconventional and elusive sort of warfare, the British and Tory leaders adopted most extreme measures. Hanging without trial became the common fate of their captives. Most of the partisans retaliated in kind, and the civil war degenerated into an affair of organized murder, robbery and plunder. On both sides, so desperate was the need of supplies in a land so nearly stripped of everything, that friends were plundered as readily as enemies. Life and property were being destroyed at such a rate that observers feared the region would soon be completely depopulated. To attract more recruits and at the same time bring a bit more order to the looting, Sumter instituted a plan which offered salt, corn and a definite share of loot, and a slave (to be taken from a Tory owner) for all who enlisted for a ten months' tour of duty. This plan had great appeal and recruits flocked to his standard.

After the battle at Guilford Courthouse, Greene moved his army southward to fill the vacuum created by Cornwallis's evacuation eastward to Wilmington. By the latter part of April, his army was back in the neighborhood of Camden where Gates had met with disaster eight months before. The British force there was under the command of an uncommonly able young officer, General Lord Rawdon. Greene deployed his troops along the brow of a long sand hill, known as Hobkirk Hill, which lay athwart the Charlotte Town road about two miles above the British stockade and fortifications. Fearful that Sumter and Marion might soon bring reinforcements, Rawdon attacked. At first success was with the Americans, but an ordered retrograde movement along a portion of the line was construed as a retreat by other sectors, and they in turn gave ground when victory was within reach. The battle was not decisive, but Greene again gave up the field.

When the Volunteers of Ireland, elegant in their scarlet coats, and their Tory companions in arms marched out of the stockade on the morning of the battle there was tense excitement behind the boarded-up windows of a nearby second-story room which was being utilized as a jail. Among the miserable prisoners crowded together in that fetid room were two half-grown boys. The smaller of the two, a wiry redhead, stood at one of the barricaded windows peering through a knothole, observing what was happening outside, relaying the sights to his fellow prisoners, many of whom were too ill with smallpox to raise themselves from the floor.

Among the prostrate ones lay the other boy, Robert Jackson, suffering from both the dread disease and infected saber slashes. It was mostly for his benefit that his younger brother, Andrew, was giving his running account of what he saw, all colored with his violent hatred for those whose movements he was watching. With intent excitement they listened to the first shots of the battle two miles to the north. With sinking hearts they heard the sounds of battle recede, rightly guessing what that meant.

After the battle the gracious Rawdon heeded the earnest pleas of the boys' mother, who had ridden the fifty miles from the Waxhaws to beg for their release. Although Andrew was also suffering from saber slashes across his arm and face, and now had smallpox too, he and his mother walked the long road back home through the rain, supporting Robert in the saddle of their single mount. A few days later, Robert became the second of the two Jackson boys whose life was taken by the war. The boys had landed in jail for being present at a Whig gathering at their church when a Tory raiding party passed that way. Robert had been wounded and captured in the fray. Fourteen-year-old Andrew made his getaway, only to be captured the next day at a kinsman's home to which he had fled. The saber scars which he carried through life on his arm and head were mementoes of the lesson the Tory officer gave him in "proper respect" when he refused to clean the officer's boots which had been spattered with the red clay of the Waxhaw hills in his search for Andrew.

Those days and those scenes fixed in Andrew Jackson that burning hatred of Britain which he carried all his days. And before the end of the energetic Carolinian's life of unmatched adventure and accomplishment, that hatred would prove very costly to its object.

While Elizabeth Jackson was getting her two ill sons back to her sister Crawford's home, where the fatherless boys had been raised and which had been ransacked and wrecked by Tory raiders but still spared the torch, Greene was moving westward to try his luck against the other principal British post in the interior—Ninety-Six, in the hills a few miles south of the Saluda near the present Greenwood. For a month he doggedly tried to capture this strong British position but its garrison, all Americans of loyalist sympathies, stoutly defended themselves behind their protecting palisades and earthworks. As June wore to a close, on the arrival of news of approaching British reinforcements, Greene gave up the effort.

Both Hobkirk Hill and Ninety-Six were useless battles. Before Greene approached them, events had already made their evacuation by the enemy inevitable. The wearing tactics of the partisans had made these interior positions practically untenable. Ironically, at Ninety-Six, Greene's men captured several couriers attempting to carry messages to the besieged garrison. The messages which were prevented from arriving at their destination were repeated orders to evacuate the fort and retire back to Charlestown—just what Greene was trying to force the defenders to do! So, as soon as the siege was lifted, the garrison moved down the river to the safety of the coast, trailed by numerous loyalists, who were afraid now to remain in the interior. Near Charlestown these refugees established a temporary town, which they called Rawdon-town, where many existed in misery throughout the remainder of the war. Rawdon had already evacuated Camden and moved his army downstate.

From these retrograde movements which left the triumphant Whigs in the saddle all through the interior of both the Carolinas, one would think that the long struggle was all but over, but the Rebel forces were so depleted and worn that it would require more than a year and a half of incessant struggle before the enemy would finally set sail from the capital.

To rest from his long and arduous campaign which, in the style of George Washington, he had won without winning a single battle, Greene moved his troops for a midsummer pause in the High Hills of Santee overlooking the wide green expanse of the Wateree swamp to the west. Supported by his position there, Sumter, Marion, Lacy and Wade Hampton, who was now back in the fight for liberty after going over to British allegiance after the battle of Camden, kept their partisan bands raiding nearer and nearer to Charlestown, keeping the enemy forever on guard and making ever more and more difficult his efforts to secure supplies from the interior plantations.

In late August, word from Virginia arrived at Greene's headquarters that Cornwallis was about to be trapped by the combined main American and French forces near Yorktown, and the fear was expressed that reinforcements might be moved from Charlestown in an effort to save him. To forestall any such attempt, Greene decided to risk battle again. Summoning all the partisan bands of the region to his assistance, he moved up and across the Wateree and then the Congaree, to gain the south side of the five-mile-wide flooded expanse of the Santee swamp so that he might march towards the enemy concentrations in the neighborhood of the capital. When on September 8, 1781, he left his camp at Henry Laurens's Santee plantation and moved downriver to the British position near the mammoth Eutaw Springs, with its sapphire waters boiling up into a crystal, cypress-girt pool (now deep beneath the tawny waters of Lake Marion), Greene had with him the cavalry units of William Washington and Light Horse Harry Lee, and the commands of Wade Hampton, Francis Marion, Andrew Pickens, William Henderson, William Polk and Thomas Sumter, although Sumter himself was absent. Greene's army of twenty-one hundred which he was leading to meet Stewart's twenty-three hundred was the most experienced ever engaged in any battle of

the war in the South, although the background of their individual experience would not bear too close a scrutiny for,
as Greene himself observed, he was fighting the British with
their deserters and they were opposing him with deserters
from his forces. In the battle which followed by the springs,
the British lost almost half of their army. Although the American losses were far less, being but a fourth of their strength,
they as usual lost the field—but, also as usual now, they won
the campaign. With a sweeping victory quite within their
grasp, whole sectors of the American line were distracted by
a quantity of captured food and rum. An enemy counter-
attack found many of the celebrants little interested in continuing the battle—and for the want of those defenders the
battle was lost. But just as in the case of the battles of Guilford Courthouse, Hobkirk Hill and Ninety-Six, where the
British had been unable to remain in the region won, the
neighborhood of Eutaw Springs now became an unhealthy
spot for the British army. With the unpredictable partisan
bands operating all about them, disrupting their supply lines
and requiring a constant vigil, to remain in the field, even so
close to Charlestown, was no longer possible.

Except for the siege at Yorktown where, six weeks later,
Cornwallis surrendered his whole army to Washington and
Lafayette, the battle at Eutaw Springs was the last important
engagement of the war. But, in Carolina there remained fifteen months of continuous small engagements both in the
neighborhood of the British-held Charlestown and against
the still unruly Tory bands in the interior; while, again at the
High Hills of the Santee, Greene tried to hold at least some
semblance of an army together under conditions of privation
and suffering comparable to those suffered by Washington's
forces at Valley Forge four years earlier. His camp there re-
sembled a vast hospital. There was a dearth of all the barest
necessities—even salt. Greene reported: "Near one half of
our soldiers have not a shoe to their foot, and not a blanket

to 10 men through the line." And it was a bitter cold winter.

But, somehow, they survived the hunger and cold of the winter, and the summer malaria of the year of skirmishing that followed—until that day of triumph and great joy, December 14, 1782, when Greene rode at the head of his somewhat refurbished army as they marched into Charlestown, while the British forces and nearly four thousand loyalist citizens boarded the great fleet which lay anchored in the harbor to carry them to a less inhospitable country.

Missing from the triumphal parade were the men of Marion, Sumter, Pickens and the other leaders of the militia and partisan forces who had dared so much and suffered so long to make that great day possible. Even the partisan leaders themselves did not receive an invitation to participate. The official explanation for the omission was fear of disorder, owing to the notoriously unrestrained hatred of the militia for the departing Tories. However, in view of the fact that even the leaders were excluded, one suspects that jealousy and the inelegant appearance of the ragged, ununiformed partisans was at least part of the reason.

So the British sailed away from their favorite and most prosperous colony, leaving it devastated and ruined far beyond any of her sister colonies. But for those who had survived the ordeal they left a challenge, the rebuilding in the face of momentous difficulties, the sort of challenge which Arnold Toynbee says is the formula for success in human society.

❦ ❦ ❦ ❦ *20. The Swamp Fox*

We arrived at the Indian towns in the month of July. As the lands were rich, and the season had been favorable, the corn was bending under the double weight of lusty roasting ears and pods of clustering beans. The furrows seemed to rejoice under their precious loads— the fields stood thick with bread. We encamped the first night in the woods, near the fields, where the whole army feasted on the young corn, which, with fat venison, made a most delicious treat.

The next morning we proceeded, by order of Colonel Grant, to burn down the Indian cabins. Some of our men seemed to enjoy this cruel work, laughing very heartily at the curling flames as they mounted, loud-crackling, over the tops of the huts. But to me it appeared a shocking sight. "Poor creatures!" thought I, "we surely need not grudge you such miserable habitations." But when we came, *according to orders,* to cut down the fields of corn, I could scarcely refrain from tears. For who could see the stalks that stood so stately, with broad green leaves and gaily-tasselled shocks, filled with sweet milky fluid, and flour, the staff of life—who, I say, without grief, could see those sacred plants sinking under our swords, with all their precious load, to wither and rot untasted, in their mourning fields!

I saw everywhere around the footsteps of the little Indian children, where they had lately played under the shelter of the rustling corn. No doubt they had often looked up with joy to the swelling shocks, and gladdened when they thought of their abundant cakes for the coming winter. When we are gone, thought I, they will return, and peeping through the weeds with tearful eyes, will mark the ghastly ruin poured over their homes, and the happy fields where they had so often played. "Who did this?" they will ask their mothers. "The white people, the Christians did it!" will be the reply.

So wrote Lieutenant Francis Marion of his service in 1761 with Colonel William Moultrie's provincial militia under the command of the shockingly ruthless Colonel James Grant during his campaign of extermination against the Cherokee Indians. This campaign, it was hoped, would push them completely out of their idyllic home in the Carolina mountains beyond the headwaters of the Saluda.

Francis Marion—hero of legend and song, idolized by his followers, magnanimous as a victor, fearless and tireless —insignificant in appearance, but possessed of a character lofty and strong as the forest giants of his river home. Like the subject of a minstrel ballad, glamour entwines his story as the vines and gray moss of his region drape the trees. Which is the man and which is the legend? But is not legend only the warm, colorful garment time weaves from the spirit of a man to clothe the skeleton facts of history, to bring to life the essential truth of the past?

Bred of the land of the lower Santee, this Huguenot farm boy was familiar from earliest childhood with the eerie gloom of the trackless swamps lying beyond the lush fields of his Santee home. Adventure touched him early—it was there to meet him when, as a small and puny boy of fifteen, he shipped to sea. His ship was wrecked by collision with a whale. For six days, the survivors drifted about in the lifeboat without water or food save the sustenance provided by their pet dog, until at last they were rescued by a passing vessel.

From the sea Marion turned to farming, first on the family plantation through which the Santee Canal would later be cut, and later on his own Santee swamp plantation near Eutaw Springs, which he called Pond Bluff. Here, with but the interruption of his service in the Indian wars, he led the quiet existence of a prosperous Huguenot planter so esteemed by his neighbors that, although by nature incapable of making a speech, he was frequently sent as their representative in the Colonial Assembly. Unwittingly these years were building in Marion the knowledge and qualities that would make him a natural partisan leader, unrivaled in the annals of America.

As the threatening clouds of the War of the Revolution moved in over Carolina from the northeast, Marion was one of the first to stand up in the sorely divided colony and be counted on the side of Liberty. So by the time the confident British fleet moved in to attack the miserable fort of palmetto logs on Sullivan's Island, it was Major Francis Marion who was there behind the makeshift fort with his old commander, Colonel Moultrie. The famous reception they gave the British fleet that day was warm enough to persuade them to eschew these parts until the Northern colonies were considered all but conquered, four years later.

When the British did return, more circumspectly by land this time, and set siege to Charlestown, Marion was again there among the town's defenders. By a fortuitous set of circumstances, which a fiction writer would hesitate to use to save his hero, Marion escaped capture when the city fell. At a gathering of his fellow officers during the siege, their host in the fashion of the day locked his guests in the banquet room to insure that none should leave until all were deep in their cups. Marion, too temperate for such excesses and too gracious to offend his host, quietly slipped from the second-story porch to the ground. Miscalculating the height of his drop, he suffered a severely broken ankle in the fall. Being *hors de combat* he was transported by litter across the harbor to Haddrell's Point and on to the temporary safety of Pond Bluff.

In the months that followed, his devoted neighbors by all sorts of ruses successfully kept the crippled officer from the clutches of Bloody Tarleton and the Tory leaders of the neighborhood, by whom he was being specially sought throughout the dreary months in which there was no resistance force in all the colony to challenge the British might.

It was well on into the summer after the fall of Charlestown before, with assistance, he could mount a horse and gain release from his frustrating inactivity in the face of his country's sore need. As soon as that became possible, he gathered a motley score of die-hards about him and headed north to join the army of General Horatio Gates which he had learned was heading south to liberate Carolina from the mounting oppression of the British occupation.

Some say that it was because the elegant Gates was ashamed of the swarthy, hook-nosed little officer and his ragged, half-starved followers that they stayed but a few days in his camp. But Gates's protagonists have it that the "Hero of Saratoga" was more astute than is generally recognized, and that he immediately saw in Marion potential "eyes" for his army and an instrument to harass the enemy

supply line between Charlestown and Camden along its route through the Santee country, where Marion and his men had the advantage of complete familiarity, and that he hurried the partisans back to their swamp country charged with those responsibilities.

As Marion was making his way back from Gates's command at Hillsborough to the Santee country, his route lay through Kingstree in the Williamsburgh district. There recent Tory outrages and the modifications of the terms of the paroles taken at the fall of Charlestown had stimulated the organization of a resistance band led by several James brothers. When they learned of Marion's assignment, they joined their band to his. Soon there were others—the Horry brothers, Peter and Hugh, the Postell brothers, Witherspoon, Conyers, Maham and McCottry, a blend of the Huguenots of the Santee and the Scots of the Peedee. Around these brave and devoted leaders was built the fabulous Marion's Brigade, that incomparable fighting unit which always bore more resemblance to a spiritual fraternity than a conventional military unit.

Isolated in a region where the only government was that of the British military, and operating close in among the enemy bases and supply lines—upon which they were heavily dependent for their own supplies and ammunition—discretion, skill and trustworthiness were prime requisites in every recruit. Since the men received no pay, for most of them it was necessary, between campaigns and forays, that they repair to their homes to tend their crops and to see to the safety of their families, ever vulnerable to Tory retaliation. These necessities made the Brigade an incredibly fluid organization. Sometimes with Marion at his forest hideout there were but a handful of men. Overnight, when the secret summons went out from the leader, several hundred would find their way through the trackless swamps to the headquarters of the moment. The mystery of the success of his men in finding their way to his headquarters is enhanced by the fact that these headquarters were forever being changed. There was but one certainty of location—Marion would be deep in a river swamp—sometimes on the Peedee, sometimes on the Black, and sometimes on the Santee. But he had two favorite spots: Snow Island, where Lynches River joins the Great Peedee, and Peyre's Plantation, a few miles downriver from his own home on the Santee. At the latter spot on the Great Bend of the Santee, he was near the abundant plantations of his fellow Huguenots from whom supplies could be obtained and was yet protected by the riverbed lakes, water-filled guts and tall canebrakes which provided both protection and forage for the mounts of his men—the right arm of his mobile striking power.

Wherever might be his camp, the initiated were guided along the paths to it by the birdcalls and whistles of sentries concealed in the treetops along the route. A different whistle from sentry to sentry back to the camp gave ample warning of the approach of the uninvited. The time was ripe for an order for the gathering of the band when ammunition sufficient for three rounds per man could be accumulated by waylaying the wagon trains of the enemy bound from Charlestown to the interior posts. Singly and in small groups they would straggle in astride their personal horses. Each brought with him his entire equipment, his rifle or fowling piece, a sword, often a homemade affair cleverly fashioned from a saw, perhaps a blanket, an empty powder horn and saddlebag to receive the carefully rationed powder and the corn meal and cold sweet potatoes that would be their fare for the expedition that might take them sixty or seventy miles through swamps and over rivers to their objective. The camp was usually only an agglomeration of rude palmetto-thatched shelters among which the men sat and talked. Here the forest gloom was made deeper by a pall of acrid smoke from the smudge fires ever necessary as their only means of combatting the ubiquitous swarms of mosquitoes and deer flies.

Browsing on the canes around the site were the horses of those already in camp—a mount for every man. There among them was Ball, the General's own fabulous mount, a horse that had become as much of a leader of the other horses as Marion had of their riders. It is said that this animal was the key to the Brigade's ability at any time to utilize the wide Santee as a barrier against the enemy, regardless of the availability of boats for the crossing. Whenever that necessity presented itself, Marion reined him right into the river and the other horses unhesitatingly followed Ball's leadership. It is even reported that Marion never learned to swim and yet was always confident that Ball would carry him on his back to the safety of the farther bank.

It was the efficiency of their eerie signal system, the inaccessibility of their campsites, their movement only under cover of darkness, their ability at any time to make a protective moat of a river—coupled with their complete familiarity with every part of their region that made Marion's Brigade so elusive. The Tory colonels, Ganey, Tynes and Wemyss, each in turn futilely tried their skill against him. Doyle and Watson, both of whom were partisan leaders of outstanding ability, met with no better success when they made their efforts to reap the glory of tracking him down. And when Tarleton finally gave up in disgust his repeated efforts to take Marion, he told his exhausted dragoons: "Let us go back, and we will soon find the game cock, but as for this damned old fox, the devil himself could not catch him." So General Sumter became the "Gamecock" and General Marion became the "Swamp Fox."

Almost as familiar as the Swamp Fox sobriquet is the story of the "potato dinner" served by General Marion to the young British officer. The story goes that the Englishman was sent from Georgetown as an emissary to arrange an exchange of prisoners with the partisan leader. Met at a pre-arranged point by partisan scouts, he was blindfolded and conducted through the intricate labyrinth of paths through the canebrakes of the river swamp to the Swamp Fox's lair. Here he found himself in the midst of a picturesque and unforgettable scene: the setting, the mysterious, dimly lit swamp, with its towering cypress and pine trees draped with gray moss; the characters, the rugged, individualistic woodsmen of Marion's matchless Brigade—hawk-eyed and lithe, as different as possible from the conventionally uniformed and formally disciplined soldiery of his experience—yet, as he well knew, formidable and fearless and utterly incorruptible. All about the strange wilderness camp lay the trappings of war—the rifle against the tree, the sabre hanging from a bough, the horses, saddled but browsing at ease—and over all, men and horses alike, brooded a strange impression of watchful waiting, of wary alertness even in relaxation.

Strangest of all to the young British visitor must have been the central figure in this swamp tableau—General Francis Marion, a name echoed with awe, by now, even in the enemy camp. . . . Could this gentle, slight, limping soldier in homespun be the great partisan leader, already successfully threatening the British hold on Carolina?

So it was! But more confusion awaited the British officer after the business of exchange was satisfactorily concluded. General Marion, with his grave courtesy, entertained the English guest at lunch, a lunch of sweet potatoes, baked in the ashes and served whole in the skin on pieces of bark. In answer to the bewildered Englishman's questions, the General replied that this was their usual fare, though often indeed in less plentiful amounts. When the British guest learned that in addition to lack of shelter and of adequate food, the partisan Brigade received no pay at all but fought only for Liberty, he exclaimed that surely England must lose the war—these men could never be defeated! It is said that the young emissary, on his return to Georgetown, retired from the service, unwilling to fight against such men of principle as those he had seen in the haunting wilderness of the swamp hideout.

From such concealed posts, the partisans emerged in endless harassing forays. In the face of Marion's constant attacks on their supply lines, the British were soon forced to send several hundred soldiers with each wagon train in an effort to foil those attacks. For additional protection fortified strong points were established along the routes inland. An especially important post was that known as Fort Watson where the roads from Georgetown and Charlestown to Camden met. The fort was a large fortified Indian mound. Then it was located near Scott's Lake, an isolated old bend of the Santee. Now the waves of Lake Marion wash close by its base, revealing here and there the hard-packed floors of long-gone Indian cabins—perhaps the same ones in which John Lawson was so hospitably received here by the Santees so long before.

The British had surrounded the mound with three rings of pointed logs or abatis, making it all but impregnable against any force lacking artillery, as there was no nearby cover for riflemen since the old Indian fields around the mound had not yet come back in trees.

It was soon after the Brigade's ammunition requirements were increased by the addition of "Light-Horse Harry" Lee's legion in the spring of 1781, that a critical shortage of it developed. To relieve this shortage, Marion decided to attack Fort Watson where according to the reports of his scouts a substantial supply was stored. Undaunted by his lack of artillery or trenching tools by which the works might be approached through protecting ditches, he invested the fort with the hope of cutting off its water supply. The garrison foiled this plan by successfully digging a well within the works.

Frustrated by this development and facing the probability that at any moment relief for the fort garrison might arrive on the scene, Marion was forced to consider some improvisation to meet the situation. As was his cutom he summoned his officers for a conference on the problem. Their several suggestions were received and weighed. Among them was Colonel Maham's plan that a log tower, higher than the mound, be erected and manned with riflemen under the cover of darkness.

With the dawn of the next day the garrison were horrified by the sight of a log tower sixty feet high erected close by their mound. In the top of the tower, well protected by a miniature log fort, were the pick of Marion's riflemen. Throughout the night while part of the besiegers distracted the attention of the garrison, others had been erecting this clever nailless structure, quietly lifting into place each pre-mortised log. Under cover of the protecting guns in the tower, which now commanded the interior of the fort, a detail approached the mound and began tearing away the abatis.

Outwitted and facing destruction, the Fort Watson garrison showed the white flag. Imagination, ingenuity, and daring had triumphed again!

A few miles northwest of Fort Watson, near where the Congaree and the Wateree join to form the broad Santee, on a high sand hill overlooking the Congaree, stood the large new plantation house of Mrs. Rebecca Motte, a patriot of great integrity and courage. This the British had seized and converted into a fortified post for a garrison commanded by the gallant Captain McPherson. The hill had been protected by a deep trench, with a lofty parapet on its inner edge.

This post was of strategic importance as a protection for convoys from Charlestown to Camden and for those headed for Fort Granby and Ninety-Six. If these supply line posts could be captured, it would force the British to withdraw from Camden and Ninety-Six and retreat to the coast. So, shortly after the affair at Fort Watson, Marion crossed the Santee and moved up the river to attack Fort Motte. Mrs. Motte had been forced to take refuge in an overseer's house on a neighboring hill, and here Marion placed Light-Horse Harry Lee's corps; while Marion took his position in front of the fortified mansion, hoping to breach the fortification with a single small cannon just received from Greene. However, before the preparations for the attack were completed, the fires of Colonel Rawdon's relief force were sighted across the Congaree swamp, emphasizing the necessity for a more speedy method of assault.

As Mrs. Motte's mansion covered most of the palisaded area, Marion reluctantly concluded that the only hope of early success lay in firing the house. When the patriotic Mrs. Motte was informed of the plan, she gave it her enthusiastic support and active assistance, she herself contributing a bow and several flame arrows, curios from India given to her by her brother, Miles Brewton. Nathan Savage, a militia private, crept close enough to the palisades to fire the flaming arrows tipped with resin and brimstone to the roof already tinder dry under the noonday sun. After a futile attempt to extinguish the flames in the face of the American rifle fire, the garrison surrendered. Both sides joined in a successful effort to stop the spread of the fire. That evening after the paroles were given by the defeated soldiery, Mrs. Motte, a gracious hostess, entertained all the officers of both sides at dinner.

During dinner Marion received word that some of Lee's men were hanging Tory prisoners. Dashing from the table, he was in time to cut the rope and save the life of one of the victims, but two were beyond help. With sword drawn and black eyes flashing indignantly, Marion threatened death to any man who persisted in such outrages.

THE SWAMP FOX

The chroniclers tell of these and many other exploits of the Swamp Fox. The details of countless more were never recorded. Cumulatively he and his forest-bound band played an enormous part in the ultimate American victory. General Greene was in the best position of anyone to know the worth of the part General Marion played. With still another year of brilliant guerrilla warfare ahead of him he received this recognition from the commander of the Southern Department:

> When I consider how much you have done and suffered, and under what disadvantage you have maintained your ground, I am at a loss which to admire most, your courage and fortitude, or your address and management. Certain it is no man has a better claim to the public thanks than you. History affords no instance wherein an officer has kept possession of a country under so many disadvantages as you have. Surrounded on every side by a superior force, hunted from every quarter with veteran troops you have found means to elude their attempts and to keep alive the expiring hopes of an oppressed militia, when all succour seemed to be cut off. To fight the enemy bravely with the prospect of victory is nothing, but to fight with intrepidity under the constant impression of a defeat, and inspire irregular troops to do it, is a talent peculiar to yourself.

As the last year of the war drew near and the British hold on Carolina was only a tight semicircle centering about Charlestown, Governor Rutledge decided that the time had come to attempt to restore a measure of civil government to the war-torn state. Accordingly he summoned the Assembly to meet in the village of Jacksonborough, not far from Charlestown, on the Edisto River. When Marion learned that his presence was necessary to make the thirteen senators required for a quorum, he reluctantly turned the command of the Brigade over to Colonel Peter Horry and departed for the makeshift capital in January, 1782.

Among the first acts of the Assembly were those to increase the stability and support of the militia and the confiscation of the estates of a list of the more objectionable Tories. Marion supported these measures, believing the latter to be a necessary war measure. He soon, however, realized the injustice of the act; that it, in many instances, penalized men solely for their honest opinions, and it did that by legislative act without the privilege of a fair trial. When he saw those implications of the Confiscation Act, he became a leader in the fight against it. He was joined in this fight for justice for the Tories by old Christopher Gadsden. There were few, if any, in the Carolinas who had fought as unswervingly for Liberty or suffered as much in the struggle, often at the hands of the Tories themselves, as these two men. But, being truly great men, they were bountifully endowed with that essential ingredient of greatness—magnanimity. Eventually, their efforts were rewarded by the gradual modification of the Confiscation Acts.

Another act adopted by the Jacksonborough Assembly provided for civil immunity for the state's militia leaders for their acts during the war, its purpose being to prevent suits against those leaders for the private property they had seized during the war. When the act was introduced Marion rose and requested that his name be deleted from its protection, stating that if he had improperly seized anyone's property, he personally assumed the full responsibility for the seizure and would personally make the proper amends.

For a century and a half, now, the Swamp Fox has slept beside the river in the half-light, beneath the towering oaks of Belle Isle. Nearby, the dense magnolias and the long-armed live oaks that once graced the lawn of a mansion long

weathered away brood over a lost and desolate scene. Far
away towards the tawny river stretches the impenetrable
swamp, silent but for the wild birdcalls, lonely and still—
save where the gray moss sways in the twilight, alive with a
haunting illusion of shadowy horsemen weaving through the
forest.

> Well knows the fair and friendly moon
> The band that Marion leads—
> The glitter of their rifles,
> The scampering of their steeds.
> 'Tis life to guide the fiery barb
> Across the moonlight plain;
> 'Tis life to feel the night-wind
> That lifts the tossing mane.
> A moment in the British camp—
> A moment—and away
> Back to the pathless forest,
> Before the peep of day.
>
> Grave men there are by broad Santee,
> Grave men with hoary hairs;
> Their hearts are all with Marion,
> For Marion are their prayers.
> And lovely ladies greet our band
> With kindliest welcoming,
> With smiles like those of summer,
> And tears like those of spring.
> For them we wear these trusty arms,
> And lay them down no more
> Till we have driven the Briton,
> Forever, from our shore.

—WILLIAM CULLEN BRYANT

❧ ❧ ❧ ❧ ❧ *21. The Santee Canal*

*T*he curb gutter along the street after a summer shower, the free flow of the untended garden hose, and the brook winding its way through the meadow are irresistibly attractive things wherever there are children at play. Nor is the challenge to childhood alone! Wherever water flows, men have been inspired to manipulate its power for pleasure or for profit. Even the Indians, in spite of their lack of earth-moving machinery, constructed some astonishingly ambitious projects to direct the river as they would have it. Across the wide expanse of the turbulent Broad they somehow built a well-constructed zigzag dam of rock to channel the water and thus facilitate their fish trapping efforts; and near Camden they dug an arrow-straight, eight-foot-deep canal extending more than half a mile across the great meander of the Wateree known as Friends' Neck.

For the first hundred years after the Europeans arrived in this country, they made no attempt to remedy the obvious inadequacies of the Carolina rivers for navigation purposes. Foremost among these defects was the fact that the Santee River flowed directly into the Atlantic Ocean over a treacherous bar, instead of into spacious Charlestown Harbor—so that boats could not travel directly between the commercial capital of the colony and the Santee back country. So sinuous was its course across the Low Country between the sand hills and the coast that its waters flowed a full two hundred twisting miles to gain the sea, a bare hundred miles away. On the line of the sand hills and on up into the clay hills, even more challenging difficulties for navigation presented themselves where the Congaree, the Saluda, the Broad and the Wateree-Catawba rush in magnificent rapids across the strata of hard rocks that outcrop directly athwart their courses.

In the face of such obstacles, the adapting of the recalcitrant Santee to human convenience was no task for puny spirits. Those who dared to take the first step in the gigantic attempt were by no measure men of puny spirit.

For years there had been talk of a great canal that would permit river traffic to leave the Santee a hundred miles above its mouth and proceed directly to Charlestown. When Lieutenant-Governor Bull made his frustrating tour of the back regions in 1770 to appease the mounting resentment there against the colonial government, he talked of such a project to people along the upper rivers. Then intervened the terrible war years, during which personal survival was the sole, all-engrossing problem. Carolina was just beginning to stagger up from its ruins when the following item appeared in the *South Carolina Gazette and Public Advertiser* of November 12, 1785:

> Thursday last a number of gentlemen met at the State house in this city, to take into consideration the proposed plan of opening a communication by locks between Cooper and Santee rivers.

Numerous meetings followed and then in the *Charlestown Morning Post, and Daily Advertiser* for March 8, 1786, there was the following:

> At a meeting of the Incorporated Company for opening the inland navigation between Santee and Cooper Rivers, held at the City-Tavern on Thursday, the 23d instant, the following officers were chosen, viz: "His Excellency, Governor Moultrie, President; Honorable John Rutledge, Esq., Vice-President; Judge Burke, Judge Grimke, Judge Drayton, Gen. Pinckney, Gen. Sumter, Gen. Marion, Commodore Gillon, Major Mitchell, Edward Rutledge, John Huger, Thomas Jones, Thomas Walter, William Doughty, Joseph Atkinson, Henry Laurens, jun., James Sinclair, Theodore Gourdin, Aaron Loocock, and Theodore Gaillard, Esquires.

Here were the leading political figures, the war heroes, brilliant judges, able merchants, Huguenot planters and even one known best as the learned botanist of the Santee, Thomas Walter. Certainly few enterprises were ever launched under better tutelage.

Fifteen years later, *The Times* of Charleston contained this interesting item:

> We are happy in being able to announce to the public that Mr. William Buford, an enterprising citizen, who lives on the banks of the Broad River, near Pinckney Court House, which is more than ninety miles above Granby [near Columbia] arrived in this city, through the Santee Canal, on Tuesday, the 26th inst. with his own boat, built on his own land, and loaded with his own crop, after having safely passed over all the falls and shoals that are between his plantation and Charleston.

The decade and a half between the latter two news items were, for those having a part in the construction of the nation's first major canal, years of struggle in the face of a multitude of vicissitudes, while its cost in human life, money and reputations relentlessly rose.

The four decades following the latter jubilant item were years of mounting disillusionment until that day in 1840 when the obituary of the canal would be written between the lines of another enthusiastic news item announcing the opening of the country's longest steam railway line, running from Charleston into the back country.

The several years before construction of the canal was actually begun in 1793 were devoted to financing and planning. Wide public enthusiasm for the project and the obvious certainty of handsome returns made the problems of financing much less difficult than those involved in its engineering aspects. Henry Mouzon, a Huguenot of the French Santee country, who had prior to the war prepared a splendid map of the Carolinas and during the war been a captain in Francis Marion's first brigade was consulted by the directors. He laid before them a map showing several practical routes for the canal. For some reason obscure to history neither his services nor his plans were accepted. Instead, Colonel Christian Senf, a Swedish engineer who had come to America with Burgoyne's Hessian troops, was employed as the project engineer. With the surrender at Saratoga he had fallen into American hands and thereafter had somehow come to the attention of Henry Laurens, who arranged for his release and sent him to South Carolina to serve as State Engineer. During the latter years of the war he had served as engineer with the South Carolina militia. Beneath the somber shade of the moss-draped forest south of the great bend of the Santee there is yet ample evidence in the great dry ditch and the crumbling masonry of its locks that Senf was a daring man and a master craftsman. There is other evidence that he was also a man of energy and drive and that he possessed a quality of magnetism that inspired confidence even when undeserved. But unfortunately for the investors in the Santee Canal he was also inordinately vain, prejudiced and overenthusiastic.

When he laid out the route of the canal between the Santee and the headwaters of the Cooper, he eschewed all the practical routes which Mouzon had suggested. Some accounts have it that his jealousy of Mouzon compelled him to build the canal along a route his rival had not proposed. Others say he was swayed by the urging of Ralph Izard, one of the directors of the company, who very much wanted to have the canal leave the Santee through his plantation, that he might there establish the town which never got beyond the dream stage and the layout of its neat blocks on the canal map, on which it is shown as "Izardtown." Be that as it may, the location he selected, running as it does across a high dry ridge, instead of up one of the Santee tributary streams, resulted in far greater construction costs and an inadequate water supply in dry years for the twelve miles of the canal on the crest of this ridge. Not only was the deficiency of water supply for the upper level of the canal a serious drawback to the route chosen, but it required a deeper cut and locks of higher lift. Also it lay almost entirely through virgin forests. The removal of these forest giants without machinery was a gargantuan task. Nevertheless, by 1793, he had won the directors' approval of his plans and work was started.

The Colonel was one of those men who are constitutionally unable to delegate to others any important phase of a job. Consequently he refused to contract to others the construction of the project in portions, by which procedure the completion of the work might have been greatly expedited. He was even reluctant to concede to others the actual field supervision of the work. So along its whole twenty-two miles he himself undertook not only the general supervision but the immediate superintendence of the laborers, and in a large measure assumed the functions of an overseer—an impossible job when it is considered that the labor force through the almost eight years of construction averaged some eight hundred Negro slaves and sometimes exceeded a thousand!

The requisite laborers were secured by renting contingents of slaves from the neighborhood planters. At first, they could be hired from their owners for about twenty cents per day each. Later, when the cotton planting fever spread through the neighborhood from its focus of infection on General Moultrie's plantation, North Hampton, near the canal route, the price of the labor supply rose and the planters refused to rent men unless the women were also utilized. This latter adverse development was largely offset by the only fortuitous assist in the entire project, and that helpful event was the consequence of the ill fortune of others. For a hundred years the French Huguenots had been reaping fabulous harvests from their incredibly rich fields in the lower Santee swamps, popularly known as French Santee. Such freshets that came, except on rare occasions, were successfully held from their fields by the low dykes they had constructed. But by 1790, the effects of the great land rush to red hills of the upper river country were being painfully felt by those settled in the river region far below. As the Upcountry settlers stripped from the land nature's protective covering of forest and grass and replaced them with their clean-tilled row crops of corn and beans, the speed of runoff of the torrential rains of summer was greatly accelerated. With increasing frequency freshets such as had never before been experienced rolled down the river over the protective dams and over the crops of the river planters. With no crops to harvest, their slaves became available to the canal builders. Many of those swamp planters were saved from ruin by the revenues they received from the canal company for the use of their slaves.

For more than seven years, through the heat and storms of summer and the bogs and mud of winter, the tireless Senf pushed his great work in the face of obstacles which would soon have beaten a less indomitable soul. Summer fevers repeatedly decimated the ranks of his white tradesmen, skilled workers and foremen. After a score or more, including two physicians, had died, it became all but impossible to get white men to work on the canal during the summer months

when most progress could be made by the laborers. The route of the canal ran across about thirty-five plantations. Of these all the owners except Ralph Izard (who hoped to make a fortune from his town), Major Samuel Porcher and General Moultrie were actively non-co-operative and demanded excessive payments for the right of way. They maintained that the slow-moving traffic through the canal would prove a distraction to their slaves, and they also regarded the canal's invasion of their isolation as dangerous to the docility of their plantation organization. Frustrating delays resulted.

At length when the new century dawned the great, thirty-five-foot wide, twenty-two-mile long ditch had been dug, the twelve substantial, artfully designed locks had been completed, the great reservoirs which had been built to catch rain water in order to supply water for the upper level were full, and the eight aqueducts carrying the canal on masonry bridges across the streams and swamps where the route crossed them were at last watertight. The nation's greatest engineering undertaking was complete. Now, the port bound boats, laden with the produce of the interior, could be lifted thirty-five feet from the channel of the Santee, navigate twelve miles, across the low ridge and then be let down sixty-nine feet in Biggen Swamp and into the Cooper River channel. Incidentally, it is this anomalous difference in level between these two nearby rivers that is the key to the power aspects of the immense Santee-Cooper development, the waters of whose reservoirs now hide most of Colonel Senf's handiwork.

When Mr. Buford brought his epoch-making cargo down from his Broad River plantation, he entered the canal through the riverbank lock and proceeded into the locks at Izardtown on White Oak plantation. After being lifted to the third level he soon entered Major Porcher's Mexico Plantation, where, between the nearby plantation house and that of the lockkeeper his craft was slowly passed through the masonry walls of the double locks, a process which consumed about an hour. He was then in the top-level, thirty-five feet above the Santee. As he was wearily poled along by his stout black crew, Upcountryman Buford no doubt enjoyed a leisurely review of the long series of prosperous plantations through which he passed, as much of a spectacle for him as his craft must have been to the field hands as they paused in their spring planting to watch it glide slowly past. After Mexico, there was Robert Marion's Belle Isle and Burnt Savanna and the houses and workshops of the canal personnel. Next came Fox Hall and then the unbroken forest of Kirk Swamp and the intake from the reservoir to the west which supplied the water which was supporting his loaded craft. From his boat he could look down on Langsford and Frierson, for there the canal was elevated above the surrounding country to cross the streams flowing westwardly through those places. Descending first at the Hipworth locks and again a short distance farther at those at the Flints, where it crossed another aqueduct, he continued through the Widow Ravenel's Chelsea Plantation and René Ravenel's Pooshee, to two more sets of locks. These locks were near the muster field of the St. John's militia at Black Oak, headquarters of the St. John's Hunting Club, which had been organized the year before. Next there was Wantoot Plantation, where the again elevated canal skirted a two-mile-long rice field before reaching the locks at Stephen Mazyck's Woodboo Plantation, where it entered the natural watercourse of Biggen Swamp. Mr. Buford must have been greatly impressed by the utter dissimilarity of these plantations and the rolling red clay fields of his own plantation which he had left two weeks before. The channel cut through Biggen Swamp passed through Somerset, Oak Fields, Wampee, Hope, Broughton Hall, Keith Field, and the plantations of Pinckney, Moultrie and Challot (where the great earth dam and the powerhouses of Lake Moultrie now stand). Finally, after passing the tide locks between General Moultrie's Kent Plantation and Grave's Fair Lawn, Buford entered the natural waterway of the Cooper River thirty miles above Charleston.

With the great work completed, a wave of exultant optimism spread throughout the state. The voices of the few skeptics of the feasibility of inland navigation were effectively quieted by reports such as that for 1830, when seventeen hundred vessels passed through the Santee Canal to Charleston. A canal-building fever seized everyone, a fever which would hold its grip on the state for nearly forty years, eventually sweeping even such brilliant geniuses as architect-engineer Robert Mills and doctor-lawyer-scientist-diplomat Joel Poinsett. Both these men were native Carolinians who had gained national reputations in various fields. Mills, a protégé of Jefferson, had designed the Washington monument in the national capital and many notable buildings in Philadelphia, Baltimore and Carolina. Poinsett, in addition to his versatile professional attainments, held responsible positions under five presidents, eventually becoming Secretary of War under Van Buren. His interest in botany is memorialized by the Poinsettia, which he introduced into the United States from its native Mexico, and to him is due much of the credit for the establishment of the Smithsonian Institution.

By 1820, these two were serving together on the South Carolina Board of Public Works, one of the principal responsibilities of which was the completion of the State's Internal Navigation System. Only partially completed was the Wateree Canal around Grave's Shoals near Camden, although it had been begun many years before. The year previously the log jams blocking the Wateree near Cook's Mountain had been cleared and similar obstructions had also been removed from the Congaree. These log accumulations had resulted from the propensities of the settlers to use these rivers as a sort of gargantuan sewer for the trees they were removing from their riverside clearings. The Columbia Canal running from the confluence of the Broad and Saluda down to Granby was under construction, as were also the Saluda and Dreher's canals on the Saluda River and Bull Sluice, a short distance above Columbia on the Broad and the canal around the Lockhart Shoals, above Fishdam Ford on the same river. Higher up the Wateree where it carries the name of the Ca-

tawba, even more ambitious projects were in the making. At
Rocky Mount and the Great Falls of the Catawba, the river
made a spectacular plunge over a series of cascades, falling
nearly two hundred feet in sixteen miles. The magnificence
of these falls, which chroniclers of the past extravagantly
extolled, can be only vicariously enjoyed by us of the twentieth century, for their turbulence has long been stilled by
the great power dams whose bulks rise at Rocky Creek, Great
Falls and Fishing Creek. That navigation might be rendered
possible around these rapids, a series of canals, largely utilizing the ravines of Rocky Creek and Fishing Creek, had been
designed and soon after the completion of the Santee Canal
Colonel Senf had carried his daring enthusiasm on to them.
There, in 1806, long before they could be completed, death
closed his tragically futile life.

Fifteen miles farther upstream, at Tivoli, General Davie's plantation to which he had retired after his rich and
varied career, a canal was being built at Land's Ford, the
beautifully fashioned locks of which today stand as one of
the few accessible, unsubmerged bits of the whole Santee-
Wateree-Catawba inland navigation works.

For a few years it perhaps appeared that all the money
and effort which was being devoted to these works were justified by the demands of commerce. For a while river traffic
burgeoned. Numerous navigation companies were launched.
When the Columbia Canal was opened in 1824, after leaving as a permanent deposit in the community the numerous
Irishmen who had been imported as laborers to construct it,
it carried as much as sixty thousand bales of cotton a year. In
1828, in one day, thirty-three boats arrived at the Camden
wharves. Those coming down the Catawba were small craft,
known as mountain boats, capable of carrying fifty bales of
cotton. Those running downstream from Camden were
double that size. Most of them were pole boats, propelled by
a crew of six men who walked the deck from stem to stern,

pushing against the river bottom with their long poles. Efforts to introduce other types were not very successful. One of these was the team boat, a craft equipped with paddle wheels, which were turned by the mule power of nine mules walking a circular path on the deck.

However, even during those years of its greatest activity, transportation on the Santee and its tributaries was painful and unreliable at best. "Normal water," the average flow, was really abnormal. Most of the time these rivers were either in freshet or too low to permit clear sailing. But it took several disastrous attempts to establish regular steamboat services along them to finally convince Carolinians that their great river system would never be an artery of water-borne commerce.

Perhaps it was Colonel Senf's boundless and contagious optimism which made their dream die so slowly. And perhaps it was those same qualities in the colonel which led men of the caliber of Mills and Poinsett and many of their able associates such as Abram Blanding and David R. Williams to take from him his high burning torch, to carry and feed it almost to the time their delusion became too apparent to question.

Carrying Senf's torch, these men seriously planned an extension of the Catawba Canal system all the way to the headquarters of the Linville River and thence, with a short portage, to the west-flowing waters of the Watauga and on to the Ohio and Missouri rivers, that Charleston might be the natural port of all that vast region. Closer to realization came Mills's plan to connect Columbia and Charleston with an almost straight grand canal, following the ridge south of the Santee, crossing by aqueduct all streams encountered en route. In this scheme there was at least a concession to the future in the form of a paralleling highway along the bank of the canal throughout its length.

Incredible as it now seems, these men were completely

convinced that the canal systems they were laboring so arduously to construct would be facilities which would be used for ages to come. In all their reports and recommendations there is not the slightest doubt of that conviction. It seems passing strange that men whose accomplishments in other fields even today demand great homage never for a moment foresaw that America would soon be done with a transportation system as slow and unreliable as rivers and canals of necessity are. Their pathetic delusion is illustrated by the reluctance with which, for the lack of good stone, they recommended the use of brick masonry instead of granite in a section of the Wateree Canal, even though its cost was thereby lessened. They said their disinclination to use any material other than cut stone stemmed from a fear that the works would thereby be less durable.

Senf, Mills and Poinsett for years gave liberally of themselves and their talents in their efforts to quiet by manipulation but a small portion of the Santee that boats might travel it. Ironically, almost all their relatively puny works, designed to attain that goal, are now obscured by the stilled water of the great stream, curbed now for industry as they strove to control it for navigation. Slaves no longer sweat and strain on the surface of that water. Instead the water itself is the slave, turning the generator turbines at the master's beck and call. No ponderous canalboats, loaded with cotton, ply those waters, to the accompaniment of a dolorous work song. Instead, every sparkling day hatches swarms of tiny craft whipping the quiet waters with the ephemeral welts of their wakes as they dash here and there with aimless frivolity to the accompaniment of the ear-splitting, oversized purrs of outboard motors.

Deep beneath those waters, coated with sedimental mire, lie Woodlawn and Hipworth, Chelsea and Pooshee, the hallowed ground of Black Oak, where the planter gentry from all around found a center for their social life and political strife; Wantoot and South Hampton, where King Cotton was wrapped in swaddling clothes; Somerset, Woodboo, Oak Field, Hope and Wampee. Not quite so completely obscured is Colonel Senf's masterpiece which attempted in a modest way what has now been accomplished on a wholesale scale by Lake Moultrie, for yet unsubmerged is the top level section of the canal and its Santee-side locks. A second generation of forest giants rear their towering bulk from the bottom of the long dry cut through which commerce once floated. In the deep funereal shade of the moss-draped, subtropical forest growth, mellowed by time to a unity with the earth itself, the colonel's lovingly fashioned masonry slowly crumbles into oblivion.

A hundred miles upstream, high on Rocky Mount, overlooking the lakes of the Catawba, which have submerged his handiwork—there, where death interrupted his work on the canal around the falls at Mountain Island—sleeps the man and his dream. No stone marks his grave.

❧ ❧ ❧ ❧ ❧ *22. King Cotton*

Considering the early format of Carolina, with its carefully devised system of nobility, it is not surprising that it should fall under the sway of a ruling King, especially after the core of the region had been accustomed to the rule of the relatively petty monarchy of the Golden Prince Rice—who had vastly extended the realm of his own predecessor, the Indigo Queen. But at the time of the unpretentious coronation of King Cotton, probably even his most ardent supporters had no suspicion that this immigrant from the Far East had brought in his fundamental genes all the makings of an Oriental potentate, who, through the years, as he exalted his authority to ever more absolute levels, would scourge his subjects to the brink of ruin.

Quietly, seductively he took his first steps to power, enlisting here and there influential henchmen in his support. First, there were a few planters in Georgia, whose slave organizations had outgrown the availability of new swamp areas suitable for rice growing; and then there was General William Moultrie, closely followed by Captain Peter Gaillard. The rich rewards that followed from their new allegiance soon brought a veritable multitude flocking to a fleecy standard, which for a century and a half would fly over an ever growing domain—even above the Stars and Stripes.

For more than a century prior to 1792, cotton had been a familiar plant throughout the Southern colonies. Some patches of it were among the first crops planted by the newly arrived settlers at Albemarle Point in 1670, but an early frost prevented its fruiting. Thereafter on many plantations

cotton was annually planted rather as a garden plant, to help supply the planter's own household fiber needs, to be spun and woven into crude cloth by his domestic staff during their idle time. Since each yard of such cloth represented an incredible investment in time, there was no economic justification for its production except that the hours devoted to its production would be otherwise wasted. The eight months of painstaking care the plant itself required before the seed cotton could be picked from the bolls, when they at last yawned open under the southern sun, were but a small portion of the over-all task. Most arduous of all was the difficulty of separating the lint from the seed to which it so stubbornly adhered. Five pounds of lint a week was about the top production capacity of one so employed. Then followed the time-consuming process of combing the fibres, both to clean them and to arrange them in parallel strands, that they might be twisted into thread. This combing or carding process was then done by working together two wooden, wire-bristled brushes, treating but a handful of cotton at a time. After that there were endless hours at the spinning wheel, slowly producing the thread each length of which would have to be individually woven into its place in the cloth by the use of both hands and feet in the operation of the hand loom. Finally came the dyeing process—boiling the cloth in great pots, charged with the dye matter, which itself had been painstakingly produced from the roots or berries of the neighborhood wild plants. At today's wage rates a yard of cloth so produced would cost literally its weight in gold. So, under such production difficulties, even with the employment of slave labor exclusively, cotton cloth production offered no commercial possibilities.

Meanwhile, back in England, while the American colonies were distracted by their all absorbing dispute with the mother country, several men with a mechanical turn of mind were creating some crude mechanical devices of enormous import to the world in general and especially to the South. During those years the Industrial Revolution was gestating through James Hargreaves's invention of the spinning jenny, Richard Arkwright's spinning machine, and the Reverend Edmund Cartwright's power loom. While these machines were built primarily for processing wool, they could easily be adapted to cotton. By simplifying the production of cloth and thereby greatly reducing its cost, they enormously increased the demand for raw fibers. But a single obstacle prevented cotton from answering that demand—the difficulty of separating the seed from the staple.

In the face of this economic situation, with the return of peace and prosperity, necessity being the mother of invention, it was inevitable that this bottleneck in the production of cotton goods would soon be removed. When economic necessity calls for an invention, it frequently happens that more than one inventor independently answers the call, and so it was in the case of the cotton gin. But, however meritorious may be the priority claims of several Georgians and South Carolinians, history has overwhelmingly accorded to Eli Whitney the honor of being its inventor.

The personalities of several people and a series of fortuitous events dovetailed to produce the cotton gin. Fresh out of Yale, through which he had worked his way by teaching, Whitney in the fall of 1792 set sail from New York bound for Savannah, from which port he expected to proceed to a school in back-country South Carolina where he had been engaged to teach. During the leisurely days of the slow trip southward, a warm friendship developed between young Whitney and a fellow passenger, the elderly widow of General Nathaniel Greene. From spending the summer season in the North, Mrs. Greene was returning to her home, Mulberry Grove plantation near Savannah, one of several plantations presented to the general by Georgia and South Carolina in grateful recognition of his services during the war. When they landed at Savannah, she invited Whitney to proceed with her to her plantation and visit there for a while before going on to his job. There Mrs. Greene soon noticed the extraordinary mechanical endowment of her guest. So, when a group of guests at Mulberry Grove were discussing the need of a machine to separate the cotton lint from its seed she suggested that Whitney be challenged with the problem. The suggestion was sufficient to set him to work in the plantation workshop. Utilizing only such materials as he could find at hand around the place, he soon contrived a combination of revolving saws or teeth, wire brushes and combs that effectively accomplished its purpose. So it came to pass early in 1793 that Whitney's cotton "engine," soon shortened to the cotton gin, threw wide the door to commercial cotton production.

One of the first to enter that open door was alert, intelligent old General Moultrie. The very next year at North Hampton, through which the Santee Canal was then being cut, he made an extensive planting of cotton. The next year his friend Captain Peter Gaillard devoted a goodly part of the river swamp fields of his Rocks plantation on the Santee to cotton. Rapidly, in the years that followed, as King Cotton quietly mounted his throne, the end of the dog days would find a blanket of white spread over the Carolina fields from the coast to the mountains and farther and farther beyond, as Carolinians in search of more and ever wider cotton fields sought the newer lands to the southwest, clear to the Mississippi and across it. With this accomplished and this vast domain in total bondage, King Cotton might well have gloated with an appropriate Mephistophelean laugh, for in all of history not even any other Oriental potentate had secured an enslavement of both the minds and bodies of his subjects on a grander scale.

Even as has been so often the case in the empires and dictatorships that have had their day in this old world, King Cotton demanded and received the absolute fealty of his far-flung subjects. Even beyond the bounds of his domain, his reign received the adulation of its superficial observers—of those who could not or would not look into the rottenness of its foundation or the sterility of its flowering, of those who profited by its export trade, and, even to this day, of a vast number of romanticists who love to visualize the wide white-flecked fields under a benevolent Southern sun with whole families of blacks, each armed with his burlap bag, happily singing through the livelong day, as the King's tribute starts its journey to the staccato and whirring bedlam of the weave room of the nearby mill and thence to the corners of the earth. For those romantics the few surviving, well-kept mansions of the cotton Bourbons are now surrounded with an aura of sanctity. The more frequent empty-eyed ruins of those mansions that still dot the countryside produce nostalgic sighs and accusations of criminal neglect. It seems to require but a recession far enough into the past to glorify even the iniquitous.

At the same time it is only fair to admit that there was and is a considerable excuse for the blindness of King Cotton's protagonists. The façade of his realm was so attractive that it tended to blind all but the most critical to the evils behind that façade. He built an elegant court of cultured gentry, spreading out through the length and breadth of the South in modern castles, tastefully designed and beautiful to see. He rapidly pushed back the frontier and in a few years wrested from the wilderness millions of acres of fertile fields, turning them to production for the welfare of all the world. He supplied America with its greatest and richest export, thereby providing a major stimulus to its rapid development. By putting a money commodity in the hands of a large section of the country and thereby enticing them to leave other enterprises alone he made a substantial contribution to the building of the industrial East. Finally, he amalgamated the South into a working unit, endowed it with a conviction of its world-wide importance, and thus planted a sectional pride the like of which, to this day, exists nowhere this side of California.

However, hidden behind this façade, suppressed as far as possible, lay a multitude of facts, the sum of which constituted a most damning indictment of King Cotton's tinseled reign. During his heyday few men were both intelligent and daring enough to raise their voices against his iniquities. Nevertheless, some did dare the ostracism which was the penalty of such treason and spoke their thoughts. In Carolina, the sterling James L. Petigru spoke out freely against the social order and the national political positions which the King required of his faithful subjects, and he paid for his temerity with a life of unremitting turmoil. Dr. St. Julien Ravenel gave up his medical practice to devote his life to chemical research and experimentation, to encourage the adoption of a more balanced agricultural economy. Voicing the postwar disillusionment of the intellectuals, Professor F. A. Porcher told the South Carolina Historical Society that

> cotton made men rich, but kept the country poor . . .
> its magic paralyzed all energy for any other pursuit. . . .
> If I were an absolute governor I would punish with
> death every citizen of the State who would plant a seed
> of it.

From time to time there were others who saw the evil fruit of King Cotton's regime and acted their protests by freeing their slaves and moving away from the Land of Cotton. But for a full century such subversive conduct did little more than flyspeck the grand façade.

By forces beyond his realm much more formidable attacks were launched against the King's regime. There was the tariff, designed to clip his power in the markets of the world. Then there was the devastation of the Civil War and the emancipation of his Negro slaves, which severely, if only temporarily, shook the foundation of his realm. Finally there was the most serious of all the attacks from outside, a wholesale invasion from Mexico—by the boll weevil. Still the old King hung on, almost as arbitrary as ever in demanding his tribute from his stricken domain.

At last, from deep within his own realm came the truly redoubtable threats to his long tyranny. From the poverty and misery of the economically prostrate land rose a mounting tide of disillusionment. With it came its usual ally—enlightenment. Together they unceremoniously deposed the

old tyrant, chained him, and set him to work for the land
he had so long dominated. So came the dawn of the New
South—at long last a Free South. And so became possible at
last the rapidly diversified economy of the Carolinas.

North Hampton lies deep beneath the Santee waters of
Lake Moultrie. Its great mansion house survives only in
photographs and memories. The bountiful fields of the Rocks
have been submerged by Lake Marion. In the Low Country,
thereabouts, cotton fields are now few and far between. And
all up the river and over its whole wide countryside there
are no longer endless fields of cotton. Four fifths of the cultivated land is now put to other uses. Yes, Carolina is free at
last—for the first time in its long history. This freedom is
something new for Carolinians. Only those of this generation
have been privileged to enjoy the new opportunities that fre-
dom offers. But even as they grasp the opportunities of their
new-found freedom they must of necessity shoulder the terrific burden of the effects of King Cotton's long misrule—of
the accumulated social, moral and economic debts and deficits
he left behind. To pay those debts and remedy those deficits
will require the best talent of the region and the concerted
action of the people for generations to come. For now, ill
concealed by its veneer of romanticism, its picturesque fields,
its gaily clad, spiritual-shouting darkies, the blythesome song
of the mocking bird, and the heavy fragrance of magnolia
and jessamine, lie evil and noisome facts of the King's awful
legacy:

He all but irreparably gullied hundreds of thousands of
acres of the rich red hills and leeched from the sand hills the
little substance they possessed;

He enslaved the minds and spirits of the whole population by inflexibly directing their thoughts and efforts into a
single narrow channel;

He undermined the stability of the most stable of professions, converting the self-sustaining Carolina farmer into a

single-crop speculator, and so weakened his traditional independence that he could soon be found in the vanguard of those demanding government pap and government regulation;

He led his devotees to substitute the economic power of their crop for moral and political rectitude; by spreading economic salve upon their consciences he seduced his minions into placing immediate economic welfare above principles; to support the protective tariff when they thought it would profit them, only to threaten to withdraw from the Union in protest against the "principle" of a protective tariff when cotton prices demanded such a reversal of principle; to recede from their progress towards the abandonment of slavery and fight a war principally for its preservation, regardless of the right or wrong involved, simply because King Cotton demanded its preservation;

By encouraging the growth of Negro slavery and its rigid caste system, he created the nation's most difficult sociological problem, which is yet far from solved;

He quite effectually extended the institution of Negro slavery for nearly three fourths of a century after the Emancipation Proclamation by adding to the planter's hold on his workers the operations of the lien merchant, the share-cropping system and a multitude of severe labor laws relating to farm labor;

He blinded his subalterns to the oft demonstrated truth that permanent economic prosperity is the product of high educational standards, and encouraged them to withhold education from a vast segment of their people that they might attain no skill beyond that of a cotton field hand;

By monopolizing all the available land, by equally monopolizing the minds of his subjects, and by preventing the accumulation of risk capital for investment in other ventures, he nipped in the bud the region's industrial development and paralyzed it for a hundred years. Before King Cotton took over, the manufactured products of the four Southern states exceeded those of all New England and New York combined;

By taking all the land unto himself and discouraging the growth of industry, for a century and a half, he banished from his realm its most valuable and most costly product —its opportunity-seeking youth;

By decreeing a subsistence level of living among his laboring class, he effectively barred from his domain the influx of the skilled workers which other sections were garnering from abroad.

Finally, with the assistance of his predecessor, Prince Rice, he laid out the tragic road that led from the early cotton patches on Albemarle Point down to Mrs. Greene's Mulberry Grove and thence to General Moultrie's North Hampton, on to John Calhoun's seat in the Upcountry, back to Charleston and the ramparts of Fort Sumter, and, finally, to the red brick farmhouse at Appomattox.

Truly, the reign of King Cotton was America's greatest tragedy.

🌺 🌺 🌺 🌺 🌺 *23. Green leaves
and bright feathers*

*N*ature ordered it that Caro-
lina should sing for her a special song, a song of varied verses,
running from that of the somber, moss-draped "lotus land"
where the Santee meets the sea, to that of the "gardens of the
gods" in the southern Appalachians where the river has its
sources; from the rapiers of the marsh grass and bullrushes
and the shields of the great pads of the yellow-flowered lotus,
the flamboyant hibiscus, the dense hedgelike masses of sweet
myrtle and cassina, the magnolias with their magnificent,
fragrant flowers, the erect, formal palmettos among the ponderous informality of the spreading live oaks—from this subtropical land to the flower-bespangled verdure of the storied
rain forests of the mountains where the tangled jungle of
rhododendron, flame azalea and stewartia grow as a mid-
story between the towering spruce, balsam, chestnut and tulip
trees, and the green carpet of oily-leafed galax, fern fronds,
ladies' slippers, carmine columbines, blue delphiniums, and

snowy trilliums. Between the seaside fringe and the mountains there are several almost equally diverse lands—the broad expanse of the pine flats, interrupted only by the traversing river swamps and the scattered elliptical "bays," a land which now widely separates the sea from its pristine beach where the extensive, rolling sand hills run across the Carolinas—which hills, in turn, are separated from the mountains by the land of the remnants of the once high Ocoees, the rich red hills of the Carolina Piedmont.

Before the white man unbecomingly modified the scene, the pine flats were parklike expanses of tall longleaf and loblolly pines rising from a lush expanse of grass, decorated in season with dainty white atamasco lilies, delicate clear pink sabbatias, and the weird yellow and red flowers and seed pods of the insect-devouring sarracenias. From the deep soft carpets of moss around the boggy edges of the "bays" of the pine flats grew smilax-draped hedges of red bay and myrtle, overtopped by sweet bays of unforgettable fragrance and the elegant gordonias, encircling and concealing the bell bottoms of the black gums and cypresses wading deep in the "pocoson's" forbidding gloom.

Cutting the pine flats from west to east were the verdant, teeming jungles of the river swamps where the tops of the vine-trammeled oaks and sweet gums, great buttressed tupelos and cypresses towered ten stories above the forest floor of impenetrable canebrakes or lawns of sweet violets.

Beyond lay the old beaches and sand dunes of the long receded sea, the wide, rolling sand hills, beneath whose cover of flat-topped longleaf pines and jessamine-decorated scrub oaks lay an incredible fairy flower garden—silenes, pink and salmon, fragrant arbutus, ethereal, white-flowered pixie moss, miniature rhododendrons called sand myrtles, bright blue clumps of lupine, the yellow glory of the cacti and the Carolina allspice, snow white stinging spurge, yellow and gold butterfly weeds, and in the fall an endless variety of asters in a showy display of blue, yellow, white and gold.

Westward, alien but adjacent, the clay hills of the Piedmont rolled away to the west—sometimes a prairie of grass and wild peas, and sometimes forested with oaks, hickories and shortleaf pines; the land of the blue butterfly peas, the yellow and red wild sweet peas, redroot and bloodroot, dainty blue hepaticas, the fabled, intricate passion flowers, the pinksters, mountain laurels and viburnums and the white-bolled sycamores—a land made brilliant in the fall by the flaming sumacs, the yellow of the sassafras, the scarlet of the sourwood and the gold of the maples and cottonwoods.

And this whole resplendent flowering wilderness was also a vibrant singing wilderness. Claiming for themselves the beaches and marshes of the coastal region, were the comical, ponderous pelicans, the ever busy piping plover, the screaming terns and the ungainly statuesque herons, blue and white; while painted buntings and wrens graced the seaside thickets along with the inimitable mocking bird, songster unrivaled, known to the Indian as the cencentlatolly, or four hundred tongues. By the river estuaries nested the noisy red-winged blackbirds, the majestic osprey, golden and bald eagles and a countless variety of gaudy, fleet-winged ducks. High in the towering cypresses the green and orange Carolina paroquets fed and nested in a forest resounding with the hammering of the great ivory-billed woodpeckers whose beaks were worth three deerskins each in the trade between the Carolina Indians and those of the Great Lakes. All over the countryside were birds of such brilliant plumage that back in England the tales of them were received as gross exaggerations until specimens were sent to prove the facts— that here were blue birds, red, scarlet and yellow birds, jays, tanagers, cardinals and warblers. Here were soarers unmatched—the tirelessly wheeling buzzards. Here were beautiful new species of the birds of prey—the strong-winged hawks and the silent-flying owls. Here through the still of summer afternoons came the mournful notes of the doves, and by night the eerie lonesome call of the whip-poor-will, believed by the Indians to be the embodiment of the spirits of their people whom the English had slaughtered. As common as sparrows in England were those birds whose palatable flesh would be their nemesis—the great iridescent turkey, the whistling quail and the grouse.

To the hundreds of species that nested in this varied garden of nature, for a fleeting while twice annually there were added hundreds more, as the feathered hoards of South America and the West Indies passed to and from the great northern land masses to breed and feed there through the long daylight hours of the subarctic summers. Carolina, from the mountains to the sea, lay athwart the world's most concentrated fly-way of the migratory birds. The flights of the passenger pigeons "blotted out the sun." The ducks, geese and swans all but choked the inland waters when they stopped to rest and feed.

The beasts that crawled and walked beneath added wonder to it all—tales of the "wondrous," terrifying rattlesnake, the clever raccoon, the repulsive, pouched oppossum, the great-antlered elk, the thundering herds of buffalo, the sly and supple panthers, the less exotic bears and the myriads of graceful little deer.

Where nature had spread her creations so bountifully, and with such diversity, inevitably her devotees would come bringing their devotion to the new and wonderful things she had here on display.

It was the enthusiastic report of these wonders, from the lips of a returning traveler, that prompted John Lawson to make a sudden change in his plans to travel on the continent and lured him to face the perils of the sea and the wilderness simply to see for himself. No doubt the publication of what he saw in the little-known interior of Carolina played a persuasive role in bringing the talented Mark Catesby to Charles Town in 1722. For years he roamed the Carolina coast and up the rivers beyond the narrow fringe of the English settlements, where he lived with the Indians and learned of birds, plants, reptiles and insects from them—years of drawing, painting, and making notes. Nine years later he laid before the Queen the fruit of those years of travel, labor and hardship, dedicating to her the first of the two magnificent volumes on the natural history of the New World, bringing for the first time into English drawing rooms the wonders of the Carolina wilderness.

In the course of the half century after Catesby came to Carolina the coastal settlements prospered and matured beyond the stage of complete absorption with the physical aspects of building a new community in an isolated wilderness. The fruit of this growing maturity was a measure of leisure, at least for the more fortunate—leisure which was beginning to make possible a polite society and intellectual pursuits. Products of that new-found leisure were the elegant Doctor Alexander Garden and simple, retiring Thomas Walter.

During the decades preceding the Revolution, during which, incidentally, he was an ardent Tory, Doctor Garden became widely known both at home and abroad for his attainments as a naturalist, particularly as a botanist. He was the Carolina correspondent and collector for the great Linneaus. By way of grateful recognition for his assistance, Linneaus fittingly named the heavy-scented gardenia for him, so that, through the ages to come, the Doctor's name would grace the flower shops of the world, to be joined there every Christmas season by the name of a Carolinian of a later date, after the versatile Joel Poinsett introduced the poinsettia into the United States from its native Mexico.

Most of the details of the life of Thomas Walter are shrouded in the mists of time. It was probably about 1760 that he came to Carolina from England where he had secured a sufficient education to write in flawless classical Latin. He acquired a modest plantation on the south side of the Santee, a little up the river from where, a half century later, the boats from the back country headed for Charleston would enter the Santee Canal. There he was one of the few Englishmen in an almost exclusively French Huguenot region. He built a simple plantation home, married three times, at least twice into prominent planter families of the neighborhood, and reared a large family. To a kinsman he writes: "The cottage I invite you to is but a homely one, but it will at least teach us to philosophize." There is ample evidence of the high esteem in which he was held in that throughout the terrible years of the Revolution he and his home were unmolested, even though his Tory sympathies were well known. His neighbor, General Marion, apparently saw to that—although he considered two of Mrs. Walter's brothers sufficiently important prizes to have them marched all the way to a suitable prison in Philadelphia.

It is a safe assumption that the talisman that protected Walter's family and property, in an area almost totally devastated by one side or the other as the swaying fortunes of war in turn presented the opportunity, was the avocation to which most of his energies were devoted—the avocation which was to become one of the important milestones in the science of botany; for all the while, during the parlous years preceding the Revolution, and throughout the terror and destruction of the war years, the modest, studious Walter was busily intent with harmless botanizing. Confining his field of study to the country within fifty miles of his plantation, he had collected more than a thousand botanical species, of which more than two hundred were new to science. Most of these he brought to his own fertile herbarium where he lovingly cultivated and studied them. All of them he carefully classified and described in a manuscript couched in classical Latin and employing Linneaus's new binomial system of nomenclature—the first such local botany in America. The manuscript so impressed John Fraser, his scientist correspondent in England, that Fraser had it published at his own expense.

Among the new species Walter officially discovered and named are Catesby's lily, the pitcher plant and the black gum. Every Christmas season, children all over the South wade through the muck and tangle of branch swamps for the lovely, bright Christmas berries of the *smilax Walteri*.

With the advent of the ever more serious freshets, which became devastating a few years after Walter's death in 1789, the planters were driven from the alluvial lands of the Santee. With his fields and gardens neglected, the plants he loved soon took unto themselves again the land he had borrowed from them that he and his family might live there among them. Now, in the wilds of the swamp forest, there is no evidence of those borrowed fields, or his "homely" cottage. There is only a weathered headstone marking his grave which had been placed in his lovingly tended herbarium. Writers have waxed eloquent on the pathos of that lonely headstone, deep in the wilds of the swamp—a sentiment which is more than likely misplaced; for Walter would probably have liked it just as it is. Far more tragic was the sale, years later, of the neglected remains of his splendid botanical collection to the British Museum for fifteen shillings. And there is tragedy, too, in the absence of any reference to him or his herbarium in the diary of the world-renowned botanist, André Michaux, even though he ferried across the Santee very near Walter's home only three years after the death of the modest student.

André Michaux had left his prosperous farm near Versailles, France, and embarked on a career of roaming the green world in response to the restlessness which possessed him after his wife died at the birth of their only child, François André. Although he gave up farming, never to return to it, he never abandoned its heritage. As he trudged the fields and forests beyond alien shores, he was ever on the alert for useful plants as well as the beautiful and unusual, and he was always collecting living plants for shipment back to the soil of his native land. In André Michaux, the farmer and the botanist were inextricably entwined.

He had reached his life's middle years when he first landed in Carolina. Behind him were perilous botanizing trips to all sorts of out-of-the-way places—to the Near East, to Persia where he cured the Shah with his herbs and was robbed by the Arabs. As he was preparing for an expedition even farther east to Samarkand and Karakorum, his King's decree revised his plans and sent him west—to America, to find useful trees, shrubs and game birds for importation into France. After two years in New York he sailed for Charleston. In Carolina the climate, the people and the variety of plants so completely enchanted him that for the remaining sixteen years of his life the region was to claim his almost undivided attention. And he passed his enthusiasm on to his botanist son, who would carry on his work here after his death.

Soon after Michaux landed, he purchased a plantation about ten miles north of Charleston to receive his collections pending shipment back to France, and, with his seventeen-year-old son, set out on his first collecting expedition to the mountains, traveling up the Savannah River to the southern end of the Appalachians. A few months later he was back in Charleston with a vast store of roots, seedlings, dried specimens and seeds, and an even greater accumulation of enthusiasm for that island of tertiary flora which the continental glacier had pushed into the Southern mountains, to become

isolated there when it receded. Ever afterwards he was far
more interested in nature's gardens in Carolina than in those
of his King back in Versailles. So, even though he was the
official emissary from Louis XVI to the plant kingdom of
America, he appears to have been very little disturbed by
the world-shaking events occurring back home which reached
their climax while he was far in the Carolina hinterland
on a second collecting expedition. That almost all the sixty
thousand living plants he had shipped back to France were
among the casualties of the upheaval at home seems not to
have deterred him from readily adopting the new order before he set out on a third trip inland. In fact, there is basis
for the suspicion that on that expedition he had extracurric-
ular activities as a secret agent for the Republic, to determine
the temper of the people in Kentucky and judge whether or
not they might be co-operative in a French move to recover
that lost territory. At least there is the inference of a more
than abstract interest in the new regime in a trip to Philadelphia to confer with Citizen Genêt, the ambassador of the
Republic, before setting out for the old Northwest Territory.
And the new order creeps into his terse diary:

> The 30th Germinal in the 3rd year of the French
> Republic One and Indivisible (Sunday 19th of April
> 1795 old style) started to go and herborize in the high
> mountains of the Carolinas and afterwards to visit the
> Western Territories.

Noting along the way alumroot, wild vetches and phlox
in bloom, he traveled up the Cooper River and on to the
Santee where he discovered a new species of elm while waiting to be ferried across to the east bank, up which he traveled
to the "Santee High-hills" and "Statesboroug." There white
and pink phlox and blue biennial lupine were in blossom.

He continued upriver to "Cambden," where he found a new species of kalmia, and thence on by Flat Rock and Hanging Rock to the "Waxsaw" hills where he lost his horse but was "overwhelmed with civilities." Here he was the guest of Colonel James Crawford, uncle and foster father of Andrew Jackson. Here the wild ginger, shooting stars and spring beauties had his special attention. A few days later he was at Colonel William Hill's ironworks on the west side of the Catawba, marveling at the Colonel's new invention of an improved water blast, his forge, furnace, rolling mill and nail factory (where now there are but forest-covered hills beside the peaceful waters of Catawba Lake). He continued on through Lincolnton to Morganton, where he was the guest of Colonel Waightstill Avery, who, years later, was to become involved with Jackson in an "affair of honor."

From Morganton he traveled up the Catawba and Linville and on over the mountains to Jonesboro, Tennessee. In the mountains, ginseng was always of particular interest to Michaux because of its commercial possibilities in the China trade, for in the Far East its tubers, thought capable of curing almost every ill of man, were then highly prized for medicinal purposes. For Michaux the mountains in May were thrilling. The aloes and wild mandrakes and yellow ladies' slippers were in flower and the slopes were a mass of color— flame azalea, rhododendron and mountain laurel. He longed to linger and "herborize" but on to Kentucky he had to go.

Three years later in the early spring he returned across the mountains to retrace the route he had traveled up the river. Now he was busy collecting living specimens for the "Garden of the Republic" at Charleston—hazelnuts, red maples, bloodroots, trailing arbutus, great-leaf magnolia, silver bells, stewartia, and the new kalmia he had discovered at Camden. As he neared Charleston, his pack train heavy laden with his live collection he made this final travel note:

Slept at house of Widow Stuard 18 miles from ferry.
. . . Tavern dirty and without supply of fodder for
horses.

On his way back to France his ship was wrecked off the
coast of Holland and much of his wilderness treasure and
part of his diaries were lost. But among those not lost was an
unnamed leaf and seed pod which were destined to set off a
botanical treasure hunt unique in the annals of botany. In
1839, long after Michaux's death, Asa Gray, a noted American botanist noticed the small, round, glossy leaf and the
lone seed pod in the Frenchman's Paris collection. Its label
stated only that it was from *les hautes montagnes de Caro-
linie*. As the plant was a complete stranger to the botanist,
his curiosity was greatly aroused. On the strength of the close
similarity of an Oriental specimen, he undertook to describe
it and he gave it the name of Shortia. There were countless
futile searches for a living specimen, extending over nearly
forty years, before a farm boy brought home to his amateur
botanist father a clump of galaxlike plants he had dug from
the banks of the Catawba near Marion, North Carolina. So
the lovely plant commonly known as Oconee Bells was redis-
covered.

Another assignment, which resulted in his death in Madagascar, prevented André Michaux from returning to Carolina; but his son and collaborator, François André Michaux,
carried on. In the years that followed he made three trips to
Carolina during which he removed and shipped back to
France most of the plants that his father had put in temporary
residence in the "Garden of the Republic." Time has obliterated all evidence of their garden, as it has that of Thomas
Walter. But some of Michaux's seeds from other lands, nota-
bly the unique Japanese varnish tree and the delicate, fragrant Persian albizzia or mimosa, took to their new environ-

ment and escaped—to write in flowers and living green across
the length and breadth of Carolina a fitting memorial to its
devoted wilderness plantsman; and the descendants of the
camellias and tea plants that he introduced still grace the sun-
drenched gardens.

It was the wild creatures of the sunny beaches, endless
marshes, gloomy swamps and wilderness forests of Carolina
that inspired one of the most devoted and fruitful collabora-
tions in the story of American natural history.

Beautiful Jean Jacques Audubon, carrying through life
an aura of mystery which encouraged the conviction of many
that he was the lost Dauphin of France, came to America
from Haiti endowed with a unique blend of abilities which
destined him to inspire in the expansion-distracted young nation an artistic appreciation of nature's bounties which its
ruthless growth was recklessly destroying. With a devotion
which led him to the brink of ruin—a devotion even rivaling
that he showed for his beloved Lucy and their children—he
followed the wilderness trails, floated down rivers and
climbed mountains, for most of a lifetime, to depict with con-
summate skill the birds of America. Although equally at
home in polite society and in the most forbidding wilderness, he had found the life of frontier merchant utterly alien
to his personality. With amazing improvidence he had
walked out on wife and family and walked into lasting fame.

It was a middle-aged Audubon whose insatiable treks in
search of every bird species of America finally led to Carolina
in 1831. In Charleston it was only natural that his host
should be Reverend John Bachman, the rector of St. John's
Lutheran Church, for the pastor was widely known as a man
who was interested in everything, especially in several lines
of nature study. Under his hospitable roof began a warm
friendship between the two nature lovers which eventually
spread to the entire families of both of them. For twenty

years, "J. B.," as Bachman always signed himself, and "Jostle," as he usually addressed Audubon, were either together or in constant correspondence.

From Audubon to Bachman there would be the plea:

> Study our *dear herons* as much as you can. Write what you know of the whooping crane, Kildeer plover, wood ibis, yellow-breasted rail, great and least terns, dabchicks, grebe, solitary sandpipers, sandwich terns, roseate terns, long-billed curlews, pied oyster catchers—send me several skins.

And the minister would answer these pleas with the accuracy of observation of a trained, professional scientist. He would write too of the kegs of whiskey and rum purchased to preserve the numerous specimens he was securing, pending the next visit of Audubon or for shipment to him.

And Bachman would urge on Audubon that he study the migrations of the birds and report his observations, for in the field of ornithology the seasonal migrations of birds was his greatest interest. Long before bird banding gave the details of that superlative among the facets of nature, Bachman, in a learned paper, had told the story of the wonders of bird migration with amazing accuracy.

The enthusiasm and absorption of the collaborators was contagious. Soon friends were bringing in specimens and observations. Bachman's sister-in-law, Maria, who would later become his second wife, learned to draw and paint, and for years she furnished Audubon with skillfully done pictures of the plants and wild flowers of the region for the backgrounds of the Southern birds. Dr. Ravenel supplied a barrel of sea shells; Audubon's sons, John and Victor, joined in the art work. Both the Audubon boys married Bachman girls, both of whom died within a few years. When the Audubons remarried, the first-born of each was a daughter named for her father's first wife. The Audubons and the Bachmans moved on through the years almost as a single family.

After the *Birds of America* was off the press and the prints all tinted and bound, and copy number one despatched to "J. B.," it was the "Quadrupeds" that engrossed the friends. It was Bachman who interested Audubon in preparing this companion work to his work on birds. This was the minister's special field. The text of the two-volume work, *The Viviparous Quadrupeds of North America,* is almost totally his work. The 150 colored plates were partly the work of John and Victor, for before this second great work was completed Audubon's life was slipping away.

All the while, for scientists, the South was a difficult environment during those years when the best talents were being lured into public affairs by the growing crisis, as the region drifted ever nearer the vortex of the maelstrom whose tragic swirl had been set in motion so many years before. More than once Bachman would write to "Jostle" in this vein:

> Oh, what an enjoyment it would be for me to escape just for one week, from the hydra-headed "Nullification" and sit by your side and talk of birds.

❧ ❧ ❧ ❧ ❧ *24. Titans from the hills*

The two dominant American personalities of the first half of the nineteenth century, the two men whose influence graved most deeply that critical and exciting period of our history, should have been kindred spirits and basically perhaps they were. For Andrew Jackson and John C. Calhoun by heritage and environment were poured in very similar molds. These two Carolinians, from their obscure backwoods homes on opposite sides of the wide Santee tributary country, moved rapidly along their separate paths to national fame; and for more than three decades they would wield influence of enormous import to the burgeoning young nation. By very different paths from their humble homes in the red hills, these two ceaselessly combative and uncompromising men would follow their intensely emotional, irrepressibly ambitious natures to the dizzy heights they reached, where, with dire consequences to the nation, they were to clash in bitter conflict. The outcome of that struggle between kindred titans was an irreparable cleavage between North and South; for Calhoun it spelled the wreck of a brilliant career just short of its goal—and a broken heart.

Before Andrew Jackson left the region of his birth, in the Waxhaw hills along the east bank of the Catawba where North and South Carolina meet, the rugged, red-haired boy

with flashing blue eyes had already crammed into his eighteen years vast excitement and action.

Via Pennsylvania, two years before his birth, Andrew's Scottish parents and their two small sons had come from a miserable North Ireland exile, down the long wagon road to the "Garden of the Waxhaws" where several of Mrs. Jackson's sisters had already settled. By their glowing accounts of the region they had induced the Jacksons to follow them. While clearing his first patches (after erecting a crude log cabin for his family), the elder Jackson died suddenly from overstrain a few weeks before the third boy, Andrew, was born at the home of Mrs. Jackson's sister, Jennet Crawford. Thereafter, the Jackson boys were raised along with the numerous Crawford children as one family on the relatively prosperous and expanding Catawba River plantation of James Crawford. A small portion of the education Andrew acquired during those years was reluctantly imbibed from the primitive school the settlers had established in the neighborhood, but more was picked up informally along the way, thanks to his sociable bent and a boundless avidity for life and action—in the fields, the woods, the cockpits and at the neighborhood kirk.

Although only thirteen the summer that Tarleton led his dragoons into the Waxhaws in pursuit of Buford, he counted himself man enough to join his brothers and the other men of the household as Rebel soldiers. During the next two years he took part in the battle of Hanging Rock and in several skirmishes including a defense of his home against a band of Tory raiders. He suffered capture, imprisonment, smallpox and the loss of both his brothers and his mother, all as war casualties. In Charleston, to which he journeyed soon after the war to collect an inheritance from a relative back in Ireland, he learned about horse racing, investing his whole inheritance in that part of his education.

With such a background, whatever determined Jackson to become a lawyer is quite a mystery. Nevertheless, in 1787 in Salisbury, to which he had migrated to read law in an office, he was duly licensed to practice. In that town, which was then the most important settlement of the Carolina hill country, he was remembered more for his roistering than for the learning his new profession implied.

Another year passed, and, with a Negro slave girl he had purchased before leaving Salisbury, he was beyond the mountains in what was then western North Carolina, having been appointed prosecuting attorney for the region now known as Tennessee. There the upstart, short-lived State of Franklin had just been outlawed and Jack Sevier had been deposed from his governorship. Embracing with impartial gusto the rough-and-tumble backwoods politics, the excitement of the constantly recurring Indian wars and land speculations on a baronial scale, Jackson was soon an important frontier figure and a very busy man—but not too busy for simultaneous involvements in a succession of personal difficulties, more than one duel, and the wooing and winning of another man's wife.

Such adventures, far from hampering the young firebrand's career, rather enhanced it. As an exaggerated personification of the raw Western frontier, he was soon its idol. So it was natural that he would be one of the prime movers in the establishment of Tennessee as the sixteenth state of the Union, with Nolichucky Jack Sevier as its first Governor and he himself as its first Congressman, only to be elevated to the Senate a few months later. Nor did it appear unseemly when the unrestrained fighter-gambler-speculator donned the judicial robes of a justice of the Superior Court. The ever truculent Jackson never felt the traditional restraint of the bench. While still serving as justice, he sought and secured his election as commanding officer of the state militia with the rank of major general. He engaged in a violent public altercation with Governor Sevier, challenged him to a duel and in a paid advertisement in the Nashville newspaper branded the hero of King's Mountain and the Cherokee wars as a "base coward." He joined posses in pursuit of desperate criminals, bet recklessly at every horse race, and spent his spare time building up large-scale, slave-operated plantations. Continually in financial difficulties, his undertakings always outstripping his capital, on more than one occasion he saved himself from financial ruin by betting everything on a horse of his choice—usually one of his own which he himself had trained. On one occasion the stakes included a substantial number of the General's slaves who from their pen at the track watched the race upon which their ownership turned.

Months before the outbreak of the War of 1812, Jackson jumped the gun he so ardently desired to hear, by a stirring call for Tennessee to mobilize and for "50,000 volunteers." By the time the war actually started he had three thousand men well trained—equipped partly at his own expense—and he was itching for an important assignment, against New Orleans or against Canada. But the authorities back in Washington had other commanders they much preferred to the border militiaman. Nevertheless, through the back door the impatient General managed to get a commission in the United States Army and an assignment to quell Indian uprisings in Alabama and western Georgia. By promptly producing a series of victories in a war which had proved but a succession of defeats, Jackson overnight elevated himself from a frontier hero to a national hero. His popularity with the populace, his forte throughout his career, sent him on to command at New Orleans where he gained both his overwhelming postwar victory against the invading British forces and his sobriquet, "Old Hickory."

Three years later, in 1818, when "Old Hickory" again went on the warpath—this time against the Seminole Indians who were raiding up from Spanish Florida—he extended his expedition on into Florida itself and precipitated the country into a new international crisis. It had all come about by the General's having put his own wishful construction upon the rather wide and indefinite instructions he had received, telling him to adopt the necessary measures to terminate the conflict. Those instructions had been sent him by Monroe's young Secretary of War, John C. Calhoun.

Although his name was Patrick and he had come to America from Ireland, the father of John C. Calhoun, and his mother, too, were Presbyterian Scots. After his family landed in Philadelphia when Pat was a small boy, they had settled on the Pennsylvania frontier. In the years during which he was growing up they kept moving southward along the frontier. By 1756, they were in the Waxhaws. Three years more and they had moved again, across the Catawba,

the Broad and the Saluda to the area between the Saluda and the Savannah, the Long Canes section of the Ninety-Six District.

When the militant Regulator movement was born of the bitterness between the back country and the coastal aristocracy, grim, roughhewn Patrick by his leadership in the frequent Indian wars of the frontier had already earned his position as one of the leading spokesmen for the neglected hinterland settlers. One election time he led several hundred of his irate, well-armed neighbors halfway across the State to the studiedly inconveniently located polling place to get himself elected to the Colonial Assembly. Thereby he attained one of the first successes in the long battle to break the political wall which the coastal aristocracy had erected against the growing population of the back country. Until he died, when John, the youngest of his four sons, was a boy of twelve, Pat relentlessly and furiously pursued this political siege.

The older brothers and a brother-in-law, Moses Waddell who subsequently was president of the University of Georgia, recognized the unusual endowments of the brooding and studious John and, being more convinced of the advantages of schooling than his father had been, undertook to provide the educational opportunities which carried him through Yale, where Timothy Dwight predicted that he would one day be President of the United States, and on through a legal education.

At twenty-nine he was elected to Congress just as the deteriorating relations with England were reaching the boiling point. Almost immediately he was the leader of the "War Hawks," a group of young Westerners of strongly nationalistic views who were bending every effort to stir up enthusiasm for war. With Britain's attention monopolized by the Little Corporal, they were confident that Canada could be easily seized and the nation's honor adequately salved by such an imperial acquisition. In spite of the disappointing outcome of the war which American school children are taught that we won (although the Canadians and British teach the opposite), Calhoun continued his stellar rise to national fame as he embraced the temper of the Western territories: nationalism, public works and a liberal construction of the Constitution. At the same time he pleased the commercial East by supporting a protective tariff to stimulate manufacturing. With these popular views, a magnetic intensity of purpose and a superb proficiency in debate, young Calhoun was a popular selection as Secretary of War in the cabinet of President Monroe in 1817—and suddenly the tempestuous Andrew Jackson was of enormous import in his life and career.

When Secretary Calhoun instructed General Jackson to "Adopt the necessary measures to terminate . . ." the Seminole trouble, knowing full well that soldier's aggressive nature and his convictions that Florida should belong to the United States, did he intend those instructions to authorize an invasion and seizure of Florida? Did President Monroe intend to reinforce those instructions by the message he sent Jackson a few days later—when he received the General's opinion that an invasion might be necessary to eliminate the Seminole trouble? In that message the President had written that

> the movement . . . against the Seminoles . . . will bring you on a theatre where you may possibly have other services to perform. . . . Great interests are at issue. . . . This is not a time for repose. . . .

Jackson thought these instructions constituted the permissive wink. Only the overcautious could have thought otherwise— and everyone knew Jackson was not in that category. Consequently when he failed to find the Seminole raiders in Georgia, he moved on into Florida, which was now a Spanish colony again, imprisoning and executing several British nationals for acting with the Indians.

So the administration immediately had a double-barreled international crisis to deal with. After a great furor, the matter was disposed of by appropriate apologies and the explanation that Jackson had acted on his own responsibility.

For years there had been a public clamor for the acquisition of Florida from Spain but all efforts to arrange for its purchase had come to naught. Jackson's "private" invasion served to shake the tree again. A few years later by dint of a nice combination of pressure and money the fruit was garnered.

The reason for mentioning these events which occurred so far from Carolina is that from them stemmed directly the ultimate tragedy of Calhoun. As the diplomatic pressure over the Florida affair reached the boiling point and the administration disclaimed responsibility for Jackson's acts, Calhoun advocated in the secrecy of the cabinet meetings that the American position be bolstered by court-martial and censure of the General. Ten years later, through political intrigue, President Andrew Jackson would learn that Vice-President John C. Calhoun had been willing to sacrifice him. Relentless fighter that he was, Old Hickory promptly sacrificed the Vice-President—who until then appeared to have the presidency almost certainly within his grasp.

Through the first ten or fifteen years of Calhoun's Washington career, during his service in Congress and as Secretary of War, he was true to his origins—his views reflected the sentiments of his neighbors back in the Carolina hill country. He was an advocate of national public works, the tariff, an aggressive national expansion, a liberal construction of the Constitution. Those were the tenets of the frontier, of the rapidly growing West—and of the less vocal masses of the old Eastern regions. His popularity in all sections, which had landed him in the Vice-President's chair in 1824, was founded on his able advocacy of those views. Those were the principles of Jacksonian democracy, so it was natural that from the time Old Hickory welded his motley support into some semblance of a party, Calhoun should be his heir apparent and his favorite, too. Could anything other than a brilliant career await the ambitious, self-confident Vice-President who had already come so far along the road of success?

That Calhoun could readily change even his basic political tenets and support his new convictions with fanatical intensity seriously impeded the attainment of his greatest ambition. That his wife, Floride, could not change hers at all, explosively wrecked her husband's career.

When Calhoun married Floride Colhoun, he married into the South Carolina coastal aristocracy. Although her father had been an Upcountry Scotch-Irish Presbyterian, a cousin of Calhoun's father, the family had retained the well-entrenched social standing of the Bonneaus, her mother's family. Floride and her Cooper River plantation were sufficient entree to Charleston society for a man of Calhoun's dignity, brilliance and education. And it meant much to Calhoun. He reveled in its elegance and dignity. He was soon convinced that it was the epitome of perfection among all societies of the world—a thing to be cherished and preserved at all costs. He looked forward to its spread into the back country and all through the South. Up at his plantation at Fort Hill he emulated it, as did many other first and second generation slaveholders.

When, following the invention of the gin, cotton culture fairly dashed from the first commercial plantings on the Southern seaboard clear across the whole breadth of the Gulf states and Tennessee, new plantations were opened up more on the basis of the fortune someone else had made from planting the crop than in sound response to the laws of supply and demand. By 1820 the market was glutted, and the price had fallen drastically. The effect was most disastrous in the less fertile and more worn lands of the coast. It was unpleasant to the coastal planters to recognize the waning fertility of their fields. It was easier to blame their troubles on the tariff than on less tangible economic laws—so the tariff became the scapegoat for all the economic and social ills of the region. As Calhoun became more closely associated with the planter society, both economically and socially, he imbibed those convictions and by 1825 he was a dedicated opponent of the protective tariff, which he now regarded as simply a means of transferring money from the pockets of the Southern planters to those of the Eastern manufacturers. But to oppose the tariff on constitutional grounds required a strict construction of the Constitution, inimicable to any federal internal improvement program—so he had to reverse himself on that score also. Fortunately the doctrine of strict construction, by seeking to preserve to the states a large measure of their sovereignty, gave maximum security to the institution of slavery against possible congressional interference. In support of these anachronistic principles Calhoun, with fire in his soul, a fire which was slowly consuming his very being, dashed himself to pieces trying to move against the inexorable evolution of modern society.

Even in the face of the fact that Calhoun was henceforth proceeding under the handicap of sociologically retrogressive ideas, he was so bountifully endowed with personal magnetism and winning powers of argument that he might have moved on to the realization of his consuming ambition for the presidency had it not been for Floride's inflexible principles. Her refusal to return the call of Peggy O'Neill Timberlake Eaton, erstwhile barmaid, cabinet wife, and personal favorite of President Jackson (a refusal persisted in even to the extreme of summoning a servant to show the President himself the door when he dared, in person, to protest her determination) loosed against the Vice-President all the renowned Jackson fury. The situation was made worse by the growing rivalry between Calhoun and Van Buren, leading rivals in the Jackson camp. From then on it was open warfare in the party between the Chief and Calhoun, the one representing the liberal democratic West and the other the waning power of the conservatives of the older regions.

With his hopes dashed for an easy succession to the presidency under the aegis of Jackson, Calhoun cast expediency to the wind and embraced the nullification movement which was then mounting in South Carolina in response to the 1828 tariff law, the "Tariff of Abominations," even though he had earlier argued that no constitutional right of nullification existed—that a state could not stay in the Union and reject the laws it found distasteful. Dissension was tearing the party asunder. In an effort to secure a greater measure of harmony within the party, a banquet to include all the party bigwigs was planned for Jefferson's birthday, April 13, 1830, at the Indian Queen Hotel. While the purpose of the banquet was peace and tranquillity, that purpose was belied by the air of tension which prevailed throughout the evening. Fireworks were expected. As the dinner wore on and toast after toast, twenty or more of them, were eloquently offered and drunk, the tension mounted. The twenty-fifth was the President's. Glass in hand, he turned and faced Calhoun. Glaring into his eyes, slowly, emphatically, he gave his toast: "Our Union—it must be preserved." So intense was the atmosphere in the room no one dared break in with a cheer or applause. The next move was Calhoun's. Every eye was on him. Would he accept the pointed challenge? Shaken, pale, with eyes blazing, the tall, gaunt figure hesitated, then raised his glass: "The Union. Next to our liberties, most dear."

In the minds of men the Confederate War was declared that night.

Taking advantage of his fall from grace, Calhoun's enemies secured statements from men who served in the Cabinet with him at the time of Jackson's Florida enterprise—revealing to the President for the first time Calhoun's proposal of a court-martial for Old Hickory. With this revelation, Jackson's fury against his fellow Carolinian knew no bounds.

Jackson was true to his Jefferson Day toast. When, two years later, in spite of being riven internally on the issue, the South Carolina Nullification Convention declared the tariffs of 1828 and 1832 null and void, and inoperative in South Carolina, the President moved firmly to preserve the Union. He employed persuasion:

> Fellow-Citizens of my native State, let me admonish you—I have no discretionary power on the subject. . . . Those who told you that you might peaceably prevent . . . [the execution of the laws] deceived you . . . their object is disunion. . . . Disunion by armed force is treason. Are you ready to incur its guilt? If you are, on the heads of the instigators of the act be dreadful consequences.
>
> Andrew Jackson

He employed a show of force. Preparations were made to send ships and troops to require submission to the laws. Back in South Carolina the Unionists were encouraged in their preparations for counterrevolution under canal-planner Joel Poinsett. "God and Old Hickory are with us," and they needed but one of the two.

He employed diplomacy and justice. Jackson set in motion a modification of the tariff law to make it more palatable and to supply a face-saving excuse for the Nullifiers to recede from their extreme position.

In the face of the President's versatile attacks, Nullification was squelched. But twenty years later it would rise again in the more consistent shape of the Right of Secession.

To lead the fight for his state, his section and his adopted class against an increasingly threatening Congressional majority, Calhoun, in the midst of the Nullification fight, resigned his vice-presidency and was promptly elected Senator. The dozen remaining years of his life were given over to a magnificent championship of the South and its institutions, appropriately tragic subjects for this frustrated genius. Far more tragic was the welling up of the slavery question as the paramount issue it became his mission to defend; and that the strict moralist son of oppression-hating Patrick Calhoun, with a tradition of generations of exile and privation, should pervert his great talents and burn himself out in a passionate fight to stem an irrepressible move for reform and for the freedom of all men, not just for the planters.

Transcending the tragedy of Calhoun as a man is the realization that but for his intense personal bitterness, born of frustration, he might have saved his country and his section, and even for a while his class, from the great disaster towards which his leadership was inexorably directing them. But it would have required compromise, and compromise was as alien to Calhoun as to Old Hickory.

However, in fighting his last losing fight, Calhoun did make one great and lasting contribution to his country. Perhaps it was an attempt to rebuild his own fortunes as a presidential prospect or perhaps it was an effort to divide the growing opposition to slavery that prompted him in 1837 to ally himself with Van Buren and his radical followers of the East in opposition to the conservatives. Be that as it may, by that move he originated the artificial alignment of the conservative South with the liberals of the North, which has persisted through all the intervening years, giving thereby a stability to the United States which is rare among the nations of the world. It is that incongruous alignment which requires of both parties a middle course.

Andrew Jackson was ever faithful to his origin. Spawn of the frontier, he gloried in it, followed it westward and eventually became the personification of both its virtues and its faults. Loyal even in death, he lies beside his frontier bride, his beloved Rachel, in their garden at the Hermitage.

Equally appropriate is the final resting place of John C. Calhoun in Charleston, the very placenta of the planter aristocracy, of Nullification, of Secession. There, in Saint Philip's churchyard, far from his family, far from the rich red hills of his origin, lies the man who had all but renounced his heritage to become the embodiment of an anachronism—the slave-supported plantation South. The story is told that a Union soldier, sight-seeing in the wrecked city after its fall in 1865, gazed on the stone marked with the single word "Calhoun" and remarked: "The whole South is the grave of Calhoun."

❦ ❦ ❦ ❦ ❦ *25. The challenge*

*W*hen the dawn haze lifted from Charleston harbor on April 12, 1861, revealing Fort Sumter's ominous bulk silhouetted against the light of the eastern sky, it marked but the beginning of another day of uneasy suspense—another day in which the fate of two nations hung on the events that might happen there. Through months of mounting tension that austere pile of masonry, rearing its mass from the shoal where the waters of the Santee-Cooper meet the sea, had become the focus of the world's attention. That morning as every morning for a long succession of weeks, as the orb of the sun peeped above the horizon, the faint notes of the distant bugle drifted across the quiet harbor while the Stars and Stripes were run up over the island fort—a routine ceremony that each day added a bit more irritation to the already tension-filled air of the restless town. No one doubted that sooner or later that air would become overcharged and the decorous restraint of the weeks gone by would be loosed in reckless fury. It was now only a question of when and how.

Following Lincoln's election in November, South Carolina had seceded from the Union on December 20, 1860. A few days later Major Robert Anderson, apparently ignorant of President Buchanan's pledge to maintain the harbor's *status quo*, had moved his small Federal garrison from Fort Moultrie to the still far from completed, but yet more easily defended, island fortress—which for more than thirty years, interspersed with interruptions and delays, had been under construction on the current-swept shoal where the *Acteon*

had run aground in its attempt to flank Fort Moultrie in 1776. The laying of its massive foundation alone had consumed six years. Just one item of its requisitions: sixty thousand tons of rock, some of it to be brought all the way from Maine. By 1861 its five-foot-thick pentagon walls towered fifty feet above the water, but only about sixty of its planned 135 guns were available. For Major Anderson this made little difference, for he had but eighty-five officers and men to man the works designed for a complement of 650.

During January and February, Buchanan's expiring administration vacillated in response to the South Carolina demands that Anderson evacuate Fort Sumter, hoping to avoid the momentous decision and pass the problem on to Lincoln. Meanwhile South Carolina impetuously mobilized. Work was feverishly pressed, with the labor of hundreds of rented slaves, to strengthen Fort Moultrie. To the cheers of the excited crowds in the streets, dashingly attired youngsters cockily paraded and drilled. Every day was made exciting by new developments—the resignation of some prominent citizen from a high Federal post, or another development in the secession parade of the cotton states, or perhaps another decision in Washington of moment in the crisis. And there were the dispatches from Montgomery where the central government of the Confederacy had been rapidly taking shape since the rash of secessions which had followed the mid-January attempt by the steamer *Star of the West* to relieve Fort Sumter—an effort which had been abandoned when one of the harbor batteries manned by the Citadel cadets opened fire on the unarmed merchantman. After that, to defer a showdown, Major Anderson had been permitted to supply his meat and vegetable needs by purchases in the Charleston market.

All the while the political and martial jubilation and excitement overflowed into every phase of the community life. The race season at the Washington race track was the finest in its long history. The pre-Lenten social season was, at least on the surface, the most brilliant ever. The full mustaches and goatee of the handsome Pierre G. T. Beauregard, the Confederate area commander, were suddenly the fashion among all the young blades, as the dashing Louisianian became the idol of the hour. The frequency of duels reached alarming proportions, adding morbid spice to the social life that had become deeply tinted by the urge to eat, drink and be merry in anticipation of the possibility of imminent death. To the perceptive Mrs. Chesnut, wife of James Chesnut, who had resigned his seat in the United States Senate to enter the Confederate Army as a member of Beauregard's staff, the gay exterior only concealed grave forebodings. To her diary she confided:

> Our hearts are in doleful dumps, but we are as gay, as madly jolly, as sailors who break into the strong-room when the ship is going down. . . . There stands Fort Sumter, *en evidence,* and thereby hangs peace or war.

Back to April twelfth and Major Anderson and his isolated garrison, encircled by the defiance to his colorful, complex banner fluttering in the breeze above his formidable stronghold—suddenly in the midst of an alien world. When the news came that President Lincoln had decided to relieve the fort by force if necessary and that a fleet to effect this was expected at any moment, an ultimatum had been delivered to Anderson demanding immediate surrender. In the early hours of April twelfth came Anderson's reply. He would evacuate by noon on the fifteenth unless he "should meanwhile receive controlling instructions from my Government or additional supplies." As Beauregard knew that the relief expedition would probably arrive before the evacuation date set by Anderson, this reply did not satisfy him and at three-thirty A.M. this message crossed the harbor:

To Major Robert Anderson,
United States Army, Commanding Fort Sumter.
Sir:

> By the authority of Brigadier-General Beauregard Commanding the provisional forces of the Confederate States, we have the honour to notify you that he will open the fire of his batteries on Fort Sumter in one hour from this time.

We have the honour to be, very respectfully
Your obedient servants,
James Chesnut, Jr., Aide-de-camp
Stephen D. Lee, Capt. S. C.
Army and Aide-de-camp.

Back in her room at the Mills House Mrs. Chesnut was making this entry in her diary:

> Anderson will not capitulate. Yesterday was the merriest, maddest dinner we have had yet; men were audaciously wise and witty. We had an unspoken foreboding that it was to be our last pleasant meeting.

And then:

> I do not pretend to go to sleep. How can I? If Anderson does not accept terms at four, the orders are, he shall be fired upon. I count four, St. Michael's bells chime out and I begin to hope. At half-past four the heavy booming of a cannon. I sprang out of bed, and on my knees prostrate I prayed as I never prayed before.
>
> There was a sound of stir all over the house, pattering of feet in the corridors. All seemed hurrying one way. I put on my double-gown and a shawl and went, too. It was to the housetop. The shells were bursting. . . . I knew my husband was rowing about somewhere in that dark bay, and that the shells were roofing it over, bursting toward the fort. If Anderson was obstinate, Colonel Chesnut was to order the fort on one side to open fire. Certainly fire had begun. The regular roar of the cannon, there it was. And who could tell what each volley accomplished of death and destruction.
>
> The women were wild there on the housetop. Prayers came from the women and imprecations from the men. And then a shell would light up the scene. . . . These women have all a satisfying faith. "God is on our side," they say. . . . I ask "Why?" "Of course, He hates Yankees, we are told. You'll think that well of Him."

From Robert Toombs when he heard the news came the despairing words: "It is suicide—it is fatal!"

In the mode of the day an elegant and glamorous society, heedless of the odds, in unequivocal terms had delivered its challenge to mortal combat because of those things it had come to believe had challenged its sense of honor—hoping thereby to stem an inexorable tide.

Thirty-four hours and three thousand shells later Anderson accepted Beauregard's generous surrender terms. The only difficulty encountered in the surrender negotiations was whether or not the garrison would be permitted a defiant one-hundred-gun salute to the Stars and Stripes before evacuating the fort. At the insistence of Anderson on this point, the salute was finally conceded. And so ended the battle which has been termed unique in military history, it being a battle wholly between forts.

As the garrison prepared to embark on the waiting steamer, *Isabel*, the guns began to boom their salute to the flag. On the fiftieth round a premature discharge set off an explosion, resulting in the death of two of the gun crew. The accident ended the costly salute with that round, and those two men became the only fatalities of the engagement and the first of the war. As the *Isabel* steamed out past Cummings Point, the Citadel cadets lined the beach, silent and with heads uncovered.

The next day President Lincoln called for seventy-five thousand men, and North Carolina, Virginia, Tennessee and Arkansas joined the Confederacy.

🌸 🌸 🌸 🌸 🌸 *26. Little David*
and the fishboat

Dr. St. Julien Ravenel, es-
teemed physician and scientist, was another product of that
small group of Carolinians, the French Huguenots, who
through more than two centuries contributed so disproportionately to the leadership and development of Carolina.
Both the St. Juliens and the Ravenels were prominent plantation families of the French Santee and Cooper River neighborhoods. Dr. Ravenel had gained an enviable reputation as
a diagnostician and national recognition for his discovery that
the ubiquitous calomel treatment hindered rather than aided
in the treatment of yellow fever. But even while he was becoming a notable in his profession, he was increasingly diverted from it by a growing interest in chemistry, especially
as it related to plants and agriculture.

In 1852 he resolved to give up his medical practice and
devote himself entirely to chemical and plant research. His
experiments soon demonstrated that crop yields could be

greatly increased by applications of the limestone which everywhere underlay the Low Country, in strata built from the remains of the mollusks of the sea floor of the ocean that had long ago flooded the Carolina coastal plain. This discovery started the lime-mining industry that was to supply most of the Confederate lime requirements.

Continuing his work with native stones and their possible use in agriculture, ten years later, he demonstrated the tremendous value of the phosphate deposits in the neighborhood of Charleston. This discovery presented the opportunity upon which later fortunes would be built. But, in 1867, in exhausted Carolina, only discouragement was in full supply and there was neither the enterprise nor the capital for the establishment of any trail-blazing industry. Undiscouraged by his failure to interest local capital in developing the phosphate deposits, he eventually got the industry under way by securing Northern capital.

By his experiments directly with the crop plants, Dr. Ravenel was able to demonstrate culture methods by which the yield of cotton could be doubled. He evolved the system of green fertilization through plowing under legumes. He experimented with grasses and advocated reduction of cotton and rice acreages and the substitution of grass culture for livestock. He convincingly demonstrated, but few followed his examples. Rice and cotton were cash crops and "Negro crops." Grasses and grains were not. It would be a half century before the agriculture bulletins and the farm agents would be heralding Dr. Ravenel's precepts as "new methods" for balanced agriculture—without giving recognition to their originator, who, as is so often the case, was too far ahead of his day to be appreciated.

It took the exigencies of war to divert the gentle, courtly doctor from his constructive dedication. Early in the war, as soon as the awful consequences of the blockade of its ports was realized by the Confederate government, it had offered half the value of any blockade ship sunk to the inventor of any contrivance effecting its destruction. As the strangle hold of the blockade tightened, John Fraser & Company of Charleston announced a reward of $100,000 for the sinking of either of the two big warships blockading that port, and $50,000 for the sinking of any of the numerous monitors stationed beyond the bar. Probably, however, it was not the lure of reward but rather the devotion of the kindly doctor to his native land that prompted him to turn his genius to implements of destruction. Be that as it may, in the spring of 1863, Dr. Ravenel laid before Captain Francis D. Lee, port engineer of the Confederate forces in Charleston, his plans for an unprecedented type of boat that was destined to take its place in history as an important link in the chain of development of the submarine, although it was not a true submersible. His plans delineated a cigar-shaped boat fifty feet long with a six-foot beam, bearing a close resemblance to the true submarines of a later date even to a rudimentary conning tower and the appearance of a periscope, which was not a periscope at all but the smokestack for its steam engine. It was to be ballasted in such a way that but ten inches of its wooden hull would cruise above water. From the point of its bow there extended a fourteen-foot iron shaft to the forward end of which was attached a copper-covered bomb charged with a hundred pounds of powder and equipped with four protruding sensitive tubes, the crushing of any one of which would explode the charge.

Although the doctor's plans received the enthusiastic approval of Captain Lee, they were much too revolutionary for official adoption even by the desperate Confederacy; and for a while it appeared that his torpedo boat would be relegated to the obscurity of a paper invention, until the faith and generosity of a wealthy friend, Theodore Stoney, rescued it from that inventors' limbo. Under Dr. Ravenel's personal supervision, in midsummer, 1863, at Stoney Landing on the Cooper River construction was begun.

Two months later the odd craft was launched and dubbed *David* in recognition of its intended challenge to the Goliaths lying at the harbor mouth. She was placed under the command of Lieutenant W. T. Glassell, who had earlier shown his interest in such contrivances and amply demonstrated his bravery when he made an unsuccessful attempt to drive a similar torpedo against one of the enemy ships from an oar-propelled canoe. Three other men completed the crew: J. H. Toombs, engineer, James Sullivan, fireman, and J. W. Cannon, pilot.

Under the cover of darkness, October 5, 1863, the *David* steamed down the Cooper and across the harbor to Fort Sumter which, after two months of relentless hammering of the heaviest siege in American history, directed against it by the Federal forces now occupying the islands on the south side of the harbor, gave the appearance of but a great jagged pile of rubble. After waiting there for the tide to turn the *David* steamed on to the outer harbor, where riding at anchor was the *New Ironsides,* the world's most powerful warship and the pride of the American Navy, appropriately nominated by Glassell "to receive the highest compliment." With the hatch open Glassell, acting as helmsman, sat on the almost submerged deck holding in his hands a double-barreled shotgun while he steered with his feet. The plan of attack called for use of the shotgun against the officer of the deck should their approach be detected, with the hope that sufficient confusion would be thereby created on the ship to permit the completion of the attack.

As the *David* steamed through the darkness to within three hundred yards of the faint outline of the bulk of the great ironclad frigate the night watch detected the sound of its engine and hailed it. Undeterred by their premature detection, Glassell continued with the attack as planned. Ignoring the increasingly peremptory hails from the deck, he steered full speed ahead straight for the looming target. At forty yards from the ship the deck officer appeared. Following his plan, Glassell dropped him with the fire of both barrels of the shotgun. A few moments later contact with the *Ironsides* set off the *David's* torpedo six feet below the water line. The terrific explosion sent a great quantity of water high into the air and into the *David's* open hatch and down its low funnel, extinguishing the boiler fire. In the belief that the craft was sinking, Glassell ordered his crew to take to the water. To the hazard of the cold dark sea was immediately added a lively fire of small arms from the battleship's decks. Glassell was soon picked up by one of the nearby enemy transports. Sullivan swam to the *Ironsides'* anchor chain from which he was rescued. Toombs started swimming towards distant Fort Sumter. After swimming a while through the murk, he noted that the *David* was still afloat, drifting away from the *Ironsides*, a welcome refuge even in the face of the rifle fire from the ship which was still being directed against it. When he reached the *David* he found Cannon still hanging on to it. Then only did Cannon admit that he could not swim. The two of them climbed back aboard, succeeded in rekindling the fire and brought their craft safely back to its secret anchorage. To their dismay, the morning light revealed the *Ironsides* still riding at anchor. The charge had not been heavy enough to seriously damage her heavy hull. However, she was injured, although to what extent is still unknown. Soon after the attack she moved down to Port Royal for repairs.

The story of the little *David* is the story of the first successful torpedo attack by one vessel upon another. For quite a while Glassell and Sullivan, as captives, stood in grave danger of execution for their part in their heroic venture. The charge against them was the "use of engines of war, not recognized by civilized nations." This threat was the price of Dr. Ravenel's failing to invent the *David* until too late in the war for the Union Navy to emulate it and thereby remove its uncivilized stigma.

While the gentle doctor was planning and building the *David*, a young naval officer, Horace L. Hundley, down in Mobile, was independently planning and building another unique vessel—a true submarine or, in the parlance of the day, a "fishboat." This fishboat, or the *Hundley* as it was later called, was twenty feet long, three and a half wide and five feet deep. Her galvanized iron hull was equipped with movable diving fins. Her motive power was supplied by eight men who had to squeeze themselves into a crouching position in the narrow hull to turn the long crankshaft that operated the propeller. The fishboat was designed to dive beneath an enemy vessel while towing a bomb, which would come in contact with the hull and explode after the fishboat had reached the safety of the opposite side of the ship.

In one of the first practice dives after her launching in 1863, she stuck in the mud in the bottom of Mobile Bay, suffocating her whole crew of nine. She was fished out and shipped to Charleston to operate against the more crucial blockade there.

In Charleston she was put in the command of a Lieutenant Payne and manned with a crew of New Orleans longshoremen. They carried her across the harbor to Fort Johnson. She was about to set out from the dock there, and all the crew had squeezed into the tight confines of their stations. Payne was climbing into the manhole, when the wake of a passing steamer rolled in from the bay. As soon as the wave rolled over the open hatch, the fishboat sank like a stone, carrying with it to the bottom all its crew except Payne. Even before the salvage workers had finished removing the bodies of the crew from the recovered craft a few hours after this second disaster, a new crew had already volunteered. A few nights later at Fort Sumter six of this third crew were drowned in an almost identical accident.

Following these disasters, Hundley was summoned from Mobile. With Hundley himself at the controls several trial dives were successfully accomplished by the fishboat's fourth crew. But then he pushed his luck too far and attempted yet another in the shallow waters of the Stono River estuary. Miscalculating the depth, he plowed the nose of the fishboat into the sticky mud of the bottom, where it stuck; and inventor and crew, unable to open the hatch against the water pressure, perished miserably.

With undaunted courage, yet a fifth crew volunteered to man the ill-starred craft. Finishing off their training preparatory to an attack on one of the blockade warships, they dived her beneath the anchored Confederate steamer *Etiwan*, only to become fouled beneath the surface in her anchor chain. And the fifth crew was lost.

As soon as she was again recovered, there were nine more courageous spirits requesting the privilege of being her sixth crew. But before this sixth crew could launch an attack against one of the enemy ships, an order from General Beauregard forbade further use of the fishboat. In response to pressure from the more daring, this order was later modified and its further use was authorized provided it did not dive. Under this restriction and equipped now with a spar torpedo, on a February night in 1864, she set forth on her great mission. She passed through the Breach Inlet and steered for the immense bulk of the *Housatonic* lying at anchor beyond. In command of the fishboat was Lieutenant George E. Dixon, who had come up from Mobile with Hundley. Although she was sighted by the *Housatonic's* deck officer at a considerable distance, he took her to be but a floating plank until it was too late. A moment later the fishboat's torpedo exploded below the water line about midship. Almost immediately the great ironclad sank, stern first, as its crew saved themselves by climbing into the rigging which remained above the surface.

Years later when the channel was being cleared of the hulk of the *Housatonic,* the workers dredged from the bottom nearby the barnacle-covered remains of the ill-fated fishboat, and the skeletons of its superbly valorous crew, who that winter night became the first men in history to sink an enemy vessel by submarine attack.

Nowhere in the press of the day are these heroic events reported. The fishboat was the Confederacy's secret weapon and everything about it was kept in absolute secrecy. There is even a paucity of detail in the official documents. Consequently, of all those who died in her six disasters, the names of but sixteen are known.

The supreme bravery of those men and their unstinting devotion to their cause illustrate emphatically why the Confederacy, with but a fraction of the Union's manpower and an even more disproportionate lack of materiel, proved so very difficult to conquer.

❦ ❦ ❦ ❦ 27. *"War is hell"*

Up until the end of 1864, there was almost no active fighting in the Carolinas. The Union forces had long been in possession of the Sound region of North Carolina and had established a beach head at Beaufort, South Carolina, in 1861, from which the only activity of consequence was the continuing attempt to capture Charleston, in response to a "morbid appetite in the land to have" that city. But, except for the relentless hammering at the fortifications of the port city, the battlefields were all far from Carolina. Nevertheless, as the dreary months formed themselves into bitter years, the war scorched its mark deeper and deeper into almost every Carolina home.

The exhilaration of action in organizing the new government and the flush of optimism which swept the South after Bull Run had been insidiously eaten away by three years of creeping disillusionment—by three long years of mounting hardship and suffering. The wishful conviction that cotton was a king who would command British aid had given way to

the bitter realization that Northern wheat was a more powerful lever in the realistic diplomacy of Britain, and that slav-
ocracy was a potent repellent to all potential allies. Then too,
contributing its portion of disillusionment, was the gradual,
painful realization that in modern warfare (and the Confederate War was the first great modern war) the means of production of war material are at least as important as the
soldiers themselves. But it wasn't such sobering developments
that brought the horrors of war into the Carolina homes
while the battlefields were still far afield. Nor was it hours of
backbreaking toil at the spinning wheels and looms which
had been retrieved from the attics, nor the dismal prospects
of the life-giving fields high in weeds, nor even the monotonous and ever shorter fare, nor the homemade shoes, nor the
chaos of inflation and the inconveniences of the primitive barter system which it eventually made necessary; it was those
awful casualty lists that had thrust the horrors of the war
deep into the heart of almost every Carolina home—the lists
that were posted after Seven Pines, Mechanicsville, Manas-
sas, Antietam, Fredericksburg, Chancellorsville, Gettysburg,
Chickamauga, Missionary Ridge, and the Wilderness and
Cold Harbor, where the Carolina sons, and fathers too as the
war wore on, were writing a chapter of history unequaled in
blood, glamour and heroism—awful, inexorable lists that
dampened the joy of the news of even their most brilliant
victories as the death lists alone approached a half of the entire Confederate Army. By 1865, an average of every third
white household had seen the name of one of its members
on those death lists—a rate four times as great as was suffered in the North.

So it was a sad, war-weary and utterly discouraged Carolina that was the subject of a letter from General H. W.
Halleck to General William Tecumseh Sherman in Savannah
where he was resting his army after his notorious march of
devastation from Atlanta to the sea. Suggested Halleck:

> Should you capture Charleston, I hope by *some* acci-
> dent the place may be destroyed; and if a little salt
> should be sown upon its site, it may prevent the growth
> of future crops of nullification and secession.

It was Christmas Eve, 1864, that Sherman penned his reply
promising to

> bear in mind your hint as to Charleston, but don't think
> salt will be necessary. When I move, the 15th Corps will
> be on the right of the right wing, and their position will
> bring them naturally into Charleston first, and if you
> have watched the history of that corps, you will have re-
> marked that they generally do their work up pretty well.
> The truth is the whole army is burning with an insatiable
> desire to wreak vengeance upon South Carolina. I al-
> most tremble at her fate, but feel that she deserves all
> that seems in store for her. . . . I look upon Columbia
> as quite as bad as Charleston.

A few weeks later, when Sherman moved his army of
sixty-five thousand men and twenty thousand camp followers
into South Carolina, he had decided to pay his respects at
Columbia rather than at Charleston. The march northward
to the capital presaged what was in store for it. One of his
officers reported that

> Over a region forty miles in width, stretching from
> Savannah . . . agriculture and commerce, even if peace
> come speedily, can not be fully revived in our day. . . .
> Day by day our legions of armed men surged over the
> land, destroying its substance . . . in all the length and
> breadth of that broad pathway, the burning hand of war
> pressed heavily, blasting and withering where it fell. It
> was the penalty of rebellion.

And a press correspondent with Sherman's army reported:

As for wholesale burnings, pillage and devastation committed in South Carolina, magnify all I have said of Georgia some fifty-fold, and then throw in an occasional murder, just to bring an old hard-fisted cuss to his senses; and you have a pretty good idea of the whole thing.

Almost everyone was deceived as to the route Sherman would take on entering South Carolina. The opinion was all but universally held that he would proceed up the coast to Charleston which was still holding on in the face of the ever mounting siege against its fortifications. Consequently, Columbia was overflowing with refugees and had become a veritable storehouse for the transportable prized possessions of the people of the Low Country when, on February sixteenth, Sherman's vanguard reached the hills opposite Columbia and looked down on the charred remains of the bridge across the Congaree which the Confederate garrison had burnt the day before. Frustrated by this inhospitality, they began throwing shells into the unresisting city, some of the marks of which remain today on the walls of the then half-built State House.

Since the rocks and swift current of the Congaree at Columbia make it unsuitable for the construction of a pontoon bridge the invaders moved on upstream (including a riverside cotton mill in their burning activities along the way), crossed the Saluda and then the Broad to enter the city from the north. During the night such Confederate forces as were in the city were being withdrawn by General Wade Hampton who was just back in his home town after building a brilliant reputation as a cavalry leader in battle after battle in the Virginia campaigns. Before leaving they had thrown open the military stores to the needy civilians and had stacked large quantities of stored cotton in the middle of the wide, tree-lined streets with the intention of burning them there, a plan which was abandoned as the wind rose to such briskness that the proposed fires might have hazarded the neighboring buildings. But, because Governor Magrath hesitated to destroy private property even under such desperate circumstances, they unwisely left undestroyed a vast store of liquor —liquor which in the next twenty-four hours would all but literally become "firewater."

Early in the morning of the seventeenth, the Union troops on the march towards the city from their Broad River

pontoon bridge were met by Mayor Goodwyn and his council. There on the outskirts of the city they formally surrendered the civil government and asked that the city be given the protection of an open city. A little later General Sherman himself was escorted to the fine home which had been reserved for him. To this courtesy he responded with assurances as to the safety of the town.

The looting which began very soon after the first troops

arrived in the city mounted apace as more and more moved in. The liquor stores were soon discovered and contributed enormously to the horror and confusion that prevailed everywhere in the town. The residences of the Confederate leaders, including both the Hampton homes, were sought out, stripped of all movable articles of value and given to the torch. These specific destructions increased in danger throughout the afternoon as the cold northwest wind kept rising until it approached almost gale proportions.

About an hour after dark into the sky from the Union headquarters three rockets ascended, the usual signal to the unit commanders to set their troops at liberty. But that night the rank and file of Sherman's army gave those rockets an added significance. Throughout the day word had leaked out to many citizens that with the evening rockets the city would be put to the torch. Perhaps by design, but more probably by rumor spreading among thousands of drunken soldiers, action quickly followed the rockets. Within a matter of minutes a dozen or more fires started along the river front, just the section from which the wind would sweep them across the entire town, ushering in a night of flaming horror as 84 of the city's 124 blocks were consumed by the holocaust. By morning almost every building of importance in the city lay in ashes—the State House, the Ursuline Convent, five churches, an equal number of banks, the two hotels, the depots, the gasworks, all the foundries and other manufacturing plants, and countless dwellings.

For days the Carolina roads were busy with the miserable refugees, streaming north, east and west from the all but obliterated capital, carrying with them such few possessions as they had been able to retrieve; desperately seeking some haven that might possibly not lie in Sherman's dreaded path; trying to keep ahead of, or by devious means avoid, the notoriously efficient bummers, who were assiduously coining for all time the contemptuous term of "bum." So complete was the destruction that even the enemy was hastened on his way, northward to Fayetteville and the final scenes of the war in the East.

Did Sherman cleverly devise the burning of Columbia, or was it some "accident" as Halleck had suggested? Historians have dug deep and sifted carefully to find the answer and have devoted endless pages to their findings. This much is definite: There is no evidence that he ordered the destruction of the city. Moreover, he apparently made a real effort to halt the burning after it had got under way. On the other hand there is ample evidence that he made no attempt to conceal his special hatred for South Carolina and its two capital cities, and he thus gave the impression among his troops that any "accident" which might befall Columbia would please their chief. And he certainly was derelict in his precautions to protect the city, for, if he did not know the open secret of the special significance of the liberty rockets on the night of the seventeenth, he should have—and would have, had he not created among his subordinates the impression that he would be happy to see the city destroyed. Blacker against him than anything else definitely established was his charge that General Hampton had carelessly burned the town by burning the cotton in the streets, a charge which he later recanted with the explanation that he had made it to discredit Hampton and weaken his leadership.

In his memoirs, Sherman wrote: "Having utterly ruined Columbia, the right wing began its march northward"—an odd way to refer to a lamentable accident, to say the least. And the plaudits for the deed were his. "Hurrah for Columbia! Isn't Sherman a gem?" wrote the Reverend Phillips Brooks, renowned Christian minister of New England.

Such was the spirit that dominated America in 1865 as the curtain rang down on its scenes of greatest travail! And that was the spirit which ushered in the blackest days of American history—the long bitter days of destruction—destruction of the spirit of a great section of the nation—ironically known to history as the Reconstruction, the venom of which, appropriately enough, was loosed amid the blackened remains of ruined Columbia.

❦ ❦ ❦ ❦ ❦ 28. Damnation
and redemption

When the Confederacy's struggle against insuperable material odds finally drew to a close, the South lay prostrate, crippled by its horrible loss of man power and very nearly stripped of its material resources. Almost half of the white male population of the Carolinas had served in the fighting forces and almost half of these were dead. The South's economy was a shambles. Vast areas had been plundered and put to the torch. Its currency and securities were worthless and its vast property in slaves confiscated, in history's most stupendous act of sequestration.

While the war had completely broken the South's physical strength, it would take the ruthless inhumanity of "Reconstruction" to break its spirit. At its inception it was but a rubbing of salt into the grievous wounds of war—that was under the humane policies of Abraham Lincoln and Andrew Johnson, both men of statuesque heart and inflexible principles of justice. But then came the tyrannical Radicals—men of intolerant, bitter hearts, overweening personal ambition and a revolting lack of principles. By them "Reconstruction" was perverted to a heartless seeking for personal power and vindictive revenge, and the wounds of war became infected from the focal infection of corruption and putridness in Washington. It was this infection and the desperate measures which it called forth to combat it that cost the South far, far more than all the devastation of the war.

With fidelity to the Constitution, Lincoln planned the first steps by which the Confederate States were to be readmitted to the Federal Union. His plans were consistent with the contention of the Unionists that secession was a nullity and that the seceded states were never out of the Union or beyond the protection of the Constitution, except for war measures during the conflict itself. Accordingly, although his Emancipation Proclamation during the war had declared the slaves free in the unoccupied areas of the South, in the summer of 1864 he had vetoed an act of Congress which would have freed all the slaves. It was his conviction that only the states had the right to prohibit slavery.

Then came the tragedy at Ford's Theatre. For Lincoln's place in history it was perhaps a fortuitous event that spared his name the unjust obloquy which was to be heaped upon his unfortunate successor, who was, in many respects, remarkably similar in character and background. For the South it spelled its most awful tragedy, for without Lincoln's prestige as the successful war president, Andrew Johnson's efforts to carry on with Lincoln's moderate and constitutional plans were doomed to failure.

For a little while the task of binding the nation's wounds and rebuilding a unified nation progressed well enough in spite of the growing opposition to the President's wise moderation. That aggressive and militant opposition was led in the Senate by the narrowly bigoted, vengeful Charles Sumner, and in the House by the utterly unprincipled, wildly fanatical Thaddeus Stevens, and was loudly cheered on by the highly vocal, bitterly partisan Wendell Phillips, Horace Greeley and Henry Ward Beecher, all men utterly devoid of magnanimity.

As soon as hostilities ceased, President Johnson had named provisional governors for the several Confederate States, charging them with the re-establishment of civil governments. In a matter of months, in both North and South Carolina, conventions had been called, legislatures elected and the Thirteenth Amendment abolishing slavery duly ratified. In spite of the overwhelming devastation of the war and the shock to its economic system wrought by the freeing of the slaves, remarkable progress was soon made towards the establishment of stable, respectable civil governments. There was even talk of enfranchising the freed blacks with, of course, proper safeguards in the form of property and educational qualifications, a right not then accorded Negroes in many of the Northern states. A step in that direction was the "Black Code" which was adopted by both the Carolinas, extending to the Negroes almost all the rights of citizenship except that of voting—a vast step forward from what had been the law in the slave states. Ignoring the social progress spelled out in these codes and seeing only their shortcomings, the Radicals seized upon them, representing them as evidence of a continuing intransigence and a flagrant lack of repentance on the part of the South. To the opportunity offered by these laws for a campaign of hate and vengeance, the Radicals added magnified and multiplied accounts of the amazingly few racial incidents which were occurring here and there through the South as it adjusted itself to its suddenly altered social system. To bring matters to a head and to prove the absence of a proper humility in the South, the Fourteenth Amendment was proposed and its ratification demanded of each of the erstwhile Confederate States. This was tantamount to a demand that they forego the constitutional rights they thought they still had as Americans and prostrate themselves before an arbitrary and vengeful Congress. Its adoption would require the duly elected legislatures of those states to abdicate their local and state governments and turn them over completely to their almost totally illiterate former slaves, for the amendment provided for the disenfranchisement of most of the leaders of the South, down even to the petty officeholders for their part in the "Rebellion," until re-enfranchised by an antagonistic Congress; and at the same time it would enfranchise all the former slaves. It meant not that the former slaves should be given a fair voice in the government, but rather that the government be turned over to them—unfit as they were to assume that responsibility. The Congressional Radicals knew that the states of the South would reject the amendment. Its rejection was part of their well-laid plans to prove that the South was still "disloyal" and therefore required government at the point of the bayonet.

So was ushered in the most disgraceful era of our national history—a decade of unparalleled corruption, while a degraded Congress, dominated by unprincipled villians, happily wallowed in the mire it created, pilloried and libeled a noble president who steadfastly fought back for the Constitution and decent government. This Congress flouted, ignored and finally intimidated the Supreme Court, and ridiculed all pleas for respect for the constitutional rights of a vast section of the nation.

Those who remove from their fellow citizens the protection of the law, inevitably remove from themselves the restraints of the law. Consequently the Radical Republican leadership in Congress was soon mired in all manner of corruption—bribery, graft and a flagrant disregard of their oaths of office, the Constitution and the laws wherever they impinged upon opportunities for personal profit or the entrenchment of their gang in the control of the land. There barely remained in Congress sufficient integrity to muster a one-third vote to prevent the removal of President Johnson from office purely on trumped-up, perjured charges.

His impeachment was the price he had to pay for integrity in a period when integrity in public office was declassé and intolerable. The long rough road which the President had traveled from the humble cottage where he was born in central North Carolina, to manhood in Tennessee, where he worked as a tailor's apprentice and was taught to read and write by the girl he later married, and on to Congress and the vice-presidency, had been marked all along the way by battles for principles. He stood firmly for the Union when both his native state and adopted state seceded. That stand had made him Lincoln's running mate. When he continued to stand for the Union in defiance of the Radicals' policies of disunion, they sought to be rid of him. But he stood by his guns and never sought cover.

Foiled in their unscrupulous effort to seize the executive department by impeachment of the president, they were forced to await the 1868 elections to complete their control of the government. After Grant, in keeping with the times, sold his integrity for the promise of the presidency, and flopped over from the Johnson camp to that of the Radicals, the Congressional infection spread on into the executive department, eventually to steep in its mire cabinet members, the President's secretary, his family and even the President himself. And so the way was paved for the infection to spread, in even more virulent form, to Raleigh, to Columbia and on to almost every capital and county seat of the South, insuring thereby almost a decade of "good stealing" and unparalleled corruption under the iron party control of the Radical Republicans, ruthlessly sustained in power by the authority of bayonets.

With executive support the plans, already under way, to return the South to the status of a conquered province, proceeded rapidly. Federal troops, many of whom were illiterate former slaves, under officers of fanatical Radical persuasion, brushed aside the civil authorities and defied the civil courts, even the United States Supreme Court itself. Soon, with the former white leaders effectively disenfranchised and the former slaves all enfranchised, organized and herded to the polls by officials of the Freedmen's Bureau, Carpetbaggers and Scalawags, the Radical Republicans held the governments of the South in an iron grip. Instead of giving the former slaves a voice in the government commensurate with their qualifications, the Radicals had turned over to them the governments of the South, lock, stock and barrel, even in states where they were in the minority, as in North Carolina. In those states, such as South Carolina, where they constituted a substantial majority of the population, the situation of the whites appeared hopeless. Orders to the puppet governments that they ratify the Fourteenth Amendment were promptly complied with, ironically creating thereby in the fundamental law of the land the special refuge of the powerful corporations of a later day; while the peonage of a later day was thwarted under the Thirteenth Amendment which had been willingly ratified by the Southern States before the Radicals took them over.

As time wore on, all across the country of the Santee waters from the mountains to the sea settled a pall of hopeless gloom. Here was a land so broken in spirit that through the heavy clouds of oppression there was even no vision of a new dawn. Here, as elsewhere in the South, ten years of intolerable present, ten years without the encouragement of a reasonable hope for a better future, effectively blocked all happy thoughts except retrospect. So was born the South's paralyzing propensity to look back to its former glory, with the past exalted to the pinnacle where the vision of the future should have stood. The "Lost Cause" was embraced with religious fervor, and there was treason in enthusiasm for the "New South." The price of this bent? A half century of apathetic stagnation.

To combat the smothering weight of the black blanket in which the Radicals had tied the South, some of the young and less broken in spirit began to use white sheets, and the Ku-Klux Klan rode in a desperate effort to offset, by surreptitious intimidation, the blatant power of the Radical bayonets. But then, even as now, the activities of the Klan, by reason of its inherent dramatics, were greatly exaggerated. It was the excuse of widespread Klan activity that, in 1870, brought on what is known as the "Kirk-Holden War" which in itself was but a page in the long black book of North Carolina Reconstruction. The murder of an official of the Carpetbagger regime and some other disorders were the ostensible excuse for Governor W. W. Holden's declaration of a "state of insurrection" in several Piedmont counties, which called for the use of troops and the suspension of the writ of habeas corpus.

Actually the declaration of insurrection was a red herring devised by the sinister Scalawag Senator John Pool (who was weak Holden's backbone), with the personal blessing of President Grant, to divert attention from the railroad swindles which were just coming to light—swindles in which the Radical regime of the State was deeply involved. Thus the inception of the Kirk-Holden War had run true to the long-familiar pattern of the endless crises of the "Conquered Provinces," when the notorious Colonel George Kirk mustered his 670 swaggering ruffians in Morganton on the upper Catawba. His army had been recruited from the pillaging scum of the countryside. Four hundred of them were illiterate, and almost none of them had any experience in military discipline. Into their hands was given the government of a large section of western North Carolina. A reign of terror ensued. By way of a return on a writ of habeas corpus issued by the Chief Justice for one of Kirk's numerous prisoners came the message that "such papers had played out." Kirk's reign of terror and the arrest of Josiah Turner, a bold newspaper editor, for criticizing the Radical regime galvanized the decent elements in the state to an all-out effort, and the next election brought to the legislature a sufficient number of Conservatives to take the first step towards the redemption of the state from the unbearable evils of Reconstruction. That step was the successful impeachment of Holden.

As bad as things were in North Carolina, downriver in South Carolina conditions were immeasurably worse. Anent the times, the New York *World* observed that "men do not grow grapes from thorns, nor figs from thistles." When the congressional "reformers" turned the State over to the Carpetbaggers and Scalawags, backed by the herded mass of blacks whose training for citizenship was mostly confined to labor in the fields, it was inevitable that only thorns and thistles would thrive.

Atop the high hill overlooking the clay-colored rapids of the Congaree stood the yet uncompleted State House, in a spacious square surrounded by the fire-blackened ruins of what had been the elegant and beautiful capital city of Columbia. Here, like buzzards to a carcass had come the boldest and most unprincipled bunch of swindlers and robbers ever to call themselves an American government. Although posing as reformers intent on reconstruction, they were infamous beyond belief. What they were doing in the name of reformation and reconstruction was so degrading that to this day those words carry for Carolinians a definitely unpleasant connotation.

In 1870 these were the central figures of the "loyal" government of South Carolina: Governor Robert K. Scott, an Ohio Carpetbagger, an incident in whose career was the issuance of several hundred thousands of dollars in fraudulent railroad bonds under the blandishments of a strumpet who was employed on a commission basis to secure his signature; Treasurer Niles G. Parker, a Massachusetts fugitive from justice; "Honest" John Patterson of Pennsylvania, who would go all the way to the United States Senate on his training in graft in the legislature of his native state and the stealing of army pay during his service as a Union Army paymaster; and the Scalawag Thomas J. Robertson, who would soon be purchasing, at $500 a vote, his re-election to the United States Senate; and, finally, there was Speaker of the House Franklin Moses, utterly depraved, but the most successful of all at stealing public funds, a success which would in a few years place him in the governorship. The absolute authority of this little group rested upon a corrupt, subservient General Assembly over which, by dint of fear or bribery, they exercised an iron control. Nine tenths of the members of the House over which Moses presided were Radicals, three fourths of whom paid no taxes. Two thirds of them were Negroes, 80 per cent of whom were illiterate. No democratic process had placed all these utterly unfit men where they were. They were there by virtue of a sinister combination of fraud, intimidation and defiance of the Constitution, backed by the authority of the rifles and bayonets of the Federal troops, and the native Negro militia, who were finding endless pleasure in lording their new-found authority over their former masters. The government thereby created reflected its source. Its corruption knew no bounds. Discretion was thrown to the winds. High officials publicly boasted of their stealing. The citizenry were lucky if more than a tenth of an appropriation was finally spent on its ostensible objective, after graft had whittled it away as it passed through official channels. With but thirty-five senate attachés, pay warrants were regularly issued for 350. Nine tenths of the enormous appropriations for furniture for the State House went into furniture for the personal use of the loyal members of the Assembly. Even the cost of lingerie for the mistresses of the members became an obligation of the prostrate state. At least a contender for the nadir was an appropriation of a thousand dollars for a member, on his own motion, to pay a horse-race bet he had lost to Speaker Moses. Two hundred of the state's trial justices were unable to read!

The sessions of the Assembly were noisy and ribald. Partly responsible for such conduct was the refreshment room operated in the State House. It daily dispensed, at the expense of the taxpayers, an average of a gallon of whiskey and forty-four cigars per member of the Assembly.

In the city an "elegant" mulatto-white society, complete with fashionable salons, sprang into being. From these salons, the policies of the government were ordained. Ironically, that white and tan society quickly developed a snobbishness towards the blacks equaling any the whites had ever entertained.

To foot the bill for this unrestrained orgy, ever mounting taxes were levied on the suffering state. As taxes multiplied fivefold, tenfold, they reached and passed the productive capacity of the lands on which they were levied. Soon, in front of every courthouse the sound of the tax collector's hammer became a familiar note. Plantations for sale—thousands of them. Who in this broken land had the money to buy them? Only those who were in on the stealing. So the more provident of those founded dynasties, some of which persist to this day, with a convenient forgetfulness of their unsavory origin.

Such was the state of affairs in the Palmetto State in 1870 —and in 1871—and on through 1875. Appeals to Washington were worse than useless, being usually construed as further evidence of disloyalty. Grant's administration had sunk to the degraded level of the Radical Congress. Grant himself had become so steeped in prejudice that when he heard the words of his own earlier report on the evils of the Freedmen's Bureau quoted by a complaining South Carolina tax-payers' delegation, he failed to recognize them as his own and irately branded them as malicious lies.

Sustained by the conviction that someday there would be nothing left to steal and that then, for lack of food, the strangling octopus would have to loose its grip, the decent citizenry with quiet desperation carried on through those terrible years. During 1875, rays of light faintly pierced the gloom. A rising tide of revulsion against the corruption in Washington and the cruel vengeance being wrought against the South was sweeping the land, weakening the long, hard grip of the Radicals, loosening its hold on the "Conquered Provinces." One way or another all the former Confederate States, except the Carolinas, Florida and Louisiana, had ousted their reeking Carpetbagger regimes. In South Carolina, the state that had suffered most from Radical iniquities, the Carpetbaggers were making their most determined last stand.

There among the more resilient of the former leaders frustrated desperation was ripening into tight-lipped determination. By revolution they would break the chains that had chafed and galled beyond endurance. To effect that revolution they would adopt such means as might be necessary to insure victory. They would fight fire with fire.

The two key figures in the carefully planned revolution were General Martin Gary and General Wade Hampton. Together they constituted a perfect combination to effect the revolution and redeem the State. Gary, the "Bald Eagle of Edgefield," a sobriquet appropriate both to his appearance and character, was a natural leader of men, a fiery and fearless fighter and a master organizer. His was the dominant spirit of the revolution.

Hampton was its symbol and rallying point. Born to a name already made notable by his forebears' accomplishments as military leaders and planters, he was the personification of the best of the prewar South. Although reared in a sumptuous plantation home and well educated, his first claim to local fame came through his physical prowess and his matchless skill as an equestrian and sportsman, coupled with his courtly manners and magnetic personality. As an obligation to the society in which he was born, he had dutifully served a term in the State Senate while he was meeting with great success as a cotton planter. He had been the adored and perfect master to his hundreds of slaves. The war had brought him wider fame as a dashing cavalry officer, hero of many a bloody engagement; but it had also brought him overwhelming personal disaster: the death of one son in battle and another grievously wounded, bankruptcy and the loss of the family's baronial estates. Perfectly he represented the glamour of the prewar South, its valor in the war, and its fortitude in the face of the adversity of the day.

Gary laid the plans for the revolution, drawing heavily upon methods which had proved successful in Mississippi, where there had been the same problem of an overwhelming Negro majority well organized to do the bidding of their Radical masters. The plans called for intimidation without violence or direct threats of violence, confronting and discrediting the Radical leaders in the presence of their constituents and a vast deal of showmanship, all organized with military efficiency.

So, throughout the long, scorching summer of '76, along the dusty Carolina roads from the mountains to the sea, bands of men in flaming red shirts were riding, riding, riding. They were riding to every crossroads to whip up enthusiasm for the cause—Hampton for Governor and Democrats for the General Assembly. They were riding to every Democratic rally to form a loudly cheering claque, to make the countryside ring again with the Rebel Yell and subtly plant the impression that the Red Shirts held an unbeatable numerical advantage. Most important of all, they were riding to every meeting of the Republicans where they gathered in overawing numbers to cheer loudly as one of their men mounted the platform and charged the Radical speakers with their crimes and the corruption of their party. Usually, the cowed Radicals took these verbal lashings meekly and thereby lost face before their simple followers. The histrionics and pageantry of the Red Shirts even attracted a substantial number of the Negroes.

Soon it became apparent to the Radicals that if they were to win the election in the face of the aggressive tactics of the Red Shirts, their only hope was to bring Federal bayonets to their aid. Military intervention could be secured only by disorders from one side or the other, and the Red Shirts had shown a firm determination to avoid violence. Nevertheless, before the summer came to a close there were incidents upon which propaganda might be hung. The first was the Ellenton riots growing out of an attempt by officers to arrest a Negro for an attack on a white farmer's wife and child. When the officers were fired on, a posse of neighborhood whites joined in the man hunt. Soon it was whites against blacks and plenty of shooting. The incident had no connection with politics and the Red Shirts were not involved. Nevertheless, it served as the excuse the Radicals longed for. Grant promptly branded the native whites as lawless bands "who ride up and down by day and night in arms, murdering some peaceable citizens." A few days later near Charleston at a political meeting, unarmed whites were fired upon by armed Negroes. In the ensuing fight five whites and one Negro were killed. But in the Radical reports it became a massacre of the Negroes by the whites. Grant ordered martial law. The Radicals were jubilant, especially when the soldiers were placed at the disposal of the Radical Federal marshal. Still Hampton and Gary ordered absolute submission. Still the Red Shirts rode and rode.

When November and election day arrived, the whole

state was grim with tension. Almost every white man except the handful of Carpetbaggers and Scalawags was at his polling place adorned with his flaming shirt. Many of the Negroes, who had in previous elections docilely supported the Radicals, as a result of the Red Shirts' revelations of the corruption of their leaders, lost their enthusiasm for them and did not go to the polls. Many of the more timorous turned back when they saw the crowds of Red Shirts gathered around the polling place. Others stayed in the fields picking cotton to earn the bonus pay their employers had offered for staying on the job throughout the day. Still others, because they liked Hampton's moderation and his record as a perfect master in slave days, went to the polls to cast their votes with the Democrats.

When the votes were counted, Hampton was the winner by a thousand-vote margin and a Democratic majority had been elected to the House of Representatives, results which were immediately challenged by the Radicals who charged frauds in the voting in some counties. The Radical-dominated Board of Canvassers met, threw out the vote of two counties which had given substantial majorities to the Democrats, and declared a Radical victory. Several of the board were candidates themselves and so were sitting in judgment on their own cases. The Democrats appealed to the Supreme Court, a court composed of a Carpetbagger, a Scalawag, and a Negro. Surprisingly the court decided against the Board of Canvassers—a serious setback for the Radicals. But they could still fall back on the President and the military.

The troops were ordered to take possession of the State House and support the Radical forces in their hold on the State. Still abiding by their determination to avoid all violence, Hampton and the Democratic House Majority organized at Carolina Hall, and for the next few months the state was in the bewildering position of having two governors and two competing lower houses. The functions of the government were paralyzed. The inmates of both the state hospital for the insane and the penitentiary were facing starvation for lack of funds.

At last Grant left the White House and President Hayes moved in. One of the first acts of the new president was the removal of the Federal troops from the State House. Without bayonets to back them, the Radicals knew full well their long orgy was over. The government was surrendered to the men who had ridden so tirelessly towards that hour in history.

The state was redeemed. The aristocracy which had ruled it for almost two centuries had reclaimed their position. However, in the process, by fighting fire with fire, they had tainted themselves. Unquestionably there had been frauds on both sides in the election of '76. The votes counted practically equaled the census figures of the number of potential voters in the State. Never again would Carolinians approach public office with the sense of high responsibility, nor politics with the freedom from demagoguery which their forebears had exhibited during those two centuries of their reign.

Meanwhile, the same election had wrought a restoration in North Carolina also, and the beloved war governor, Zeb Vance, was back in the governor's office. The Carolinas were at last restored as free partners in the Union from which they had sought to withdraw fifteen years before. Now reconstruction, which was to be largely the undoing of Reconstruction, could begin.

❧ ❧ ❧ ❧ ❧ 29. The "New South"

*B*orn of a long and painful travail, the New South was the woods colt of the old order. Desperate necessity had compelled the mesalliance between the aristocracy, suddenly bereft of its slave-supported economy, and the Poor Whites, who had long before been excluded socially, robbed of dignity and reduced to abject poverty by the indirect competition of slave labor. Of that surprising and sudden mating, in hundreds of spinning and weave rooms throughout the Carolina Piedmont, the New South was born. As the white-pillared mansion symbolized the Old South, the symbol of the New South was the textile mill—a plain red brick box with a homely square tower, a concession to aesthetics in a period when the mansard roof and the gingerbread motif were pleasing to the cultured eye.

Long before the gestation of the New South began, there had been textile mills in Carolina. In the early days of the Revolution a Mrs. Ramage, of James Island near Charleston, had a "regular cotton mill," powered by mules, which ante-dates America's so-called "first factory" at Beverly, Massachusetts. A dozen years later, coincident with or perhaps antedating the famous Slater Mill at Pawtucket, Rhode Island, there is a contemporaneous account that

> a gentleman of great mechanical knowledge and instructed in most of the branches of cotton manufactures in Europe, has already fixed, completed and now [has machinery?] at work on the high hills of the Santee, near Stateburg, and which go by water, ginning, carding and slubbing machines with 84 spindles each, and several other useful implements for manufacturing every necessary article of cotton.

Far up the Catawba at Lincolnton, about 1815, Michael Schenck and Absalom Warlick had a water-powered mill which operated for several years. But these ventures were actually of little importance, for they did not live long and left no direct descendants.

Far more significant were the mill built in 1837 by Edwin Michael Holt on Alamance Creek in North Carolina and that of William Gregg built in 1845 at Graniteville near Aiken, South Carolina, for these mills continued to operate through the years and served as valuable demonstrations that cotton manufacturing could be profitably undertaken in the South. Even more important was the influence of Gregg, himself, backed as he was by the object lesson of his successful Graniteville Mill, the first large-scale textile mill of the region. It was that mill which greatly influenced the pattern of the mills of a later day, replete as it was with its village of shanties, company-supported schools and a paternalism that made possible the enforcement of local prohibition by the buggy whip, an instrument likewise employed to enforce what was probably the country's first compulsory education system—company promulgated and company enforced.

As a young man Gregg had come to Columbia from his native Virginia. He later moved to Charleston. A man of unique ability, he rapidly amassed a fortune in the jewelry business. A successful investment in a small mill fired his interest in the possibilities of cotton manufacturing in the South. The large, carefully designed Graniteville Mill was the outgrowth of that interest. When success crowned the venture, he launched an aggressive campaign to convince the South that its future lay not with Calhoun's abjuration of manufactures, not in the aristocrats' disdain of any pursuits but the professions and agriculture, but rather in a more balanced economy with a strong system of manufacturing enterprises. Another motive which drove him to seek factories was the desperate condition of the poor whites, whose salvation he saw flowing from mill wages. He argued that the fertility of the new lands to the west was reducing the South's agricultural prosperity, that there could be no prosperity as long as all useful articles were imported, that cotton processing gave a community more wealth in added value than the growth of cotton itself, that the wealth in the region's water-power sites was being wasted, that Charleston, with its ordinance against the use of steam engines, stagnated, while its sister cities grew and prospered. "The hand of enterprise is not among us," he bemoaned. He suggested that the South Carolina politicians who regarded their state as the paragon of perfection give their attention to its prostrate agriculture, its vast white illiteracy, its poverty, and the means, ready at hand, of correcting them. Preached Gregg:

> It is only necessary to build a manufacturing village of shanties in a healthy location in any part of the state to have crowds of these poor people around you, seeking employment at half the compensation given to operatives in the North. It is indeed painful to be brought into contact with such ignorance and degradation; but, on the other hand, it is pleasant to witness the change, which

soon takes place in the conditions of those who obtain employment. The emaciated, pale-faced children soon assume the appearance of robust health, and their tattered garments are exchanged for those suited to a better condition.

Although it made abundant good sense, the preaching of Gregg had little effect. Frozen into a rigid defensive mold by Calhoun's retrogressive philosophy, few were the minds

which could be turned from the narrow road to inexorable disaster—even sufficiently to provide clothes for the gallant soldiers who would soon be suffering on the battlefields for want of adequate cover, while the bales of unprocessed fleece piled ever higher and higher. It took the shock of disastrous defeat, with the lesson it had taught of the importance of material in modern warfare, a long and bitter Reconstruction and the desperate poverty it brought, the sharp depression of 1873, and the shock of Hancock's defeat by Garfield which shut the door on the possibility of redemption by political means, to gain for William Gregg's gospel of the New South sufficient attentive ears for his message to begin to bear fruit.

If William Gregg was the prophet of the New South, his disciples were F. W. Dawson, H. P. Hammett, G. A. Gray, D. A. Tompkins and Henry Grady. All of them were of the Santee country except Henry Grady, who played a major role in this industrial revolution of the South by eloquently proclaiming the new gospel through the columns of his *Atlanta Constitution*.

London born and educated, Dawson was writing for the London stage when the news of the fall of Fort Sumter rocked the western world. It fired the ardent, romantic Dawson to enlist in the Confederate Navy from which he later transferred to the Army of Northern Virginia. Upon his release from the army after being three times wounded, he decided to cast his lot with the conquered South. In but a few years his rare talents brought him the editorship of the *News and Courier*. For fifteen years, until he was murdered on a Charleston street, he waged an unremitting campaign for the social recovery of the South through industrialization, diversification of crops, and the immigration of artisans. More than anyone else he was the leader of the deliberately planned revolution which was inaugurating the New South, for, although Grady surpassed him in eloquence and forensic ability, Dawson built a powerful, devoted following, and it was the men who followed his clarion call who made the New South a reality.

Hammett, born near Greenville and scantily educated in a country school, was introduced to the textile industry by marrying the daughter of William Bates who, as an orphan boy with experience in Slater's Pawtucket mill, had walked from Rhode Island in 1819 to seek his fortune in the

South. Bates had intended to farm but he soon found himself back in cotton manufacturing. He had established a small mill near Greenville, which Hammett joined when he joined the family. After the war and a digression into railroading, Hammett determined to build a big modern cotton mill primarily to give employment to the large numbers of destitute poor whites of the neighborhood. After overcoming all manner of difficulties, by 1876 he had completed at Piedmont a modern mill of 5,000 spindles and 112 looms, operated by the waters of the Saluda. His company village, his wise and benevolent paternalism and the great financial success of his mill made it the pattern for scores of others. Piedmont became the nursery of the textile industry of the New South. Dozens of mill superintendents learned the business at Piedmont under the tutelage of big, dignified, high-silk-hatted Hammett, and from him they learned the business well.

George Gray was all but born to a cotton mill. He was the youngest of seven children of a poor Mecklenburg County farmer who died when George was a small boy. To carry his part of the family burden, he went to work in a small cotton factory at Pinhook, near what is now Gastonia. It is said that he started in the mill at the age of eight as a doffer boy and that at ten he was earning ten cents a day. At that age he had the good fortune to get his arm caught in a pulley and badly crushed, requiring ten months of absence from his job. It was during those months that he got all his formal education. His driving energy and unflagging interest in machinery carried him (while still a boy in years) to the position of superintendent of the little mill. Incredible as it seems, he had saved money methodically through his years at Pinhook. At nineteen he had accumulated several hundred dollars although he had never received more than seventy-five cents a day. By 1888 he had persuaded enough people to back him and he had his own mill. He had built this mill at Gastonia, a railroad junction, where at the time only a dozen families lived. This first Gastonia mill was a great success and it thereby spawned many more, nine of the next eleven being mills organized by Gray himself. At his death he was president of sixteen mills in the region.

D. A. Tompkins was a lad of ten living on his family's large cotton plantation in Edgefield County, South Carolina, when the Confederate War began. In spite of the hardships of Reconstruction he managed to get an engineering education at Rennsselaer. After years in the North and abroad, he returned to Carolina in 1882, settling in Charlotte, where he set himself up as an "engineer, machinist and contractor." A tinker's shop could have handled his first jobs. As he built up confidence in his work, his business grew. Before long he was busy designing, building and shipping the machinery for mills all over the Carolinas. Supremely articulate and persuasive, Tompkins promoted the organization of new mills wherever the need appeared. Through the zeal of his writings he whipped up enthusiasm for the gospel of the New South. He was responsible for the organization of so many mills that sociologists have concluded he did more for the South than all the widely touted officeholders of the region—however spectacular and however idolized those officeholders may have been.

By seizing and carrying on into a receptive period the torch which Gregg had lighted, Dawson, Grady, Hammett, Gray and Tompkins inspired the New South. First the term "New South" was a rallying cry, a call to work, a call to look forward. Later it was a state of mind. Finally that state of mind by its tangible results became a period in the history of the South—and the nation.

The tangible results of that rallying cry were spectacular. To prepare for the planned industrial New South, a Sunday in 1886 was set aside to pull in the gauge of all the Southern railroads to match the "standard" gauge of railroads in the North. On that spring day thirteen thousand miles of rail were removed from the ties and inward three inches, and the axle lengths of two thousand pieces of rolling stock were shortened to match.

Less dramatic but of vastly more consequence was the capture of the textile industry. Never before or since has an agricultural population so suddenly and so successfully turned to industry. Starting with but a 5 per cent share of the country's textile industry in 1880, the South, in the years that followed, raised that share to 80 per cent—most of it concentrated in the Carolina Piedmont, where Gregg's disciples carried the gospel. Dawson's persuasive editorials and Hammett's success at Piedmont led the well-to-do Charleston cotton factor, Francis J. Pelzer, to back Confederate veteran Captain Ellison A. Smyth in the construction of a model mill a few miles below Hammett's mill on the Saluda, where the only signs of civilization were three or four miserable log cabins. Those successes, plus the equally successful ventures of Gray at Gastonia, led others to heed the words of Dawson, Grady, and Tompkins. Leroy Springs, in order to feed his mercantile business and to keep Lancaster the trade center of the neighborhood, started a mill there which eventually evolved into the largest single unit cotton mill in the world and later became the nucleus of a vertically expanded textile empire, carrying the risqué-ly advertised Springmaid cotton products through all the processes from the farmers' wagons to the merchants' shelves.

Commenting on the news that a mill had been organized in Columbia in 1881, Dawson wrote:

> It will be a happy day for the whole State when the hum of a myriad spindles is heard on the banks of the historic Canal. . . . The *News and Courier* busies itself with every enterprise, big and little, that will turn a dollar's worth of raw material into more than a dollar's worth of manufactures. . . . We confess a weakness for

Columbia, which suffered so sorely at the end of the war. . . . But cotton mills will soon make amends for the vicissitudes and hopelessness of the past.

Forwarded by such faith, over and over, with variations, the story repeated itself until almost every Carolina Piedmont crossroads community had at least one textile mill. Gray's initial Gastonia mill bred 125 more to make Gaston County the leading textile county of the nation. The success of the southern leaders in mixing philanthropy for the Poor Whites with fat dividends for themselves and their investors soon began to tell in the flagging prosperity of the heretofore dominant New England textile regions. Adopting the age-old policy of discretion which decrees that you "jine 'em if you can't beat 'em," the New England mills began a full-blown migration southward by 1900—a migration which has continued to this very day, even after the wage differential that started the migration has largely disappeared.

The slogan of the publicists had been: "Bring the cotton mills to the cotton fields," a slogan which at first blush appeared to make good sense and consequently was a weighty factor in the campaign. However, since most of the early Southern mills had to ship their yarns or gray goods North for finishing, there was obviously no merit in that attractive argument. And as more and more mills were powered by coal instead of water, and the coal had to be shipped in at freight costs far exceeding the freight on the cotton if it were shipped North, the slogan became patently specious. But the merit of the slogan's argument was beside the point. The important thing was that it aroused the apathetic and the discouraged, brought them to confident action, and brought manufacturing to a land in desperate need of emancipation from a one-crop agricultural economy.

As fast as the drab rows of characterless shacks of the company-owned village could be completed, as each new mill was built, the Poor Whites flocked in, avid for employment, regardless of the wage offered. "Dirt-eaters," "Hill-billies," "Sand-hillers," "Tar-heels" and "Crackers," from destitution, hopelessness and abandonment, from a standard of living lower than that of any Anglo-Saxon people since the Norman conquest, they flocked to the mills as they might have to eternal salvation. These were the people who inspired the term "the forgotten man," seized upon a half century later as a political campaign phrase. It gave them no pause that the work week was seventy hours and the top wage for men was fifty cents a day, and was usually much less than that, while the children, down to the age of eight years, got about one cent an hour. That the competition for these jobs was keen is shocking evidence of the plight of the white Southern populace in the postwar decades.

Softening somewhat the harshness of the picture were the numerous paternalistic benefits allowed the operatives such as nominal rent, the right to gather fuel and graze a cow on the company land, free schooling in primary grades, a community house and park, company bands, company baseball teams and usually a company store extending limited credit. All this seemed natural and proper to the erstwhile slave masters who in the beginning controlled most of the mills and set the pattern of paternalism which the Northern mill men had to adopt when they came South to compete with the Southerners. So, for decades, in the drab mill villages of the New South a social system but a degree removed from slavery prevailed. Low wages perpetuated the institution beyond its philanthropic inception stage, while the mills prospered by those same low wages that held their operatives captive. Rescue by labor movements was impossible, for the operative could see no conflict of interest between the mill master and himself. Together they had presented a solid front against the Carpetbaggers and the Negros; together they were united to keep the mills exclusively white, and the workers were boundlessly grateful for the opportunity the mill provided for their release from abject, hopeless poverty. They were grateful to the mill owners even for the opportunity provided for their children to put in ten or twelve hours a day for a ten or fifteen cent wage. It was a great help to a family that had rarely seen that much money per day before the mills came. Child labor was a privilege; consequently it was long before a voice was raised against it.

About the reality of this latter-day white "slavery," there was sometimes a naive frankness. When communities sought new industries they offered to serve up Poor Whites on the auction block in a manner reminiscent of the days of black

slavery. "Native-born English speaking Anglo-Saxon labor in ample supply—tractable, willing to work for little." The admission is made that the New South is successful because it has "a supply of native American labor which is still satisfied to work at a low wage." In truth, it took starvation wages and long hours to start the broken-down economy of the South rolling again.

While the outstanding feature of the New South was the rise of the textile industry, the years of its birth also witnessed great progress in other industrial fields. In the upper Piedmont of North Carolina, tobacco manufacturing rapidly evolved from a farm adjunct to a major industry, and the manufacture of furniture was growing by leaps and

bounds. At the same time the South's bountiful timber resources began contributing heavily to the economic recovery
of the impoverished region. The burgeoning postwar North,
having exhausted its principal timber supply, the Lake region, turned to the South for its lumber needs. All up and
down the river and across the South great, largely Northern-
financed lumber companies began their frenetic "cut out and
get out operations" on the remaining original-growth timber
stands of both the swamps and the uplands. With these industries added to its textile manufacturing, North Carolina
was well launched on its transformation from an agricultural
to an industrial economy—a remarkable development for a
region that had so long stagnated that it had earned the title
of "the Rip Van Winkle State."

All together the story of the earlier years of the New
South's changing economy is a dynamic one—but it does not
make a pretty picture. Socially and politically it presented
much the same aspect—dynamic, but ugly, even revolting in
spots.

The poverty of the postwar South that made an able-
bodied man grateful for fifty cents a day in return for a
twelve-hour day in a cotton mill and placed halos of philanthropy around the heads of the mill owners for giving ten
cents a day for the labor of his small children was not confined to the poor whites. A long period of depressed farm
prices, worn-out and eroded fields, the one-crop system, ignorance of good farm methods, and the competition of the
richer, newer lands to the west combined to make the situation of the small farmers of the older regions of the South
unhappy indeed. By 1885 all that was needed for a pitchfork revolution was the leadership. The small farmers and
the poor whites had so long accepted the leadership of
the planter class that they had none of their own. Consequently those who rose up from among them were bizarre
political figures without precedent in the land. Pre-eminent

among these grass roots leaders was Benjamin Ryan (Pitchfork Ben) Tillman. A violent man, scion of a violent, guntoting, fairly well-to-do but uncouth middle-class family, of Edgefield, South Carolina, Tillman rose to power by dint of a clever combination of intelligent reform demands and extravagant demagoguery. His dynamic support of more agricultural education, more regulation of the railroads, and more farmers in government appealed to the dissatisfied of higher intelligence. To gain the blind loyalty of the ignorant, he turned his unbridled tongue against Charleston, the Negros, Grover Cleveland, the "Bourbon" government of the state and the State University, upon which he poured unmatched invective, while he ardently supported lynching for rape and complete disenfranchisement of the blacks. By such methods he was soon invincible at the polls. The "Bourbon" government, which had already met most of his reform demands, was swept from power. Even the political life of the idolized Wade Hampton was summarily given the ax as the farmers climbed into the saddle. The primary nomination system was established, the Negroes disenfranchised and segregation laws enacted. Among the numerous subjects of Tillman invective was the "damned factory class," as he termed the textile workers. Being for some unknown reason an object of Tillman prejudice, they were still without the fold when the Tillmanites took over. However, the removal of their farm isolation and their concentration in tight little villages made it inevitable that someone would soon be seeking their support. To seize that opportunity, from within the Tillman ranks came the archdemagogue, Cole L. Blease, not even bothering to propose reform, while he built his power over the lower classes solely by feeding numerous scapegoats to his ignorant followers. On race prejudice and class prejudice he built his power. His only positive accomplishment was the arousal of the "lintheads" to political consciousness, awakening them to political activity as Tillman had the farmers, and thereby giving them a new sense of equality as they climbed into the saddle with the farmers.

The long dominance of upper classes was at an end. The white masses had completed their revolution, ill equipped as they were for the responsibility. In those years and in the years that followed, there were disgraceful examples of ignorance and prejudice in power. However the masses were entrenched beyond recall, and the hope of the land became mass education, that even the masses might have the training to govern well.

Soon after Tillman's name was being shouted across South Carolina, that of Tom Watson was being heard in Georgia, and James K. Vardaman was capturing Mississippi. And as Blease followed Tillman, a degenerated Watson, hitching his campaign to verbal lashings of the Pope, succeeded the reformer Watson of an earlier day; Bilbo succeeded Vardaman; and government in the South reached its nadir.

Off pattern and far less unsavory was the North Carolina phase of the revolt of the masses. There Leonidas L. Polk, a tireless reformer, effected the agrarian phase of the revolution by the power of the press and the pressure of the Farmers' Alliance. Charles B. Aycock, his successor in influence, who completed the revolution, contradictorily combined his disenfranchisement and segregation of the Negroes with the inauguration of a universal public school system which included the Negroes in its benefits—regardless of the inevitable consequences of Negro education—Negro suffrage and participation in government.

Tillmanism, Bleasism and the kindred movements that sporadically grew like rank, foul-smelling weeds across the South for four decades were ugly phenomena. To the ill informed and the unsympathetic they held the South up to endless ridicule. To those critics of little understanding, to those who fail to appreciate the condition of the land that nurtured those weeds, suffice it to say that the phenomena were not nearly so ugly as the conditions that made them possible—and for those conditions Carolina and the South were not wholly responsible. Tillmanism and its kindred "isms" were the birth pangs of a better day.

There are those who have no good word for the New South, who are critical of the long hours, low wages and child labor which were associated with it. For those critics to be consistent, they should also look down their noses at the frontiersmen and the low standard of living to which they subjected themselves in order to build a better society from what they had at hand. And to pity the Poor Whites who flocked to the mills because they received there but half a loaf is to overlook the fact that until then they had had no loaf at all. There are those who hate the New South because it jars with their idyllic conception of the romantic Old South. They like to forget that the miserable, illiterate Poor Whites were part of that Old South, a far more numerous part than the planters with whom those of nostalgic bent always associate themselves. Those critics are the same ones who confuse leisure with culture in the Old South of their mind's eye. They are the same persons to whom tumble-down Negro shacks and mud-daubed mountaineer cabins are picturesque and romantic, rather than objects of shame and pity. As a powerful force starting the crippled South on the road to the elimination of those objects of shame and pity, the New South, with all its faults, was magnificent. Centered as it was in the Santee country, the same region which had repeatedly suffered disasters unparalleled anywhere else in the country, its success created a new and vital confidence, a confidence that spread out from Carolina to make the South once again young, strong and confident.

❦ ❦ ❦ ❦ ❦ *30. On the importance of a sore foot*

One of "Buck" Duke's feet, already famous for their outlandish size, was giving him a lot of trouble in the late summer of 1904; so much so that by early fall the restless, aggressive tobacco magnate was forced to call in a doctor to treat it. From his humble origin on a small tobacco farm in the hills of central North Carolina, red-haired, raw-boned, fifty-eight-year-old James Buchanan Duke had come a long way. By dint of ceaseless work, a boundless thirst for power, an uncanny ability to seize opportunities before others saw them, all coupled with an ample share of the ruthlessness of the day, he had already become the tobacco tycoon of the world, counting his riches in hundreds of millions—when, to his disgust, his sore foot began seriously to hamper his activities.

The doctor he summoned to treat his foot was another transplanted Carolinian, who in his profession had also achieved great fame. The amazingly versatile Dr. Walker Gill

Wylie in 1904 enjoyed an international reputation in the fields of surgery, gynecology, and hospital design. Since treating sore feet, erysipelas as it turned out, was not among the doctor's specialties, it is likely that he was Duke's choice because they were both of that numerous group of Carolinians who had physically transplanted themselves from the "tight-belt" post-war economy of their native section to the greener fields of New York but had never succeeded in entirely moving their hearts from the farms of their boyhood. Be that as it may, it is certain that when Dr. Wylie called on Duke, although both men had long been nominally New Yorkers, both were still essentially Carolinians with plans to return "home."

So it was natural that when the doctor came to Duke's house day after day to change the dressings on the ailing foot much of their conversation carried them back to their Carolina hills. It was also natural that they talked of another common interest. Both men as a hobby were experimenting with the possibilities of using water power to generate electricity. Duke had built a small hydroelectric plant to light the buildings of his country estate on the Raritan River in New Jersey. Dr. Wylie had employed a young engineer, William States Lee, a kinsman of his who lived in Lancaster, across the Catawba from the doctor's home in Chester, South Carolina, to build a small hydroelectric plant on his plantation. He told Duke of Lee's boundless enthusiasm for the possibilities of hydroelectric power. George Westinghouse and Nikola Tesla, a few years before, had demonstrated the possibility of transporting electricity over long distances by stepping the voltage up very high, so in the future the plants consuming the hydroelectric power would not have to be located at the powerhouse. The limitless opportunities offered by this discovery had been quickly grasped by Lee. With enthusiasm he had told Dr. Wylie of a future day when up and down the whole Catawba-Wateree there would be a series of great dams with their powerhouses all linked together by high tension lines, with other lines carrying the power to factories and towns all over the Carolina Piedmont. Duke was fascinated by the doctor's account of his kinsman's dreams. This sort of thing was just his meat—building on an imperial scale. His reaction was immediate: "Get that young fellow up here."

A few days later Lee returned to South Carolina with two checks, each for $50,000—one from Dr. Wylie and one from Duke—to purchase the site for the Wateree Dam near Camden. He had also a verbal promise from Duke of all the millions necessary to develop the Catawba-Wateree from the mountains to the fall line. Thus was born the Southern Power Company, the world's pioneer major hydroelectric, superpower system, which in the next two decades transformed the turbulent Catawba-Wateree into the country's most highly developed major power river, a distinction it would carry for years—until the free flow of government money and the Tennessee combined to give that river the crown.

Arrangements were soon made to take over the languishing small-scale development at Catawba, near Rock Hill, and a little later construction was begun on a dam to provide a seventy-one-foot head at Great Falls. Before the latter was completed, a dam to create a fifty-eight-foot head at Rocky Creek was under way. Others undertaken in that first busy decade of the mammoth plan were the seventy-eight-foot project at Lookout Shoals east of Hickory, a sixty-eight-foot one at Fishing Creek below the old Catawba project, a seventy-two-foot one at Wateree near Camden, and the hundred-thirty-five-foot one up against the mountains near Morganton. At this last site a great lake of extraordinary beauty, then known as Bridgewater but later called Lake James, was created by three towering dams, one across the Catawba River, another across Paddy Creek, and the third across the Linville River where the powerhouse was located.

By 1926 the harnessing of the Catawba-Wateree was completed (except for one potentital site above the Mountain Island Reservoir which remains undeveloped) by the addition of a seventy-eight-foot project at Mountain Island near Charlotte, and a seventy-one-foot one at Dearborn near Great Falls, a sixty-foot-one at Rhodhiss, northwest of Hickory, an enlarged seventy-foot dam at the original Catawba site, an additional 45,000 KW powerhouse on the Cedar Creek side of the Rocky Creek dam, and a ninety-foot dam at Oxford above the Lookout Shoals project. The combined heads of all these projects utilized 768 of the 1,051 feet which the river falls in its course from the headwaters of Lake James to the tailrace at Wateree. The chain of lakes created by these dams transformed more than 140 of the once turbulent 215 miles between these points into quiet hill-girt lakes, individually varying in length from a few miles to more than twenty-five for the larger ones.

Meanwhile to the westward on the Broad at 99 Islands, a seventy-five-foot dam had been built and incorporated into the system.

The combined generating capacity of the completed hydro system was a whopping (by the standards of the day) 460,000 KW. Almost from the beginning the company had been confronted with the problem of getting customers for the power it had for sale, a problem which kept growing in magnitude as each new generating plant was completed. Duke himself substantially assisted in solving this problem by building electrically driven cotton mills near several of the hydro installations, and by engaging in a widespread pump priming in the form of financial assistance to and investment in many others in return for contracts to use his electric power. His activities in that field provided a substantial added impetus to the already rapidly growing textile industry of the Carolina Piedmont. Widespread extensions of the high tension transmission lines fully solved the customer problem so that by 1925 when the last of the dams was completed there were customers waiting for its power.

That same year there came a record-breaking drought and a drastic shrinkage in the flow of the river. In an effort to meet the customers' power demands, the water level in the chain of reservoirs kept dropping lower and lower until thousands of acres of sun-baked, stump-studded mud surrounded the diminished reservoirs, and a lesson was emphatically driven home to those who had placed too much reliance on nature's staying "normal" over an extensive period: That without reservoirs of impractical hugeness rivers cannot be relied upon to produce a steady "normal" supply of power. The drought had demonstrated that, to produce a dependable supply of power, auxiliary generating plants would have to be added to the system. Although the company had at the time two small steam generating plants, the unified system of mutually supplementing steam and hydro plants of today's system was born of the 1925 drought. Larger steam generating plants were soon under construction to bear the load in times of low water. By 1930 a fourth of the power sold was produced in steam plants.

In recent years with the coming of accelerated prosperity and rapid industrial expansion in the Carolinas the demand for electric power has multiplied phenomenally. Since the power output of an already harnessed river does not grow, all the added generating capacity necessarily was provided by steam power plants. By 1953 but a ninth of the power produced came from the hydro installations. They had become the auxiliaries of a gigantic steam generating system. Now any one of four of the steam plants of the company produces more power than all the eleven great dams of the hydro system. Although the water-power system is now but a relatively small auxiliary to a great steam-electric system, it is still essential for the production of electricity at a minimum of cost. Water power is capable of almost instantly

answering a call to inject additional power into the transmission system. The operator has but to open the gate to
start the turbine which turns the generator at full speed
almost immediately. On the other hand it requires nine
hours and an enormous consumption of fuel to heat a boiler
of a modern steam plant before it can operate at all, for
the steam has to first be heated to 950 degrees. So water
power facilely and economically takes care of the above-
normal fluctuations in the power demands made upon the
system such as occur during those hours when housewives
are cooking and ironing and the factories are at the same
time making their top demands for power.

Similar efficient, dovetailing dual generation systems
utilize other parts of the Santee system. Involving other
rivers and other power companies, these systems, all con-
nected and dovetailed, are in operation all over the Carolinas.

With the final evolution of the dual hydro and steam system came great changes along the river. As long as water was
the primary source of the required power, the reservoirs were
called upon to supply that water even when the river flow was
insufficient to replace the demand. The lake levels then rapidly fell, exposing the sediment clay so that the slightest wave
action against that mud soon reddened the entire lake expanse. The turbid waters and the repeated exposure of their
breeding beds made fish life almost nonexistent. In spite of
the attractive surroundings of all those reservoirs, few people
were attracted to them. Now, with a full or almost full head
of water being carefully maintained that the maximum power
may be obtained during the relatively few hours of peak demand, the reservoirs stay filled. Except in times of flood they
are beautiful clear green lakes, meccas for tens of thousands
of fishermen. On sites liberally leased by the power company,
thousands of summer cottages have suddenly dotted their

shore lines. Now, all over Carolina, boat and trailer rival television antennae in their ubiquity.

However, the river yet remains an essential ingredient of the region's electric-power system—even of the now primary steam generating plants. The steam plants themselves are tied to the river they invariably stand beside, for they require enormous quantities of water for their operation. A large modern steam plant, such as the Lee Station on the Saluda, Cliffside on the Broad or Riverbend on the Catawba, uses daily for cooling its steam condensers about the same amount of water required by a city of two million people.

There is one more episode in the story that started with Mr. Duke's sore foot. In 1924, shortly before his death, he set up the Duke Endowment Fund, starting it with $40,-000,000 in assets—much of which was stock in the power company, which had by then become the Duke Power Company. Consequently most of the profits of that momentous involvement of an industrialist, a doctor, a young engineer and a river flow back to their fellow Carolinians in the form of charitable and educational works in the two states.

The hydroelectric story of the Santee only begins with that of the Wateree-Catawba tributary. Even the Broad, the least developed of the Santee tributaries, has its notable installations. In the Blue Ridge is the three hundred-foot dam across the Green River which creates Lake Summit and on the Broad itself is one humdred-foot-deep Lake Lure at the mouth of spectacular Hickory Nut Gorge. Below these on the Broad and its tributaries, the Second Broad, the Pacolet, the Tyger and the Enoree are the 99 Islands and Parr Shoals projects and some eighteen more installations, most of them supplying the power for a single cotton mill.

In point of time the story of the hydroelectric development of the Santee system should have begun with the Saluda, for far up that tributary, at Pelzer, stands the first dam

to generate electricity for transmission elsewhere for use. In 1882 a group of Charlestonians had built a water-powered cotton mill in an all but unpopulated spot near Wilson's Bridge. The venture prospered greatly and kept expanding. A dozen years after the first plant was opened the fourth and largest unit was being planned. Its power was to be furnished by a damsite about three miles below the existing mills and village. Up to that time it had always been necessary to set the mills close by the power supply. Since the Pelzer officials very much desired to locate their new plant alongside their village, the best electric power talents of the country, among them being Charles Steinmetz, were called on for a solution to the problem. In 1895, the same year that Westinghouse was demonstrating the feasibility of cross-country transmission of electricity, the new fifty-five-thousand-spindle, electrically operated mill was built several miles from its powerhouse, a feat made possible, in the absence of step-up transformers, by directly generating high voltage current. So in 1895 on the banks of the Saluda stood the world's largest electrically operated cotton mill, receiving its hydroelectric power from one of the first, if not the first, cross-country industrial electric-transmission lines.

A score of miles downstream from Pelzer begins the twenty-five-mile long reservoir of Lake Greenwood, the "Buzzards' Roost" development of Greenwood County.

Below Lake Greenwood is the Dreher Shoals development of the Lexington Water Power Company. Here the mile-and-a-half-long, 211-foot-high Saluda Dam, having a base 1,100 feet thick and covering 100 acres, is one of the largest earthen dams in the world. It impounds the Saluda to form Lake Murray, one of the world's largest power lakes, covering 50,000 acres and having a shore line of more than 500 miles. Its 175,000 horsepower plant more than doubles the capacity of any other hydroelectric installation on any of the Santee tributaries.

All these power developments add up to a bountiful supply of electricity in the Carolinas with rates substantially below the national average. Consequently Carolinians, although they are still near the bottom in per capita wealth, regularly use in their homes half again as much electricity as does the average American—an intimate factor and boon in everyday living in which Santee waters have played a major role.

One would think that to look for hydroelectric plant locations amid the swamps and pine flats of the Carolina Low Country would be about as profitable as a search for snakes in Ireland. And certainly no one looking on the Santee slowly flowing its sinuous way from its source to the sea would have been inspired with visions of a gargantuan power development which would make those lazy waters generate nearly a quarter-million horsepower. He would not have been inspired by visions of such a gargantuan project, that is, unless he knew some figures which had come to light when surveys were being made for the Santee Canal back at the time of the Revolution. The levels run for the canal had revealed a unique phenomenon—that the headwaters of the Cooper River which rises but a few miles south of the course of the Santee lay thirty-five feet below the level of the Santee. So if the level of the Santee were raised forty feet by a dam and the river diverted through the low ridge into the Cooper River a seventy-five-foot head could be obtained. With the enormous average flow of the Santee such a head had great power potential. The idea was an old one. For many years private power companies had toyed with the project. In the twenties a license was issued to one of them but it could never get the development under way. There was too much question of its business and engineering soundness, and the great depression soon dried up all sources of big money—except public funds.

Soon, under the sponsorship of the State of South Carolina acting through the South Carolina Public Service Authority, the project was made part of the antidepression "pump priming" program. There was bitter opposition from many directions, from the power interests, the owners of the lands which would be inundated, conservationists and from level-headed businessmen. But the desire for projects heavily freighted with labor, the public power policy of the New Deal and, on the state level, the backing of politically powerful groups overcame all objections, and the mammoth navigation and power project was begun in 1939. Three years and sixty-five million dollars later, impounded by forty miles of great dams and dykes, newly created Lake Marion, its one hundred thousand-acre expanse making it the largest artificial lake east of the Appalachians, had submerged the sites of the plantations of the once glorious English Santee, and Lake Moultrie's sixty thousand acres had covered most of the glamorous Cooper River plantations. Except for a pittance discharge of five hundred cubic feet per second required to be released through the Santee dam, the lower hundred miles of the Santee in times of normal water had become an abandoned river, its great flow being deflected by the Santee Dam into Lake Moultrie and from thence through the Pinopolis powerhouse into a ship canal following closely the route of the old Santee Canal to the Cooper River and thence into Charleston Harbor—a mouth seventy miles from its erstwhile junction with the sea. For navigation, the historical but anachronistic excuse for state ownership of the project, a ten-foot channel was provided from a remote spot in the wide Congaree swamp down to the deep water channel of the lower Cooper. To lift and lower the hypothetical commerce into and from Lake Moultrie, a ship lock with a lift of seventy-five feet, the highest in the country, was constructed at the powerhouse tailrace.

The Santee-Cooper project's protagonists painted glow-

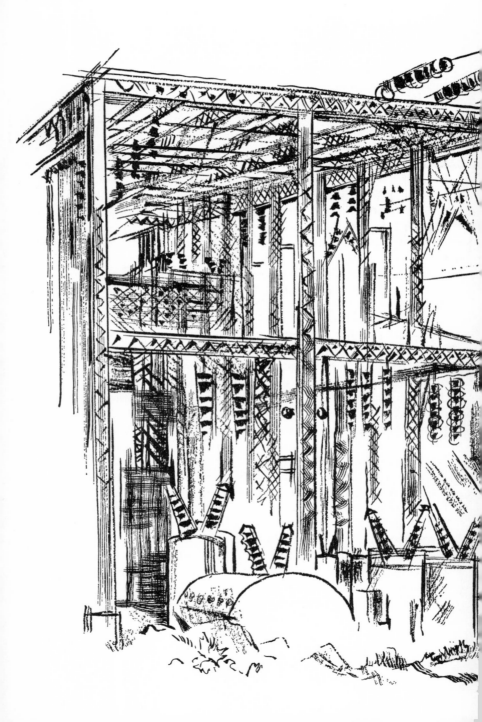

ing pictures of the industrial progress which the development would bring to the Low Country. The Santee-Cooper waterway would be busy with shipping all the way to Columbia in the heart of the state. Industries would flock to the region to use its power. Although the project's supporters still hold to their blind faith in the wisdom of the undertaking, the facts of the intervening years have long since convinced the unprejudiced that the whole project was a monstrous error, the product of anachronistic enthusiasms.

When the project was conceived, practical inland navigation on the Eastern seaboard had been dead a hundred years, and only a wishful romantic could seriously visualize painfully slow barge traffic in an age of high-speed highway and rail transportation. And, except as a subordinate auxiliary to steam-electric generation, hydroelectric plants had become almost as passé as inland navigation, at least in the East where land costs are high and coal is relatively near at hand. When the Santee-Cooper project was undertaken, it had been years since a private power company in the Carolinas had constructed a hydro plant, although they already owned several excellent undeveloped sites. Electricity could be produced more cheaply and more dependably by modern steam generating plants. It is all but strictly true that the expensive "highest navigation locks in the United States" have had no beneficial use during all the intervening years except to lift fish from the Cooper River to the lake level. The middle and Upcountry regions continued to attract the great bulk of the new industry coming to the state—to buy its power there from private power companies. The enormous fluctuations in the generating capacity of a hydro plant standing alone on a temperamental river were soon apparent. But a small percentage of the total power which could be generated during a year could be sold as dependable prime power and secondary power, which might or might not be supplied, was worth little to anyone. Some months the plant could produce only a fourth the current which it might supply during other months. So a steam auxiliary became a necessity, and the state soon found itself in competition with its private tax-paying power companies, manufacturing power, not from its own water resources, but from oil brought in from far distant sources.

In an unceasing effort to conceal the fact that their great project has proved itself a monumental white elephant, the men in charge of operating Santee-Cooper, ever on the defensive, are shameless in their official propaganda. They repeatedly represent it as a "taxpaying project" although no taxes whatsoever are paid on the development. A pittance, the amount of the land taxes at the depression rate on the undeveloped swamp lands it acquired, is paid the counties in lieu of taxes. Even the smaller of the Duke installations up the river pay a multiple of Santee-Cooper's "taxes" and license taxes, income taxes and power generation taxes to boot. Grossly slanted figures are a common tool of the project propaganda. The enormous "savings" being enjoyed by its customers are calculated by comparing its average rates against the national average (which is much higher than the Carolina rates) instead of using the rates being charged by the private power companies of the region which are substantially the same even without an allowance for the tax portion of the private rate. If the Santee-Cooper rate is compared with a private rate, the tax portion of the private companies' rates is not mentioned. "Savings" to customers are demonstrated by comparison of present average rates against the private utility rates in effect when Santee-Cooper started, with no explanation that a similar "saving" is being realized by the customers of the utility companies because greater use means more power purchased in the cheaper brackets of the rate schedule. Much is made of the "profits" from the project which are paid into the South Carolina treasury, payments which have been running about $200,000 per annum, or less than one third of one per cent on the cost of the project. Forestry studies indicate that if the state owned the swamp area from which the forest was removed for the reservoirs it could perpetually realize at present values about $1,500,000 per annum in timber stumpage alone, and the manufacturing of that timber would add several times that figure to the wealth of the state—and taxes would be coming in from the power company which would be supplying the customers now supplied by the unfortunate project.

In one respect, however, and for one class of people the Santee-Cooper project has proved itself successful beyond all expectations. For fishing, its reservoirs are unsurpassed. Almost seventy-five thousand fishermen were licensed to fish those waters last year. As a fishpond and recreation area the Authority has no need for official propaganda. The fishermen take care of that.

The building of the Santee-Cooper project had scarcely begun when the United States Army Engineers were on the scene making plans for more public power projects on the Santee system under the guise of navigation and flood control projects.

Largest of these proposals was a seventy-five-foot impoundment of the Santee by a six-mile-long dam at Buckingham Landing, just below the confluence of the Congaree and Wateree. This $60,000,000 project would have pushed the still water of its 186,000-acre reservoir up to Columbia and Camden by flooding practically the entire rich forest land of the Wateree and Congaree swamps. Together with the other five proposed projects which extended up the Broad from Columbia to the mountains the whole plan of the Engineers would have provided 750,000 h.p. of power at a cost of $158,000,000. From a flood control standpoint a remarkable proportion of the Wateree, Congaree and Santee swamp lands periodically subject to inundation by floods would have been protected from flood damage by being permanently submerged. And the great plan was rolling along towards final authorization.

But Santee-Cooper had already proved a sufficient demonstration to educate. Consequently as soon as the Engineers' plans were made public came a spontaneous and overwhelming opposition—especially to the Buckingham Landing scheme. When the public hearings required by law were held, those opposed appeared in such numbers and vehemence that the few proponents were cowed by the powerful voice of an aroused public into keeping a chagrined silence. Consequently the hearing officials were compelled to report a lack of local sentiment for the proposed developments—and the grand plan died.

Locally the fight is known as the Battle of Buckingham Landing. The signal victory gained in that battle made it likely that, with the demise of that plan, the superior economy of steam generation and the prospect of atomic power, there will be no further hydroelectric development of the river—at least in the foreseeable future.

❦ ❦ ❦ ❦ ❦ *31. Because of the*

climate

*A*bout five years after the
close of World War II, the municipal authorities of Camden
decided to move the town's Confederate monument from the
center of Main Street and place it in a nearby park. The brief
report of that decision which appeared in the local paper
created scarcely a ripple of interest. It seemed the only sensi-
ble thing to do. Standing there at a busy intersection, it had
long been a traffic hazard; and since DuPont was then
building a giant chemical plant on the nearby Wateree, on
the heels of the coming of several smaller manufacturing
plants, the hazard the monument created was becoming more
and more serious. Those of us who had a part in making
that decision had no thought that we were performing a
dramatically symbolic act. Perhaps we just couldn't see the
forest for the trees, for the incident was seized upon and
dramatized in magazine article after magazine article, until
we felt almost as though, by that simple act of local civic

improvement, we had participated as pallbearers for the Old South—that we had relegated its remains to the peaceful obscurity of a wooded park.

Perhaps there was in the moving of that monument all the symbolism that was attributed to it by those writers, all from other sections, and we here in the South were too engrossed by what was happening to us to see it. Perhaps we were standing too close to a picture of monumental proportions, depicting action on a vast scale, to grasp more than the details immediately before us. For if one stands back and looks, there is the picture—monumental and dramatic. Coming up from far behind, with a speed and vitality no one suspected, the South was rapidly closing the wide, long-retained economic lead of the other sections of the country. Suddenly released from the long-confining prison of its past, the South, led by the Carolinas, was involved in a headlong industrial development unmatched anywhere before, except perhaps in the relatively small oil regions of Texas and Southern California. Telephone installations give a good indication of the situation. During the first eight post World War II years, there was a nation-wide 100 per cent increase in telephones, while the increase in the South was 135 per cent. In the Carolinas the increase was more than 160 per cent. During that period while the national per capita income rose 194 per cent, in the South the rise was 254 per cent. In terms of manufacturing plants and capital invested, the figures are even more impressive. South Carolina's 1,300 plants of 1945 had been augmented in those few years by 1,100 new establishments costing a billion dollars, twice the accumulated total investment in all the state's manufacturing plants up to 1945, a $5,000,000-a-week capital expansion. The Atomic Energy Commission's billion-dollar atomic materials plant is not included in those figures. North Carolina's 1945 census of 4,029 manufacturing plants had, by the summer of 1954, grown to more than 7,500, carrying its industrial pay rolls to well over four times the figure for the former year. In a decade the number of Carolinians employed in industry jumped 70 per cent while their pay rolls increased fourfold.

Reflecting all this activity, the once busy but long since stagnant port of Charleston suddenly came to life. In seven years its customs receipts multiplied sixfold.

The economic picture indicated by these figures is too current to be history and too rapidly developing to avoid being quickly stale. Within a few days of this writing, news stories have told of Charleston's decision to proceed with the development of its multimillion-dollar Bushy Park industrial site area, where the great fresh-water supply of the Santee will make available a daily supply of a billion and a half gallons of industrial water where ocean-going ships can dock —a concomitant of industrial assets unmatched elsewhere in the country. There was the announcement of the awarding of a contract for a three-million-dollar wool-scouring plant near the Santee at Jamestown, where the Huguenots built their first village. On the banks of the Congaree, near old Fort Granby, American Cyanimid completed the acquisition of a site for a proposed fifty-million-dollar chemical plant for the production of an acrylic fibre. A hundred miles to the east a big community celebration, with all the state's bigwigs in attendance, was being staged for the opening of a new tufted-rug factory. Up the Catawba, the State's Water Pollution Authorities, the City of Rock Hill and the officials of the Rock Hill Printing & Finishing Company were in conference on the ways and means of permitting that plant to build a two-million-dollar addition to its existing facilities. Higher up the Catawba, near the mouth of South Fork River, according to the newspaper announcement, Duke Power Company will presently start construction on the largest steam power plant in the Southeast, the first unit alone to cost more than twenty-five-million dollars. All these news stories appeared within a single week!

While this new industrial growth was still predominantly in the textile field, a healthful diversity was beginning to take shape. In the textile field itself, which the South now completely dominates with 80 per cent of the nation's spindles, a wider diversity began to appear. New printing and finishing plants greatly reduced the northward movement of the region's gray goods, which had long been finished in the North. The lion's share of the synthetic and glass fiber plants are located in the region, giant plants, each of which produces as much fiber as several cotton counties. The woolen industry gave every indication of a wholesale trek southward, mainly to the Carolinas where it was spilling over from the long-dominant Piedmont into the all but unindustrialized Low Country, a harbinger of the industrial development that will surely take place as industry seeks out the resources of that region—water, and a bountiful supply of Negro labor which will even more warmly welcome industrial employment than did the Piedmont Poor Whites of the New South. In lesser numbers but in wide variety were the new plants in other than the textile field. In South Carolina, the variety spread was all the way from cement to sewing machines and glass fishing rods to electric irons. In North Carolina, the manufacturing of electrical products suddenly joined as a major industry the already established furniture, tobacco and textile industries, to lend further diversification to its better balanced economy. In both states long idle deposits of a wide variety of nonmetallic minerals began to be developed in substantial quantities. The new pulp and paper industry expanded enormously, to such an extent that its demands began to approach the capacity of the forests to produce its raw material requirements without depletion. And these are but the high lights of a decade of frenetic activity which, at this writing, shows no signs of waning.

So rapid and overwhelming has been the region's conversion from a farm economy to an industrial economy that most Carolinians, even though they are witnessing the changes on every hand, are finding it difficult to readjust their thinking to fit the facts. Even in the face of statistics showing that their industrial pay rolls alone now more than double the region's total income from agriculture, they still find it difficult not to consider their economy as predominantly agricultural. The politicians in both states continue to give far more heed to the demands of the farmers than to those of the industrial society.

Although evidence of the rapidly changing South is observable everywhere, the factors that have been sparking those changes are not so obvious. Hundreds of economists have put forth their views on the subject, some emphasizing one set of facts while some were giving primary credit to others. Beyond question there is no simple answer, for it lies in the interaction of numerous, almost simultaneous, developments.

Unquestionably, first in time and foremost in importance was the desperation of abject poverty to which a single-crop economy had reduced the people of the Southeast during the Great Depression. The conditions prevailing in those austere years firmly planted in the minds of the region's leaders a conviction that cotton, corn, mules and starvation wages could only lead to an ever mounting misery. Then, even while the dark clouds of depression hung low over the land, a bright ray of hope suddenly broke through. The pulp and paper industry rushed for the door which the research of Dr. Charles Herty had opened, when he demonstrated an economical process by which Southern pine could be utilized for paper manufacturing. The pay rolls provided by the great mills themselves were the least important result of their great southward migration. Of more significance was the desperately needed money which started flowing back into the hinterland to the small farmers and relief-supported laborers as they began to supply the daily requirement of thousands of cords of wood for the mills to chew into pulp. Most important of all was the rapid rise in land values that soon followed, as the mills showed their eagerness to buy vast tracts of land for pine growing, at several times the price it had been bringing. Since land was still the region's principal asset, its tangible wealth multiplied almost overnight.

Then came the war. Because of its climate, the South was selected as the location for a heavily disproportionate share of the training camps and airfields. From them, vast sums of tax money flowed out into the region. Those were lush times also in the temperamental textile industry. In spite of controls, wages skyrocketed until they almost closed the traditionally wide difference between the rates prevailing in the South and East. Perhaps it was of even more significance that the wartime labor shortage jumped common labor rates from a dollar a day to a dollar an hour. For the first time in modern history, Southerners had money in their pockets and could forget their colonial status, their poverty and economic inferiority. The cockiness and self-confidence of the *nouveau riche* suddenly became almost as much a regional attribute of the older South as it is of Texas.

It was during those war boom years that the South built up an impressive record of industrial peace which would later serve as a great attraction to industry. It may have been simply that those wartime wages, by constrast with what Southerners had been used to, seemed too generous to impair by absenteeism or strikes. Be that as it may, the record was impressive enough to plant throughout industrial circles the impression that Southern labor had all the virtues a demanding employer could desire—steadiness, adaptability, intelligence and a deep-seated distrust of labor leaders and Northern labor organizations. Moreover, the wartime economic convulsions had brought the realization that there still remained on the worn-out farms of the Southeast and among the numerous progeny of those already in industry a vast number of potential industrial workers imbued with the industrial climate of the region, who would be deeply grateful for a steady job.

Lastly, soon after the close of the war, with the drive and temerity born of these new conditions, a final organized assault was made upon the discriminatory freight rates which had existed since rate regulation was first undertaken. By long-established precedent those rates, which had been established to perpetuate a colonial type economy in the South, in effect exacted an export tariff on Southern manufacturing by prescribing low rates on raw materials and high rates on manufactured products traveling north, without similar exactions on southbound traffic. By a series of tilts, concessions were gradually gained, culminating in the late forties, when the last of the most glaring discriminations was abolished. Soon afterward, the great Northern steel companies who controlled the Southern steel industry centered in Birmingham found it discreet to abolish the notorious colonial "Pittsburgh Plus" pricing system which had required of Birmingham steel, even if delivered in its own back yard, an additional charge equal to the freight charge from Pittsburgh, thereby protecting the Northern steel industry against Southern competition.

Into the hospitable atmosphere created by all these almost simultaneous developments, industry came to be welcomed with open arms. It came because of the climate. But the climate the Lord created here had little to do with it. Plant location engineers are not taken in by chamber of commerce brochures reciting some delightful-sounding figure as the region's mean annual temperature, and they are not frightened away by an admission that in a given year the temperatures ran the gamut from zero to well above a hundred—indicating a climate far from ideal. No, the climate which has been proving so irresistible to industry is rather that created by the people, the traditions, and the institutions of the South. Many people have the impression that, among the institutions luring industry into their midst, their state chambers of commerce and development boards loom large —an impression which is obviously specious when one realizes that practically every state has such organizations, busily canceling each other out. And many better-staffed and better-financed development boards in other sections are proving themselves helpless to stem a migration of industry away from their states. Moreover, the larger industries usually do not consult these development boards until they have selected their new plantsite. Nevertheless, while these organizations cannot be credited with accessions of new industry, they play essential parts in attracting it. They prepare and widely distribute information on the location and attributes of possible sites and on the state level they spread the official welcome mat.

Of immeasurably greater effectiveness in luring new industry is the welcome mat displayed at the grass roots level, by the communities themselves. That this is true is clearly indicated by incidents in connection with the selection of the sites of two of the largest new enterprises of the Carolinas. To entice one of them, the people of the community under consideration quickly raised $100,000 by voluntary subscription that the proposed site might be offered to the company as a gift from the community. The gift was gratefully accepted. Shortly afterward the local hospital received a $100,000 donation from the new plant. Unquestionably, that donation by the community brought the decision to locate the plant there, not because of the financial benefit inherent in the gift, but rather because of the tangible evidence of warm welcome it bespoke. In the other case, the community under consideration had a local law which granted new industries a five-year exemption from property taxes, other than those for school purposes. After the site was acquired and the plant was under construction, an official of the company reported that, although the tax exemption statute had been a salient point in the selection of the site, the company did not desire to claim the exemption if its taxes were needed for essential community functions. Again the important factor was the tangible evidence of welcome. So it has been, over and over again, that company after company has picked its site for its new plant in response to local welcome mats. Assuming, of course, that the proposed site meets the basic requirements of the plant, all other considerations are of minor importance if the plant is sufficiently desired by the community, for, if the industrial climate is favorable at the grass roots level, that climate will inevitably be felt in the higher levels of government, there to serve as the best insurance against discriminatory taxes and burdensome and costly regulation.

Northern critics of the South persistently overlook the paramount importance of the welcome mat when they charge the South with securing new industries by means of low taxes, low wages, and an absence of labor unions. Officials of DuPont, Westinghouse, General Electric and Celanese know full well that the low tax rates they find in the rural or small town locale of a proposed site will not persist after their plant has converted that community into an urban center. Also they know that the small and steadily diminishing wage differential between the North and the South will probably not be an important factor for long. And, since the labor-cost portion of a manufactured article steadily falls as machinery is improved, wage rates become steadily a less important element in the cost of the product, while other expenses such as machinery costs, taxes, and insurance become increasingly momentous. Consequently, efficiency, steadiness, loyalty and a minimum of absenteeism are becoming more sought after attributes in labor than low wages. And those qualities are much more likely to be found among men who highly value their jobs, are grateful for them and intend to run no risk of losing them. And in a contented and appreciative labor force and community, unprejudiced by a long siege of anti-industrial propaganda, unionism will long find the going rough—the climate unfavorable.

If I am correct in my belief that the conditions most sought for by industry are an ample supply of labor with those qualities and a genuine welcome from the community itself, and I think I am, it would explain why the Carolinas have experienced such a relatively enormous influx of industry in recent years. No other section had suffered comparable economic distress and privation. No other section was so convinced that it would have to alter its whole economic life. And no other section had a comparable supply of naturally steady, intelligent, but poverty-stricken and all but unemployed workers who stood ready to jump at an opportunity for steady industrial employment. Consequently, no other section could as convincingly, from laborer to chief executive, put out the welcome mat. That is why more than forty-five hundred new plants were established in the Carolinas during the first eight postwar years, lured there by the industrial climate.

But the story of this influx of industry is far from the whole story. The lush profits of the war years stimulated the long-established textile industry to undertake a widespread improvement and expansion program. Many expanded laterally, simply doing more of what they were already doing. More important were the vertical expansions, the installation of bleacheries and finishing plants to end the long-standing necessity of shipping gray goods north for finishing. Another widespread change was taking place in the old mills of the New South era. In their dealings with a new generation of better-educated, relatively prosperous, more independent and self-respecting labor, those characterless mill villages were proving embarrassing, and expensive too, now that the demands of a higher standard of living were having to be met. Village after village was put up for sale, the operatives being given the first opportunity to buy the houses they were occupying. While most of those villages have not yet been sold, the handwriting looms large on the wall; and there is every reason to believe that, before many years have passed, the company village will be as definitely in the historical past as the "street" and quarters of a Santee rice plantation.

So America finds itself in the mid-twentieth century still with a frontier—an industrial frontier with its foci in the Carolinas and in Texas. If it is argued that a term with such an aboriginal connotation is not properly applicable to what is happening in the South today, I will point out that here we find people long socially stranded, leading a rugged existence in the face of all manner of adversity, but inspired with a determination to build something better with what they have at hand, people possessed with a limitless enthusiasm for what they are accomplishing. If in the face of such a response there is still an insistence that there can be no frontier in an old region like Carolina, I will surrender the term and say that Carolinians today have the optimistic outlook of a sorely tried traveler, who has finally reached the highroad to his destination, after many a false turn down tortuous and agonizing dead end roads. To me there seems to be little distinction between the spirit inspired: in either case, a robust, confident optimism.

❦ ❦ ❦ ❦ ❦ *32. Green gold*

*F*our centuries ago, the hope of finding yellow gold led the intrepid De Soto and Pardo expeditions far into the trackless hills and mountains of Carolina. Had they found some of the great gold nuggets, running up to twenty-four pounds, the discovery of which in the region between Charlotte and Salisbury was to set off a gold rush in the late eighteenth century, the whole course of American history might have been greatly altered; for it was only Spain's distraction by gold-rich Mexico and South America that made possible the successful establishment of Carolina as a British domain. Within a few decades after their discovery, the promise of those rich nuggets had proved disappointing, and, when the California gold rush started, the Southern Piedmont ceased to be the nation's principal gold-producing area. Its mining operations soon languished and finally died.

Almost another hundred years were to pass before Caro-

linians would discover the true gold of their countryside—
rich, extensive, regenerating lodes of green gold—the wealth
inherent in the chlorophyll cells of the leaves and needles
of the forest giants, and the grasses and pea vines of the
prairie hills through which the gold-hungry Spaniard pressed.
They had seen the forest only as an obstruction to a wide
view of their route, the grass and native peas only as a
hindrance to their progress. That men in quest of quick
riches should have so regarded our native trees and plants is
easily understandable, for it took two and a half centuries
and many wide and disastrous discursions to demonstrate
even to the more patient and less avaricious British that the
wealth of this region lay largely in the plants with which nature had endowed the land. These were its regenerating
lodes of green gold, and through their utilization the region
could at last come into its own with a stable, diversified and
prosperous economy. Back into history from that recent realization stretches a long story of tragic misuse of those resources.

That story begins with the first months of the settlement
at Albemarle Point. Twelve cedar planks, which were received in the Barbados from Carolina, were sent on to England in the fall of 1670 "as the first fruits of that glorious
province." Thereafter the Proprietors demanded that the
ships sent over with colonists and supplies be returned laden
with cedar, "pyne," "cyprus," or poplar, thereby working
at cross-purposes with their colonial officials who complained
that the immediate profits offered by the products of the
forests distracted the settlers from planting crops for their
own sustenance. Many were soon supporting themselves by
the cash returns of the colony's first manufacturing—the production of pitch, tar and turpentine from the apparently
limitless stands of longleaf pine, extending across the pine
flats far into the interior. The green gold of the forest kept

the ships coming to the colony, kept them bringing supplies and settlers.

Even so, except where the timber could be readily loaded on boats, it was generally a liability, an impediment to settlement. Consequently, removal by destruction soon became the rule, and removal for manufacture or export the exception. As the settlements pushed up the river and the land clearings multiplied, there was no market for the bulk of the timber being removed. The timbers resulting from the clearings near the river were disposed of by dumping them into the stream. But the convenience of that natural conveyor belt was only available near its banks. Elsewhere the task of land clearing was far more arduous. The trees had to be felled, rolled together in great piles and burnt— a gigantic undertaking in a land where animal power was scarce. In the uplands the more common practice of the early settlers was simply to girdle the trees and leave them standing, to be gradually removed through the years as they were needed for firewood. The value of such lumber as was produced was little more than the labor cost of its production and transportation. It included little or no stumpage value to the landowner. Too often he was glad to get rid of the timber as an obstruction to his cultivation of the land. It was a long time before Carolinians began to think of their standing timber in terms of potential wealth. Even down to days within the memory of some still living, when farmers desired to clear new ground, they frequently staged "log rollings," to which friends and neighbors came with their teams, to help pile and fire the host's obstructing forest cover and to receive payment in barbecue and "likker." By the time Carolinians began to entertain a suspicion that their timber perhaps represented the region's greatest natural resource, the Confederate war had come and gone. Gone also was perhaps three fourths of the original timber stand.

The next significant development in the story of Southern timber stemmed from the coincidence of exhaustion of the Northeastern and Lake timber supplies, the demands of a rapidly developing postwar North and a South whose people stood in desperate need of profitable employment and of returns from the property that was almost their only remaining asset—land. To answer these needs Northern capital, Southern labor and Southern timber combined to create the era of the large-scale lumber mills, intent upon cutting and marketing what remained of the Southern forests—to cut and get out when the job was done. Raw lumber mill towns sprang into being, and old towns were given a new lease on life as the big mills got into operation. Railroads were pushed out from the mills into the vast timber holdings the sawmills had acquired at ridiculously low prices. Into the hungry mills came what remained of Carolina's original growth timber— cypress, sweet gum and oak from the swamps, pines from the uplands—cypresses that showed by their growth rings that they were seedlings when the armies of Charlemagne were unifying Western Europe to check the encroachments of the Moors through Spain, pines that were saplings when Columbus first sighted Hispaniola. For some four decades centered on 1900 this large-scale stripping of the land continued. Careless of the future, the methods employed in these operations were perhaps the most wasteful and destructive of any logging operations in the history of the country. By the time the first world war came along most of the big mills had seriously depleted or exhausted their timber supply. The lumber demands of the war served to give the forests of Carolina and the South their *coup de grace*. A few years of active demand and most of the saw-log size second growth was gone. Uncontrolled fires swept the cutover forest areas killing most of the trees left by the loggers. With fatalistic apathy, Southerners saw those fires, year by year, sear their countryside, killing the seedlings and saplings of the commercial species while

sparing the weed varieties such as scrub oaks or "blackjacks."
Most of the once exalted forests of Carolina presented a desolate, lifeless, fire-blackened picture during those years. Carolinians had written off their forests as an exhausted resource,
as completely gone with the wind as their glorious past.
They were gone, but the sorrow of their passing was tem-
pered by gratitude for the mighty part their harvesting had
played in assisting the defeated and discouraged region to
gain its economic feet once again.

Then, fitfully at first, a fresh breeze, from a new direction began to blow through these fallen forests. To the
astonishment of those who had written off Carolina timber as
a depleted asset, lumber kept coming to market. Little porta-
ble sawmills were finding good, if limited, stands of pine
that had somehow got started in spite of the regular fall
and spring wood fires, stands that had started where the big
mills first operated and had attained sawmill size by the
time they moved out three or four decades later. And in the
wide swamps of the Santee, Congaree and Wateree where
fires rarely penetrate, the small operators were finding good
hardwood veneer blocks and flooring logs, sometimes within
a dozen years of the time big mills had cut them over. These
were exciting, thought-provoking facts; especially so, coming as they did when Gifford Pinchot was attaining national
fame through his ardent advocacy of forest conservation and
protection. Almost overnight Southerners awakened to the
fact that their forests were far from done for, that, on the
contrary, they held immense promise for a bountiful future.
In response to this sudden awakening, the states established
forestry departments; forest fire towers were suddenly part of
the landscape and the once ubiquitous autumnal smell of
burning woods soon became all but a memory. That was in
the late twenties and early thirties. In the little better than
two decades that have passed since that awakening, the face
of Carolina has vastly changed. Life and vigor have returned

to the forests. Nature has softly carpeted its once fire-blackened floor. Hundreds and hundreds of miles of neatly planted young pine forests stretch back from the road where the outlook had been a depressing expanse of worn-out and abandoned fields.

Last year the forest services of the Carolinas supplied at cost almost fifty million pine seedlings for such plantations. Every year this figure jumps substantially. This rising demand for seedlings is understandable, for those pine plantations will grow a cord of wood per acre per year until they are saw-timber size about twenty-five years after planting. In dollars and cents that annual increment is about the market value of the land itself before it was planted in pines and before the general public awakened to the tree-growing potential of Southern land, good and poor. When their tree-growing potential was realized, the price of Southern lands rose more rapidly than those of any other region. When those plantings reach twenty-odd years old they grow on the average some 350 board feet of timber per year, an annual added value of twice the prewar market value of the land itself. Nowhere in the country, except in a small rainy section of the Pacific Northwest, can forests produce at a comparable rate. The only commercial forests which exceed the Southern pine plantations in rate of production are the hardwood forests of the big rivers of the South such as those of the Santee. In those swamps, logging operations commonly follow each other at twenty-year intervals, with an incredible harvest at every cutting.

A generation ago many Southerners had never even heard of foresters and few had ever seen one. Today the South is the largest, richest, most diversified and fastest growing field of forestry practice in the country, with the greatest area of privately owned forest lands under professional forest management—and more practicing foresters than any other section. Quickly they have become an essential ingredient of the economic life of the South, for no longer can a sawmill man buy "all the timber, both standing and fallen" on a tract of land. Instead he is offered the trees marked for removal by a professional forester, who has marked them with the purpose of keeping the forest reproducing itself at its maximum capacity. Consequently, as this selective cutting practice becomes increasingly widespread, the volume added by growth in Southern forests becomes greater and greater. A few years ago the annual growth lagged far behind the timber removal rate. Today the growth exceeds the harvest. So the story of Southern forests has completed a full cycle. To the early set-

tlers their forests were "inexhaustible." A generation ago they were "exhausted"—gone forever. Today they are again "inexhaustible"—provided only that they are protected, properly managed and selectively harvested.

These developments have added up to some phenomenal facts and figures. They now enable the South with less than a fifth of the country's land area (and much of that fifth in cultivation) to produce almost half of all the timber needs of the nation, and, at the same time, to maintain a timber growth rate which already equals the harvest drain and will soon exceed it. For the Carolinas these developments laid a firm foundation for their wood-using industries, now grossing well over a billion dollars a year. These developments irresistibly beckoned to the pulp and paper industry and resulted in a headlong rush of that industry to the South with rapidity of pace and capital investment unequaled since the days of the railroad building boom. Overnight, while still in the grip of the Great Depression of the thirties, the South became the principal pulp and paper producing section of the country. A few miles north of the Georgetown mouth of the Santee, the International Paper Company built the world's largest kraft paper board plant. On the Cooper River above Charleston, the West Virginia Pulp and Paper Company put another huge pulp mill. Together these two mills daily consume the annual growth on five thousand acres of timber land, and yet they have no fear of a failure of their supply of pulpwood, for already the South has amply demonstrated that it can cut from its forests a greater volume of wood than was ever produced in the days of the big mills and that it can continue to do so indefinitely without ever again depleting its forest resources.

After touring the South a few years ago, a former chief of the United States Forest Service said:

The Southern forests are supplying now a greater volume—and a far greater value—of forest products than they ever yielded in the heyday of virgin timber. The yearly growth of Southern forests, in all sizes and grades of wood, is six billion cubic feet. Their overall growth is enough to supply, in cubic volume, all the products now cut, and still pay toll of 14 percent to forest fires and other destructive agencies. . . . I know of no parallel in world history of a forest recovery so rapid and carrying with it such industrial progress as that of the South during the last 30 years. . . . The golden age of the American forest industry has just begun. Look ahead to the industrial future of the South when all its forest lands are producing full crops of wood and employment and carrying their potential of plant investment.

Symbolizing this forest epic is the famous color photograph of a pine seedling seen against the protecting hand of a forest ranger, a photograph which has been reproduced millions of times, to become the top symbol of forest conservation. Appropriately, this picture was taken in the pinelands a few miles north of the great bend of the Santee, in the region that learned well (by long and painful experience) the lesson told in its brief symbolism.

For two and a half centuries after that early day when the colonial governor complained of the distraction of the settlers by the cash returns from logging, the story of Carolina agriculture was composed of a succession of money crops, ever luring the Carolina farmer away from balanced sustenance farming. Lumber, pitch, tar and turpentine were followed by indigo from the West Indies and rice from Madagascar, tobacco from tropical America and cotton from the Orient. The cultivation of rice required conditions and capital which were not available to most farmers. It was exclusively a planter's crop and not a farmer's crop. And yet it was the only one of all the Carolina money crops that was edible, a fact which added a special hazard to the economy of the Carolina farmer, for, when prices failed, actual want was frequently his lot, even with a bountiful crop mature in his fields. But the lure of occasional big cash returns was such that year after year he was willing to stake everything on his money crop. Other aspects of good husbandry were so neglected that the Carolina farmer eventually came to deserve his reputation for being the poorest farmer in the land.

Of these false gods of the soil, cotton was far the worst offender, for only cotton captured the whole of Carolina from the sea islands to the mountains. Its early offering of returns so bountiful that the Carolina farmer could easily buy those necessities of life which farmers elsewhere had to struggle to produce fixed its slavery on the land for generations.

Year by year as the fertility of the soil diminished, the cash returns became ever smaller and smaller. Year after year the soil was exposed to erosion by the clean tillage not only of the cotton fields but also of the cornfields, which produced the food for the mules needed to till the cotton. Especially in the Piedmont, the region's richest section, lands which had once been such that "a walking stick might then with care be thrust far into the ground, and a wild turkey could be tracked a whole day, so mellow was the soil, and the peavines, which grew thick, could be tied over a horse's back," by the end of the nineteenth century were all too often eroded hillsides with the red subsoil, hard and sterile, exposed, stripped of its fertile topsoil. From the Confederate war on, well into the twentieth century, year by year, as yields diminished, more and more Carolina farmers gave up the struggle and abandoned their worn-out acres to the elements and moved into one of the new mill villages, or departed westward in search of fresher, less manhandled soil.

For those who stayed on the farms, each successive year averaged a smaller cash return and a lower standard of living. The prophets of the New South clearly saw that a single cash crop was the road to ruin and boldly directed their attack against it. Dramatically, Henry Grady illustrated the lost independence of the small farmer with this description of his economy:

[He] gets up at the alarm of a Connecticut clock. Puts his Chicago suspenders on a pair of Detroit overalls. Washes his face with Cincinnati soap in a Philadelphia wash pan. Sits down to a Grand Rapids table and eats Indiana hominy fried in St. Joseph lard, bacon from Kansas City, and biscuits made of flour from Tennessee all cooked by a St. Louis stove. Drinks a cup of coffee from Brazil or a cup of tea from China. Goes out to a lot fenced with Pittsburgh woven wire. Puts a St. Louis bridle on a Missouri mule, rides to the field in a Kentucky wagon. Hitches up to a Syracuse plow. Works all day on a farm covered by an Ohio mortgage. Comes home that night and reads a chapter of the Bible printed in Chicago. Says a prayer written in Jerusalem. Crawls into a Grand Rapids bed and covers himself with a blanket from New Jersey, only to be kept awake by a hound dog—the only home raised product on the farm.

The plight of the farmer Grady pictured was bad enough; but, multiplied by hundreds of thousands, his lost independence and his sad plight spelled for the whole of the old cotton section the same sad fate. In hopes of solving the problem, a "live-at-home" and diversification campaign was inaugurated as a companion to the aggressive campaign for industrialization. But the counsel of the wise fell mostly on deaf ears and cotton continued to hold ruinous sway until the thirties, when the Great Depression stalked the land and the South was designated as the nation's "Number one economic problem," largely because of that ruinous rule. However, by the time that phrase was coined, the processes which would bring about a cure of the sick section were already at work. Soil exhaustion, the advent of the boll weevil from Mexico, depression prices and the competition of the newer fields of the Gulf States so completely prostrated most Carolina cotton farmers that little choice was left them. The necessity that they turn to other crops was at last too patent to avoid.

Sheer necessity spoke with an authoritative voice where precept could not be heard.

Hesitantly, with misgivings at first, but with gradually increasing definiteness Carolina turned from its dependence on cotton. That is not to say that cotton is gone from the region. Cotton fields are still a familiar scene in Carolina, but the crop no longer dominates the farm economy as it did for so long. In two decades—suddenly, by comparison with cotton's long sway—Carolinians have equipped themselves with many baskets for their eggs.

In South Carolina two thirds of the area once in cotton is now devoted to other crops. In much of the Low Country, tobacco has taken over as the dominant crop, and vegetable produce is rising in importance. South of the Santee, where a generation ago the scene was a monotonous expanse of cotton and corn, now lush pastures, wide fields of grain and extensive groves of pecan trees dominate the scene. In the sand hills, where the view had been a depressing picture of poverty supported by "bumblebee" cotton, stunted corn and blackjack oaks, now grow miles upon miles of thrifty young pine plantations, giving a new hope to a naturally sterile region. Pulpwood and lumber production on a tree-culture basis have supplanted cotton in importance in the rough hill country of the lower Piedmont. South of the Saluda, broiler production was suddenly a multimillion-dollar business, but even so it lagged far behind the proportions attained by poultry production in the North Carolina reaches of the river. Concentrated there, North Carolina's broiler production increased sixfold in a decade, to become a twenty-five-million-dollar crop. Up between the Broad and the Catawba, Chester County went heavily into dairy cattle. Of the seventy thousand acres of Greenwood County formerly in cotton but five thousand remain loyal. Clover and grain have taken over thirty thousand acres. There the price of beef is of far more consequence than the cotton market. York turned to turkeys and peaches. The picturesque foothills of Spartanburg County are now each spring blanketed with pink peach blossoms. Almost suddenly that county found itself the foremost peach-producing county of the nation, contributing heavily to South Carolina's position as the leading peach-producing state—that in the county whose mills consume more cotton than any other in the country. Vineyards, truck farms and apple orchards extend on up into the mountains. In all the wide region of the upper Catawba, row crops are fast being pushed from the scene by pasture lands and grain fields. And many, if not most, of these pastures are not ordinary pastures. They have been specially prepared and seeded for maximum nutrition and year-round grazing. The development of these seeded pastures is perhaps the most significant aspect of the entire agricultural revolution which is taking place in the Carolinas. It has put the region into the cattle business with a substantial competitive advantage over the Western range country. And Carolina farmers are fairly jumping at the opportunity these pastures now offer. In the past three years the area devoted to developed pastures has doubled. Even down in the Low Country, great tractors are everywhere clearing away the forests from extensive areas for new pasture lands. Up in Iredell County, where the Catawba turns south (in the depression years one of the most stricken regions), the farms have gone to grass, with three million dollars a year in milk sales as the result.

There is yet another change in the Carolina countryside that is worthy of mention. In the past few years more than fifteen thousand farm ponds have been built in the two states, usually for the dual purpose of supporting water for livestock and for growing fish. The application of commercial fertilizers to these pond waters, to stimulate scientifically their fish production, is an accepted practice. Fish culture is the latest, and undoubtedly the most pleasant, facet of diversified farming. Now, with irrigation looming large on the horizon, these farm ponds, and the countless more that will soon be built, will take on the added function of serving as reservoirs for irrigation water.

If this account of the changing face of the earth in the country of the Santee waters has given the impression that poverty has been suddenly banished from that region and all there is now "peaches and cream," such an impression would be far from true. There are still many poor whites, mostly in the lower Piedmont sections, and a vast number of Negroes, mostly in the Low Country, who have been completely unaffected by the agricultural revolution taking place around them. They live in abject poverty from cotton picking to cotton picking, with their next crop always mortgaged for their current subsistence rations. Limited in education, trapped by their environment and inured to an abject existence, only death will free most of them from their slavery to cotton. So, on the average, as the statistics show, the Carolinas are still down near the bottom in per capita earthly goods. But the changes which have been related here are having their effect on those statistics. They show that while the Carolinas are still poor they are becoming less poor far faster than the nation as a whole. Even the most rapid of agricultural revolutions is a slow affair. The improved methods and new crops spread by example and not by fiat; and there is a long lapse of time between the seeding of a pasture or the planting of an orchard and the publication of the statistics reflecting the steers and the fruit sent to market.

Mention of the New South brings cottonmills to mind. Lately one hears much of the Changing South, and those words suggest grain fields, pastures, orchards and protected forest lands. Of what is happening, there is a saying abroad in Carolina that everything is on the move—cotton going west, cattle coming east, Negroes going north and industries coming south.

❦ ❦ ❦ ❦ ❦ *33. River lure*

*O*rion high in the sky, Venus shining jewel bright above the faint outline of a hill across the river to the west, and a faint pink promise of dawn creeping up under the tall hilltop pines to the east—all enhance that otherworldly atmosphere of the predawn stillness as the expectant fishermen start down the steep rocky path towards the blood-quickening roar of the river far below. For hundreds of years, naked red men, no doubt with kindred expectancy, had scrambled down this same hill from their high perched camp, with traps and spears, for then as now this was a favorite spot of the prized striped bass or rockfish (*roccus lineatus*). To this section of the river, where the rapids begin, from time immemorial has come this beautiful game fish, up from the sea in the early spring, to spawn in the swift flowing waters among the rocks. And here the rock bass linger, throughout the summer, before returning in a leisurely way to the ocean 150 miles or more down-stream.

The foot of the path reached, our fishermen proceed cautiously to the rapids upstream through a maze of slippery rocks, which during the daylight hours are deep beneath the river waters—as long as the turbines are running at the upstream power dams. But when evening brings a lessened demand from industry, the penstocks are closed and in the hours that follow the river diminishes to but a wraith of its daytime robustness, leaving wide bands of wet rocks exposed along either bank. The rapids reached, each fisherman goes into a prayerful huddle with himself, asking himself what he would be attracted by today, if he were a not very hungry striper. Now this indecision is quickly ended by a rapid series of "champs" and splashes, startlingly loud above the tumult of the rapids. Every heart doubles its beat. Trembling with excitement, each sportsman fumblingly puts on the same old lure he always uses and casts towards the continuing slaps and splashes. Muffled oaths from one, as spray erupts once, twice, and again, as a big one persistently follows and strikes, each time a little short of his incoming plug. Another cast back to the same spot and a hungry one lunges at it, seemingly before the plug hits the water. A whoop, a long, singing whine from the reel and the fight is on. Two hundred—three hundred feet of line gone and the reel still sings. Somewhere downstream and towards the far side of the river there's a burst of spray visible through the gloom. There's a moment of incredulous amazement before the realization that that's his fish way over there surfacing at the end of its first frantic run! Follow the fish down the river so that he won't peel off all the remaining line with his next run. Weak-kneed, recklessly heedless of the slippery rocks, our angler stumbles along the water's edge, all the time pulling and reeling to build up a reserve of line for the next run. Suddenly, the reel's singing again as Roccus makes another run for it! "Lord, don't let him wrap that line around that snag out there! Don't let him break this taut, singing line!" Again he's pulling and reeling in, bit by bit. Now he's safely by the snag. Nearer and nearer in, after each less determined run. Finally, the beautiful striped silver form is visible through the current a few feet from the bank. Tenterhooks! A last minute prayer: "Don't let him get away now!" A sigh of gratitude and relief as the big fish flops helplessly out of his element among the rocks high above the water's edge. Other fishermen are now coming downstream in similar maneuvers. Smaller fish are being landed above with less finesse, amid intermittent silver sprays of fleeing, fingerling shad.

Full daylight dawns and the resounding splashes of the feeding "rocks" move down out of the shoals and along the farther bank of the calmly flowing river below, like a dancing chorus leaving the stage. Soon there is only the roar of the rapids, an occasional show of gold as a playing carp rolls on the top, and here and there a gar breaking the surface, opening and shutting aimlessly the long, toothed scissors of his beak.

Experience has taught the fisherman that fishing is over for the day, that it is highly unlikely that schools of little shad will run back up to the rapids, bringing the stripers in pursuit. Still they linger, to drink in the peace and beauty of the first hour of daylight on the river. They stay on to see the careless echelons of the snowy egrets dropping individuals here and there along the riverbanks as far as the eye can follow them downstream, to hear the sweet, resonant "tea kettle—tea kettle" of the Carolina wren, with wonder that a creature so small can produce sound in such volume. They stay to see a lone great blue heron in ponderous flight go by upstream, to thrill at the vibrant whistling wings, as a flight of summer duck streaks by, and then to watch, with

amusement and intellectual admiration, a great flock of crows
on their way from their roost upriver, becoming raucously
communicative and wheeling to pick up safer altitude as
their vedettes spy those suspicious characters on the rocks
below. Finally, they stay to see the sun strike, first the tops,
and then down the green forest wall along the far bank,

to admire the great snowy trunks of the sycamores, the
majestic bulk of the vine-draped cottonwoods with their
leaves quivering discordantly in the first morning breeze.

Suddenly they are conscious of change in the splashing
background roar of the rapids. It has grown in tempo, volume and liquidity. Upstream, frothy waves span the whole
breadth of the river. Seven fifteen: the river has gone to

work. The workaday demand for power is being answered. The penstocks have been opened, and the turbines have begun to spin. The world's work has begun and is summoning those truants there on the riverbank.

Set late for the reluctant, nature's summer alarm clock, the thorax of an unseen cicada, goes off with the vibrant sound of a high-pitched buzz saw—and tapers off to stillness.

❧ ❧ ❧ ❧ ❧ 34. Living waters

*A*t Old Fort, up under the shadow of Mount Mitchell, the townsfolk get their drinking water from the sparkling Catawba as it rushes by, a clear mountain stream. There it meets its first duty as a workaday river. After giving the town its water supply, it furnishes the large industrial water requirements of a rayon-finishing mill, receives that water back with its burden of industrial waste, picks up the town's sewer effluent and flows on through Pleasant Gardens, to Marion. There it picks up the wastes from that town, a yarn bleaching and dyeing plant and nine hosiery mills. After resting in the sparkling blue body of Lake James, it takes a hundred-foot fall through the power generator turbines, to add another to its multiple services to the industry it has already twice served. As it passes Morganton and Lenoir, it receives in Lake Rhodhiss the creeks bearing the industrial and domestic wastes of those towns and of Valdese; it gives Granite Falls its water supply, turns the generators of the Rhodhiss powerhouse, and carries away the waste of the large cotton mills below the dam. As the Catawba flows slowly through Lake Hickory, its services measurably increase. It provides the water supply and receives much of the waste from the industrially active city of Hickory, and contributes yet again to the region's power supply. Twice more in the next dozen miles it performs that latter service—at the Oxford and Lookout Shoals powerhouses.

Forty miles farther downstream, after serving cotton mills along the way, the Catawba enters Mountain Island Reservoir where it is called on to perform an entirely new industrial function. There it supplies one hundred thousand gallons a minute of its cool water to operate the condensers of the great River Bend steam-electric generating plant. After giving up Charlotte's water requirements and passing through the turbines of the Mountain Island powerhouse, the river enters its most burdensome and hazardous reach, a thirty-five-day hesitation in Lake Catawba. Almost every tributary entering that lake bears a heavy pollution burden from the highly concentrated industrial region surrounding it. Into it comes also the South Fork Catawba with the waste loads of the Hickory-Newton-Lincolnton manufacturing region. The lake directly receives quantities of acid from a dye plant, caustic soda from the same plant and from a cotton-mercerizing plant and from a woolen-blanket mill. And it gives water into the water system of Belmont and the neighboring mills. Soon its waters will be doing the second big cooling job. When Duke's new steam-electric plant is constructed, more than a hundred million gallons a day will be pumped from the lake's Catawba branch, through the plant's condensers, and released into the lake's South Fork branch.

After again turning the wheels of industry as they pass out of Lake Catawba, the waters of the Catawba supply water to Fort Mill and receive its wastes. As the river passes Rock Hill, it supplies that city with its water requirements, the Celanese acetate rayon plant with some fifty million gallons a day and the Rock Hill Printing and Finishing Company with twelve million gallons a day, and receives the heavy pollution of the latter plant and of the city's sewers at nearly the same point that it receives Sugaw Creek, with the effluent from Charlotte's sewers and industries.

A score of miles farther downstream, Spring's Grace Bleachery takes 7,500,000 gallons a day from the river and gives it back with a further burden. The resting periods which follow in the Fishing Creek, Great Falls and Rocky Creek reservoirs permit the digestion of the vast amount of organic matter which the river has received after leaving Lake Catawba. By the time its waters reach Wateree Pond, they have purified themselves sufficiently to permit that twenty-five-mile-long lake to become a water-sports and fishing resort of considerable proportions. Fed by the wastes the river has received along its course, much as a farm pond is fed by commercial fertilizer, Wateree Pond has become a fishing Mecca. Each season some twenty-five thousand fishermen purchase licenses to fish its waters.

After dropping seventy-eight feet through the Wateree powerhouse, the Catawba waters, which have now become the waters of the Wateree, receive the effluent from Du Pont's acrylic fiber plant and the sewage of Camden. In the next hundred miles, as it leisurely flows through the Low Country, the river is relatively free of its man-imposed duties. It has but to turn Santee-Cooper's generators, before approaching Charleston, in the Cooper River's bed. In the Charleston neighborhood, it rounds out its work by receiving the untreated wastes of eight sewer systems and the industrial wastes of the great kraft paper mill of the West Virginia Pulp and Paper Company.

Much of the work of the tributaries of the Catawba-Wateree-Santee-Cooper has been, of necessity, omitted from this account. Entirely omitted also, lest this account become too tedious, is the at least equal performance of the Congaree-Broad-Saluda portions of the Santee system. In the reader's mind these works of the river should be added to those recounted.

That a river can take unto itself these functions and burdens and not become a foul open sewer is one of the more important wonders of nature. The key to that wonder is its living water.

It is that living water with which an unviolated river is naturally endowed that gives it a remarkable resemblance to a living creature. Nature has filled every drop of its life-giving waters with myriads of living organisms. In fact it is the actions and reactions of these organisms that endow a river with most of the qualities that make it useful to man. It is those bacteria and plankton that sustain the aquatic insect life which in turn supports the fish life of the stream. And those same microscopic animals and plants are in turn supported by the organic matter they consume from the water, whether it be the deceased generations of the animal and plant life of the watershed, or the human industrial wastes that find their way to the river. Mile after mile, as the river flows towards the sea, constantly picking up contamination, those organisms are equally constantly at work, consuming, digesting and altering the polluting substances—rejuvenating and purifying its life-giving waters. They are as essential to the health of a river, as essential to its digestive processes as bacteria are to human digestion. A river devoid of them would have little utility for man or beast, for, beyond the use of its water for the power inherent in its falling weight, it could only serve as a vehicle to carry waste matter, in undiminished foulness to the sea. Thus, in this "best of all possible worlds," rivers are naturally endowed with a wide variety of those beneficial organisms and it is their presence which makes the river act like a living creature—their absence, like a dead thing, albeit still writhing.

Like a living creature, a river in its natural state is capable of consuming, within limits, variable quantities of organic matter. But, if either is pushed beyond those limits, its digestive food becomes a poison, and death will result. From a river, so overtaxed, will arise the malodorous aroma of death, and except in name it will be no longer a river. Despoiled, it has descended to the status of an open sewer. That has been the sad fate of too many of our country's rivers. Many of them, honored in song and romance, are better avoided if those pleasant associations are to be retained.

Twice in our times the Santee system itself was threatened with the destruction of its vitality as a living water system. Both times a series of fortunate developments barely saved it.

The first time was during the second and third decade of this century. That was the period of the high tide of cotton and corn culture, when those crops reached their maximum acreage throughout the drainage area. The major threat then was the choking effect of the red clay washed from the hills of the extensive Piedmont area drained by the river. From those hills, no longer protected by forest and grass, every rain swept vast quantities of fine ground substance into the Santee tributaries and on into the river itself. The particles that make up most of that soil are so fine that they remained suspended in the water, even throughout its more sluggish reaches, and rivers with the relatively great fall of the Saluda, the Broad and the Catawba are too active in their natural flow to permit the sedimentation of even the larger suspended particles. So, during those years when the erosion of the Piedmont country was at its height, all those rivers ran as red as the clay hills through which they flowed. Into such turbid water the life-giving sunlight can pierce but a little way. Since without sunlight most beneficial bacteria and algae cannot survive, the living attributes of the streams declined to the vanishing point. Mud coated the larger aquatic plants, smothering them. With like lethal effects, it coated the spawn of most species of fish, preventing incubation, and further unbalancing the river life. Game fish disappeared, leaving the river to the carp, catfish and eels, for the game fish are sight feeders, and in such silt-laden waters they could no longer see their prey.

Weakened by this excess turbidity, the rivers of the Santee system were in no state of health to cope with the additional burdens which were just then being dumped into them in the form of the raw sewage of the fast-growing Piedmont towns and the industrial wastes of the region's early cotton finishing plants. It was at that critical time that the boll weevil came to the rescue. By discouraging cotton growing on marginal lands, the steeper and more gullied fields were given back to forest and grass. Better culture methods were required on the fields which were retained. Terracing, contour plowing and strip planting practices were increasingly adopted. The combined effect of these developments was a greatly decreased soil erosion and an enormously reduced silt load in the rivers. Contributing also to the threatened rivers at the same time were the construction and filling of the numerous great power reservoirs, the still waters of which permitted much of the river's burden of mud to settle to the bottom—a process costly to the power company in storage capacity, but a salvation to the health of the river itself. The wider aeration area provided by the surfaces of those lakes enhanced the river's capacity to assimilate its ever growing industrial and municipal pollution burden.

So it came to pass, in the years that followed, that gradually olive green displaced red clay as the characteristic hue of the Wateree-Catawba and the Saluda; and only the Broad continued to carry an undue burden of silt from the hills along its relatively lakeless course. The retrieved green of those waters was the green of the essential vitality they had recovered. Back came the game fish and back came the fishermen.

The next threat to the Santee as a vital living force was much more recent. It was an insidious threat born of the influx of water-dependent industry during the years since the close of World War II. With the water requirements of the nation increasing far faster than its population, and with many of the rivers of the older industrial sections already too polluted for further economical utilization by industries with exacting water requirements, it is understandable that the rivers rising in the high rainfall regions of the relatively lime-free, time-mellowed Southern Appalachians should be avidly sought for industrial use. Unquestionably, no other physical factor has played a more important part in the recent southward trek of industry than those bountiful, chemically hospitable waters. And the great Santee carries between its banks more of that luring resource than any other river of the Southeastern seaboard. The innate industrial hospitality of its waters is enhanced by the enormous spread of that hospitality—two thousand miles of river front encompassed in it and its major tributaries.

When one considers the fact that the waste matter of a single textile-finishing plant in some instances equals the pollution burden of the sewage of a city of 100,000 people, and that the manufacture of a ton of wood pulp requires 70,-000 gallons of water, that a pound of rayon requires 150 gallons and a yard of woolen goods 200 gallons, it gives some conception of the enormous added burden of the recent industrial influx all along the river from the mountains to the sea. This increased demand could not have been met except for the Santee System's decreased turbidity and its enhanced digestive capacity, resulting from the extensive power dam reservoirs, each of which serves much the same biological functions as the ordinary waste treatment plant. Those changes in the shape and condition of the river enabled it to receive and assimilate a far greater pollution load than most other rivers of comparable volume. But even so its ever growing pollution load was fast approaching its assimilative capacity. The awful threat posed by that approach brought legislative action in both the Carolinas—laws which will protect their rivers from new, untreated sources of infection, and gradually reduce the load they are already being called upon to bear. Thus an enlightened, conservation-minded public came to the rescue of the Santee waters just as the second threat to their vitality was reaching critical proportions. Already, in Lake Catawba, pollution was occasionally killing fish near the mouths of the more heavily contaminated creeks, and its waters were no longer safe for swimming. In the Rock Hill neighborhood the river was carrying a top pollution load. Without the installation of more and better waste treatment facilities, any increase in the river's work there might turn a local infection into a general infection with which the river might be unable to cope. At any time its burden might overreach its vitality, permitting the infection to spread from its focal point there on downstream into the lakes below, with widespread and disastrous results. The river's very life had been threatened.

It was to answer those challenges to the regenerating powers of our yet vital Carolina rivers that our new water-pollution laws were enacted—that those rivers might be kept alive.

Thus protected, the industrial potential of the bountiful waters of the Santee system has been enormously enhanced. And this is true even in the face of an almost certain widespread additional drain on its watercourses to provide for farm irrigation on a scale unprecedented in the East. Recent studies by Clemson College revealed that the annual increase in net returns from irrigated fields runs from $60 per acre of corn and $65 per acre of pasture to $275 per acre of tobacco—yield increases so great that in many instances the cost of the requisite irrigation equipment was recovered in a single season. The report of those amazing returns from irrigation was made just at the onset of the 1954 drought, the worst in the history of the Southeast. The lesson of the report was thus emphatically driven home. That is why widespread irrigation with Santee waters is a practical certainty of the immediate future.

Supplying life, by itself remaining vital—that is the story of the Santee's living waters.

❧ ❧ ❧ ❧ ❧ *35. The river remembers*

*T*his has been the story of what an old river remembers as its waters flow on through the ages. Today I stood upon a gentle hilltop beside the river at a spot where the evidence of time has lent the special charm of a fourth dimension. This hilltop, long an abandoned cotton field and now green with neat rows of head-high young loblolly pines, commands a magnificent view of the wide, turbulent shoals of the Wateree. In the peaceful meadow, between the hill and the river, white-faced cattle graze placidly, belly-deep in Johnson grass. Wheeling and screaming overhead, a flock of terns, far astray from their usual seaside abode, flash in the sunlight, while below stately snowy egrets lend elegant decoration to the numerous rocky islets which dot the wide frothy shoals.

Upstream nature's priority ends. There looms the austere concrete bulk of the eighty-foot-high Wateree Dam, athwart the whole valley, dwarfing the red brick powerhouse and its companion weird array of transformers and switches. Above the roar of the rushing water and the raucous screams of the fishing birds is heard the monotonous, high-pitched whine of the whirring generators, providing a tonal accompaniment to the scene as nature and industry harmonize in a strange duet.

Here, through the ages, men have written their story, a story still faintly legible in the earth itself, turning memory back, through the full sweep of time and man since he first came to this place by the river.

Here on the ground are fragments of handmade brick, once the foundation of a rude cabin whose long-forgotten tenant, in tilling his cotton patch, turned these furrows still discernible beneath the young pines. Here and there are piles of field stones he and his forebears painstakingly grubbed from the fields to spare their plowpoints. In a nearby old hedgerow bloom peach trees and chinaberries, descendants of those long ago planted near the shanty and shed.

A little way to the west, through the woods beyond the pine plantation, now all but hidden by briars and sumac thickets, runs the earthwork of an old railroad bed, abandoned for almost a half-century. For a while this was a busy route, as the work engines shuttled trainloads of rock from the quarries to the concrete mixing plant, and hauled the matrix on to be poured into the cofferdams at the damsite. For four years there was a ceaseless hum of activity, as the great dam slowly rose and took shape, to an accompaniment of a din of shrill whistles, grinding ratchets and the explosive popping off of safety valves, as the steam and compressed air construction monsters volubly bent to the task. Hidden in the woods beyond the old railroad bed are a group of great concrete monoliths, the old foundations of the concrete mixing plant of the project, resembling, strangely, but for their forestbound loneliness, the remains of an Assyrian temple.

If it were possible to stand here among these young pines and turn time back yet another hundred years, the southwest breeze would bring far different sounds: the heartfelt, sad melody of a gang of blacks at work, its rhythm undisturbed by the stonecutter's hammers. For in the woods behind the pine plantation, almost alongside the railroad of a later day, lies the great dry cut of Mills' and Blanding's Wateree Canal, with its expertly fashioned granite locks, all now indiscriminately repossessed by the forest. For then it was that their ambitious internal navigation system was being rushed up this river—the project of the day! Easing their backbreaking work with song, gangs of rented slaves struggled and strained to drag the great stumps from the route. Others interrupted their songs only to gee and haw at the

mule teams as they loaded and dumped the primitive drag pans with which the big ditch was cut. Yet others were heaving away at the block and tackle, hoisting heavy granite blocks into place in the locks. Perhaps, singing his heart out there among the sweating blacks, labored some undeveloped genius of music or poetry, unlettered and unknown, chained to a lifelong burden of physical toil, doomed to oblivion—his only monument his anonymous contribution to this all but forgotten cut across the red hills of the Wateree.

For a tragically ephemeral interlude the riverbanks continued to echo African melody, as the long narrow "mountain boats," laden with the produce of the stump-studded fields of the new plantations of the hill country, drifted slowly past down the new canal bound for the trading wharves of Camden or for transshipment upon larger river craft for Charleston. Soon the boats stopped passing. Through the neglected lock gates the water leaked out of the canal and the inexorable forest crept back.

Here on the ground beneath my feet these potsherds and bits of fashioned stone in evidence on every bare spot of this old field turn time back yet another two centuries or perhaps even half a millennium to the day when a cluster of Indian huts stood here and the Indian women skillfully fashioned the clay pots from which these fragments came—pots used, it may be, to prepare the warriors' paints for the fertility festival of spring planting season. For that occasion all the villages of the region would be gathering two miles down the river on the opposite bank, where the group of wooden temples stood, each on its great earthen mound, high above the river.

Where the cattle now graze in the river meadow below would have been the village cornfield, where the strong-limbed, naked, copper-skinned children played among the brown stalks of last year's generous crop. Beyond, the great wide river ran free and clear. This land was then so wide and bountiful that no man felt the necessity of calling any part of it his own. Here, reflecting on those simple days, the mind digresses—tempted by a doubt of the validity of our conception of progress.

The river remembers! But life, like the river, flows on and man, obsessed with immortality, looks ever forward into an uncertain future—uncertain in all but the certainty of change. Into that future I dare not push my imagination, limited as it is by the fetters of this our twentieth century. But, surely, as time moves on, as inexorably as these waters follow their age-old course to the sea, this old river will yet witness here as varied scenes as these it remembers from time long past.

☙ ☙ ☙ ☙ ☙ *Acknowledgments*

The dedication of this volume to my wife is insufficient recognition of the great assistance she has been in every aspect of the writing of it, from research to index.

Numerous others have helped in one way or another during the more than three years this book has been in preparation. To them all I am grateful indeed. The historical articles of A. S. Salley, W. D. Workman, Jr., Henry Lesesne and Douglas Summers Brown, as well as the newspaper feature stories of Lathan Mims have been most helpful. I am indebted to Mr. H. P. Kendall, who generously made available to me his Caroliniana library and map collection.

Valuable assistance was also received from Fred Seeley of Beaufort, N. C., Major Daniel Adams of Old Fort, N. C., Dr. A. R. Kelley of Athens, Ga., Colonel Clifford L. Miller, L. A. Savage, and Mrs. Priscilla Oliver of Camden, Mrs. W. S. Lee, John W. Fox and Herman B. Wolf of Charlotte, N. C., and W. T. Linton of the South Carolina Water Pollution Control Board.

Many public agencies and business concerns also assisted in various ways. Among these are the Duke Power Company, South Carolina Electric and Gas Company, West Virginia Pulp and Paper Company, International Paper Company, The Kendall Company, Southern Bell Telephone and Telegraph Company, and The Mill-Power Supply Company, The Corps of Engineers of the U. S. Army, The North Carolina Department of Conservation and Development, The South Carolina Development Board, North Carolina Board of Health, North Carolina Department of Labor, South Carolina Department of Labor, South Carolina State Ports Authority, South Carolina State Commission of Forestry and The Southern Pine Association.

The Charlotte Observer, The Columbia State, The News and Courier, The South Carolina Magazine and The *State Magazine,* of Raleigh, were constantly found useful as were also issues of the *Manufacturers Record* and *Fortune.*

To those in charge of the several libraries I used I owe special thanks. They frequently went to much trouble to assist me. Especially helpful were Dr. and Mrs. Robert L. Meriwether of the South Caroliniana Library.

Finally I wish to express my appreciation to Carl Carmer and to Miss Jean Crawford for entrusting me with this assignment and for contributing their valuable suggestions and criticisms.

❧ ❧ ❧ ❧ ❧ *Bibliography*

ADAMS, JAMES TRUSLOW, *The March of Democracy.* (2 vols.) New
York: Charles Scribner's Sons, 1932 and 1933.

ALLEN, HERVEY AND HEYWARD, DUBOSE, *Carolina Chansons.* New
York: The Macmillan Company, 1922.

ALLEN, WILLIAM CICERO, *North Carolina History Stories.* Richmond, Virginia, 1901.

ANONYMOUS, *Liste des François et Suisses 1694-1695.* Charleston,
1868.

ARTHUR, JOHN P., *Western North Carolina, 1730-1913.* Raleigh,
1914.

BACHMAN, C. L. *John Bachman.* Charleston: Walker, Evans and
Cogswell Company, 1888.

BAILEY, J. D., *Commanders at Kings Mountain.* Gaffney, South
Carolina. Ed. H. DeCamp, 1926.

BALL, WILLIAM WATTS, *The State That Forgot.* Indianapolis: The
Bobbs-Merrill Company, 1932.

BARNES, FRANK, *Fort Sumter.* National Park Service Historical
Series No. 12. Washington, 1952.

BARRY, RICHARD, *Mr. Rutledge of South Carolina.* New York: Duell, Sloan and Pearce, 1942.

BARTRAM, WILLIAM, *The Travels of William Bartram.* Macy-Masius, 1928.

BEARD, CHARLES A. AND MARY R., *The Rise of American Civilization.* New York: The Macmillan Company, 1927.

BOWERS, CLAUDE G., *The Tragic Era.* Cambridge, Mass.: Riverside Press, 1929.

BRYSON, HERMAN J., *The Story of the Geologic Making of North Carolina.* Raleigh, 1928. North Carolina Department of Conservation and Development.

CATESBY, MARK, *The Natural History of Carolina, Florida and Bahama Islands.* (2 vols.) London, 1771.

CARROLL, B. R., *Historical Collections of South Carolina.* (2 vols.) New York: Harper and Brothers, 1836.

CHESNUT, MARY BOYKIN, *A Diary From Dixie.* New York: Peter Smith, 1929.

COIT, MARGARET L., *John C. Calhoun.* Boston: Houghton Mifflin Company, 1950.

COKER, WILLIAM C. AND TOTTEN, HENRY ROLAND, *Trees of the Southeastern States.* Chapel Hill: The University of North Carolina Press, 1934.

COOKE, C. WYTHE, *Geology of the Coastal Plain of South Carolina.* Washington: U. S. Government Printing Office, 1936.

CRANE, VERNER W., *The Southern Frontier, 1670-1732.* Durham, N. C.: Duke University Press, 1928.

DOAR, DAVID, *Rice and Rice Planting in the South Carolina Low Country.* Charleston: The Charleston Museum, 1936.

DRAPER, LYMAN C., *Kings Mountain and Its Heroes.* New York: Dauber, 1929.

DUBOSE, SAMUEL, *Reminiscences of St. Stevens Parish.* Charleston: A. E. Miller, 1858.

FEDERAL SECURITY AGENCY, *Southeast Drainage Basins.* Washington: U. S. Government Printing Office, 1951.

FISHBURNE, ANNE SINKLER, *Belvidere, A Plantation Memory.* Columbia, S. C.: University of South Carolina Press, 1950.

FISKE, JOHN, *The Discovery of America.* (2 vols.) Boston: Houghton, Mifflin and Company, 1901.

BIBLIOGRAPHY

FOOTE, WILLIAM HENRY, *Sketches of North Carolina.* Historical and Biographical. New York: Robert Carter, 1846.

GIBBES, ROBERT W., *Documentary History of the American Revolution.* (3 vols.) Columbia, 1853.

GREGORIE, ANNE KING, *Notes on Sewee Indians and Indian Remains of Christ Church Parish.* (pamphlet) Charleston, 1925.

———, *Thomas Sumter.* Columbia, S. C.: The R. L. Bryan Company, 1931.

HARRIS, SEALE, *Woman's Surgeon: The Life Story of J. Marion Sims.* New York: The Macmillan Company, 1950.

HENDERSON, ARCHIBALD, *The Conquest of the Old Southwest.* New York: The Century Company, 1920.

HEYWARD, DUNCAN CLINCH, *Seed From Madagascar.* Chapel Hill: The University of North Carolina Press, 1937.

HIRSCH, ARTHUR HENRY, *The Huguenots of Colonial South Carolina.* Durham, N. C.: Duke University Press, 1928.

HEWATT, ALEXANDER, *Historical Account of the Rise and Progress of the Colonies of South Carolina and Georgia.* (2 vols.) (London, 1779) Reprinted in Vol. I of Carroll's *Historical Collections of South Carolina.* New York: Harper and Brothers, 1836.

HUGHSON, SHIRLEY CARTER, *The Carolina Pirates and Colonial Commerce, 1670-1740.* Baltimore: The Johns Hopkins Press, 1894.

IRVING, JOHN BEAUFAIN, *A Day on Cooper River.* Columbia, S. C.: The R. L. Bryan Company, 1932.

JAMES, MARQUIS, *The Life of Andrew Jackson.* New York: The Bobbs-Merrill Company, 1938.

JAMES, WILLIAM D., *A Sketch of the Life of Brig. Gen. Francis Marion.* Marietta, Ga.: Continental Book Company, 1948.

JENKINS, JOHN WILBUR, *James B. Duke, Master Builder.* New York: George H. Doran Company, 1927.

JOHNSON, DOUGLAS, *The Origin of the Carolina Bays.* New York: Columbia University Press, 1942.

JULIEN, CARL AND MILLING, CHAPMAN J. *Beneath So Kind a Sky.* Columbia: University of South Carolina Press, 1948.

KIRKLAND, THOMAS J. AND KENNEDY, ROBERT M., *Historic Camden.*

(2 vols.) Columbia, S. C.: The State Company, 1905 and 1926.

KOHN, DAVID, (Editor), *Internal Development in South Carolina, 1817-1828*. Washington, 1938.

LANDERS, H. L., *The Battle of Camden*. Washington: U. S. Government Printing Office, 1929.

LAWSON, JOHN, *History of North Carolina* (1714). Richmond: Garrett and Massie, 1952.

LEDERER, JOHN, *The Discoveries of John Lederer in Three Several Marches From Virginia to West of Carolina, etc.* Privately printed ms. 1912.

LEFLER, HUGH TALMAGE AND NEWSOME, ALBERT RAY, *North Carolina*. Chapel Hill: University of North Carolina Press, 1954.

LOUNSBERRY, ALICE, *Southern Wild Flowers and Trees*. New York: Frederick H. Stokes Company, 1901.

MERIWETHER, ROBERT L., *The Expansion of South Carolina, 1729-1765*. Kingsport, Tenn.: Southern Publishers, Inc., 1940.

MILLING, CHAPMAN J., *Exile Without An End*. Columbia, S. C.: Bostick and Thornley, Inc., 1943.

———, *Red Carolinians*. Chapel Hill: University of North Carolina Press, 1940.

———, (Editor) *Colonial South Carolina*. Columbia: University of South Carolina Press, 1951.

MITCHELL, BROADUS, *The Rise of Cotton Mills in the South*. Baltimore: The Johns Hopkins Press, 1921.

———, AND MITCHELL, GEORGE SINCLAIR, *The Industrial Revolution in the South*. Baltimore: The Johns Hopkins Press, 1930.

MOORE, JAMES H., *Defense of the Mecklenburg Declaration of Independence*. Raleigh: Edwards and Broughton Printing Company, 1908.

MORRIS, JAMES A., *Woolen and Worsted Manufacturing in the Southern Piedmont*. Columbia: University of South Carolina Press, 1952.

MURRAY, CHALMERS J., *This Is Our Land*. Columbia, S. C.: The R. L. Bryan Company, 1949.

McCRADY, EDWARD, *History of South Carolina*. (4 vols.) New York: The Macmillan Company, 1897-1902.

McMASTER, ELIZABETH WARING, *The Girls of the Sixties*. Columbia: The State Company, 1937.

North Carolina, A Guide to the Old North State. American Guide Series. Chapel Hill: University of North Carolina Press, 1939.

North Carolina Stream Sanitation Committee, *Study of the Pollution in the Catawba River Basin.* Raleigh, 1951.

Palmetto Place Names. Publication of the South Carolina Education Association. Columbia: The Sloane Printing Company, 1941.

PEATTIE, DONALD CULROSS, *Green Laurels.* New York: Garden City Publishing Company, 1938.

PORCHER, F. A., *The History of the Santee Canal.* Charleston: The South Carolina Historical Society, 1903.

RAMSAY, DAVID, *History of South Carolina.* Newberry, S. C.: W. J. Duffie, 1858.

RANKIN, WATSON S., *James Buchanan Duke.* Princeton: Princeton University Press, 1952.

RAVENEL, MRS. ST. JULIEN, *Charleston, the Place and the People.* New York: The Macmillan Company, 1906.

RAVENEL, HARRIETT HORRY, *Eliza Pinckney.* New York: Charles Scribner's, 1896.

Ross, MARY, *With Pardo and Boyano on the Fringe of the Georgia Land.* Savannah: Georgia Historical Quarterly, XIV, 1930.

ROURKE, CONSTANCE, *Audubon.* New York: Harcourt, Brace, and Company, 1936.

RUTLEDGE, ARCHIBALD, *Home By the River.* New York: The Bobbs-Merrill Company, 1941.

SALLEY, ALEXANDER S. (Editor), *Narratives of Early Carolina, 1650-1708.* New York: Charles Scribner's Sons, 1911.

SCHLESINGER, ARTHUR M., JR., *The Age of Jackson.* Boston: Little, Brown and Company, 1946.

SHETRONE, HENRY CLYDE, *The Mound Builders.* New York: D. Appleton and Company, 1930.

SIMKINS, FRANCIS BUTLER, *Pitchfork Ben Tillman.* Baton Rouge: Louisiana State University Press, 1944.

SIMMS, WILLIAM GILMORE, *The Life of Francis Marion.* New York: George F. Cooledge and Brother, 1846.

————, *The History of South Carolina*. Columbia, S. C.: The State Company, 1940.

SMALL, JOHN KUNKEL, *Manuel of the Southeastern Flora*. New York, 1933.

SMITH, HUGH M., *The Fishes of North Carolina*. Vol. II of the North Carolina Geological and Economic Survey. Raleigh: E. M. Uzzell and Company, 1907.

SNOWDEN, YATES, *History of South Carolina*. (5 vols.) New York: The Lewis Publishing Company, 1920.

South Carolina, A Guide to the Palmetto State. American Guide Series. New York: Oxford University Press, 1941.

SQUIER, E. G. AND DAVIS, E. H., *Ancient Monuments of the Mississippi Valley*. New York: Bartlett and Wilford, 1848.

STOKES, THOMAS L., *The Savannah*. New York: Rinehart and Company, 1951.

SWANTON, JOHN R., *The Indians of the Southeastern United States*. Bulletin 137 of the Smithsonian Institution. Washington, 1946.

TAYLOR, ROSSER H., *Ante-Bellum South Carolina: A Social and Cultural History*. Chapel Hill: University of North Carolina Press, 1942.

TURPIN, EDNA, *Cotton*. New York: American Book Company, 1924.

WALKER, C. IRVINE, *The Romance of Lower Carolina*. Charleston: Art Publishing Company, 1915.

WALLACE, DAVID DUNCAN, *The History of South Carolina*. (4 vols.) New York: The American Historical Society, Inc., 1934.

WATERMAN, THOMAS T., *A Survey of the Early Buildings in the Region of the Proposed Santee and Pinopolis Reservoirs in South Carolina*. (Illustrated ms.) Washington: National Park Service, 1939.

WAYNE, ARTHUR TREZEVANT, *Birds of South Carolina*. Charleston: The Daggett Printing Company, 1910.

WELLMAN, MANLY WADE, *Giant in Gray, A Biography of Wade Hampton of South Carolina*. New York: Charles Scribner's Sons, 1949.

WHEELER, JOHN, *Historical Sketches of North Carolina From 1584 to 1851*. New York: Frederick Hitchcock, 1925.

WHITLOCK, BRAND, *La Fayette*. (2 vols.) New York: D. Appleton and Company, 1929.

BIBLIOGRAPHY

WINKLER, JOHN K., *Tobacco Tycoon, The Story of James Buchanan Duke.* New York: Random House, 1945.

WILLIAMS, SAMUEL COLE, *Early Travels in the Tennessee Country, 1540-1800.* Johnson City, Tenn.: The Watauga Press, 1928.

WOODMASON, CHARLES, (Hooker, Richard J., Editor), *The Carolina Back-country on the Eve of the Revolution.* Chapel Hill: The University of North Carolina Press, 1953.

WOODWARD, C. VANN, *Origins of the New South, 1877-1913.* Baton Rouge: Louisiana State University Press, 1951.

Index

Acteon, the, 168-72, 295
Adair, John, 205
agriculture, 301, 383-389; *see also* cotton, rice, indigo, cattle
Alamance, 140, 141, 150, 203
Albemarle Point, 53, 55, 255, 264, 376
Anderson, Major Robert, 295
Anson County, 132, 138, 139, 158
Appalachia, 10, 80
Appalachians, 10, 16, 28, 76, 265, 272
Archdale, Governor John, 87, 88
Ashley River, 53, 55, 177
Audubon, Jean Jacques, 276-278
Augusta, 175, 183, 203
Aycock, Governor Charles B., 344

Bachman, Rev. John, 276-278
back country, settlement, 85, 124-135; neglect by colonial
    government, 137 *et seq.*
backwoodsmen, 124-135
Barbados, 44, 52, 55, 91, 376
bays, 29
Beauregard, General Pierre G. T., 297, 299, 306

Cuningham, Colonel William, 185, 186
Cusabos, 16

David, the, 303-305
Davidson, Colonel William, 129, 187, 202
Davidson's Fort, 24
Davie, General William, 129, 187, 188, 202, 203, 215, 250
Dawson, F. W., 335, 337, 338
Dearborn Reservoir, 23, 350
de Ayllón, Lucas Vasquez, 18, 32, 34, 35
de Kalb, General Baron, 189-194
DeSoto, Hernando, 18, 36, 375
de Villafane, Angel, 37
Dixon, Lt. George E., 306
Doak, Rev. Samuel, 205
drainage area, 20
Drayton, Gov. William Henry, 153, 155-6, 163, 182, 242
Duke Endowment Fund, 353
Duke, James Buchanan, 346-353
Duke Power Company, 346-353, 366, 396
Du Pont, Gideon, 109
DuPont de Nemours and Company, 364, 372, 397

Eden, Governor, 91, 94
Edgefield, 337, 343
Edisto River, 21, 76
Ellenton riots, 328
English Santee, 106, 108, 357
Enoree River, 25, 131, 196, 353
Eutaw Springs, 108, 129, 222, 223, 227; battle of, 222, 223

Fairforest Creek, 131, 176, 196
fall line, 11
Fanning, Colonel Edmund, 139-141

Housatonic, the, 306
Huck, Captain Christian, 185, 186, 187
Huger, General Benjamin, 106, 156
Huger, Daniel, 178, 195
Huger, Colonel Isaac, 106, 178
Hughes, Price, 78 *et seq.*
Huguenots, 43, 55, 60, 61, 100-110, 230, 231, 245, 270, 300
Hundley, Horace L., 305-307
Hundley, the, 305-307
hurricanes, 57, 118, 119
Husband, Harmon, 139, 141
hydro-electric developments. *See* water power

Indians; buildings, 62, 67, 69; burials, 63; food, 63, 64, 67; hunting, 60, 64; names, 20; hospitality, 62, 69, 70; marriage, 66, 68; population, 17; trade, 56, 58, 72-85
indigo, 54, 106, 108, 109, 156, 383
industry, 331-345, 364-374, 401. *See also* manufacturing
Inman, Captain Shadrack, 196
Iredell County, 387
iron mining, 131
Iroquois, 16
irrigation, 388, 402

Jackson, President Andrew, 128, 188, 220-1, 274, 279-293
Jacksonborough, 237-8
James, Major John, 186
Jamestown, 100, 103, 366
Jasper, Sergeant William, 171-2
Johnson, President Andrew, 316, 317, 318, 320
Johnson, Sir Nathaniel, 80
Johnson, Governor Robert, 90-97

Kershaw, Joseph, 182, 191
Kiawah, 53

INDEX

Siouan Indians, 16, 84
slavery, Indian, 32, 34, 36, 54, 56, 61, 83; Negro, 34, 45, 95,
117, 122, 125, 127, 159, 165, 219, 245, 246, 254, 260, 263,
283, 309, 317, 318; white, 98, 341
smallpox, 17, 56, 66
Smyth, Captain Ellison A., 338
source, 19, 21, 22, 23
South Carolina Public Service Authority, 356-363
South Fork Catawba, 396
Southern Power Company, 346-353
Spangenberg, Bishop Augustus, 125
Spaniards, 19, 32-41, 42, 52, 54, 78, 83, 94, 99
Spartanburg, 177, 387
Springs, Leroy, 338
Stamp Act, 145, 151-52, 157-8
Star of the West, the, 296
Stateburg, 273, 332. *See also* Santee, High Hills of
State House (Charleston), 155; Columbia, 311, 313, 323, 324
steam power plants, 350-3, 360, 396
Stoney, Theodore, 302
submarines, 300-307
Sugar Creek, 397
Sugaree Indians, 71
Sullivan's Island, 95, 161-172, 227
Sumter, General Thomas, 129, 180, 186, 187, 188, 191, 195,
197, 209, 214, 215, 218, 219, 222, 224, 232, 242
Swannanoa Creek, 24, 131

Table Rock Lake, 25
Tarleton, Colonel Banastre, 178, 181, 185, 197, 206, 214, 215,
216, 228, 232, 281
tea tax, 154, 157-8
Textile industry, 256, 331, 350, 355, 373; *see also* manufacturing
Thatch, Edward. *See* Blackbeard

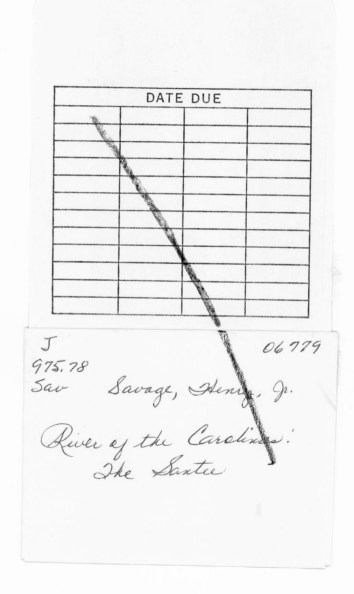